# Making an AMERICAN WORKFORCE

# Making an AMERICAN WORKFORCE

## The Rockefellers and the Legacy of Ludlow

EDITED BY

**Fawn-Amber Montoya**

University Press of Colorado
*Boulder*

Published by University Press of Colorado
5589 Arapahoe Avenue, Suite 206C
Boulder, Colorado 80303


Printed in the United States of America
First paperback edition 2019

The University Press of Colorado is a proud member of the Association of University Presses.

The University Press of Colorado is a cooperative publishing enterprise supported, in part, by Adams State University, Colorado State University, Fort Lewis College, Metropolitan State University of Denver, Regis University, University of Colorado, University of Northern Colorado, Utah State University, and Western State Colorado University.

∞ This paper meets the requirements of the ANSI/NISO Z39.48-1992 (Permanence of Paper).

Library of Congress Cataloging-in-Publication Data

Montoya, Fawn-Amber.
Making an American workforce : the Rockefellers and the legacy of Ludlow / by Fawn-Amber Montoya.
pages cm
ISBN 978-1-60732-309-9 (hardback) — ISBN 978-1-60732-310-5 (ebook) — ISBN 978-1-60732-900-8 (pbk.)
1. Industrial welfare—Colorado—Ludlow—History. 2. Colorado Fuel and Iron Company—History. 3. Americanization—Colorado—Ludlow—History. 4. Rockefeller, John D., Jr. (John Davison), 1874-1960. 5. Ludlow (Colo.)—History. I. Title.
HD6490.W42U65 2014
331.7'6691420978855—dc23

2014010475

Cover photograph credits: "Finale" Trinidad Field Days, 1915 (front); Women's Heavyweight Contest at the annual field day in Trinidad, 1919 (back). Both images courtesy of the Bessemer Historical Society / CF&I Archives.

To my Children, Teodoro and Cecilia

To my brother Ammon, 1975–2007,

and to CL—we still laugh when we think about you

And to Shawntinice "Polkey" Polk, 1983–2005

# Contents

# Illustrations

# Tables

# Acknowledgments

This collection started as an academic symposium sponsored by Colorado State University, Pueblo, in April of 2009. The symposium was part of the Ludlow Memorial Labor fest that CSU-Pueblo had hosted for a number of years. The Labor fest was possible due to the work of Jonathan Rees, Cora Zalatel, and Scott Whited. The symposium was funded by the College of Humanities and Social Sciences, Provost's Office, History Department, and Chicano Studies program.

The contributors to the collection were patient over this five-year journey, responding to numerous e-mails, revising their pieces, and enthusiastically encouraging its publication. I am sure all of the contributors would agree that at the top of the list of the people to thank is the staff at the Bessemer Historical Society and Colorado Fuel & Iron Archives. I started my research there over ten years ago, and in 2007 I was lucky enough to come back to Pueblo to work more closely with all of the staff members. Beverly Allen, Jay Trask, Victoria Miller, Stacy Comden, M'lissa Morgan, Maria Sanchez-Tucker, Tim Hawkins, and Sara Szalsky spent many hours assisting researchers and answering those last-minute phone calls and e-mails.

Special thanks to the University Press of Colorado editor Darrin Pratt, for asking about the manuscript, and Jessica Arbonne for helping to calm my nerves and for making this an enjoyable process.

This collection would not have been written if it were not for Sarah Deutsch, whose work inspired me as an undergraduate student, who I was blessed to study with as a graduate student, and who is the person I still call to ask for advice on my personal and professional life.

My colleagues Lydia Otero and Patricia Trujillo have listened to me in moments of crisis, called to wish me congratulations, and continue to be people with whom I share my highs and my lows.

I have had the pleasure to work with an amazing group of individuals on the Ludlow Centennial Commission and the Ludlow Statewide Committee. Their scholarship laid the groundwork for this collection, and their collaboration has been inspiring. A special thanks to Bob Butero, who has planned the commemorations at Ludlow for many years.

The journey to publishing this piece started many years ago in my high school and university classrooms. I have been lucky enough to be taught by the men I refer to as the Three Garcias. To Vic Garcia, my high school history teacher—I wonder if he ever thought that I would become an historian. His love of teaching and history was not wasted. To Juan Garcia, a great mentor and advocate, and to Ignacio Garcia who inspired me to go to graduate school in the first place. Ignacio: This is a book, but not *the* book.

To my colleague and friend Victoria Obregon, who has taught me how to be a better person, to understand my students, and to live life for all it has to offer.

In the process of putting this collection together, Teodoro and Cecilia have joined me on speaking engagements, meetings, and drives to Ludlow. I hope they come to love the history of Colorado even half as much as I do. Lately when I think about their futures, I wonder if it is too harsh to send them to the coal mines after high school so that later in life they can be the United Mine Workers of America president.

Throughout my professional career I have had the support of my siblings, Melissa, David, Jared, Ammon, and Joseph, who have provided me with many laughs and who miss Tripod as much as I do. Without my parents, whose roaming lifestyle and love of the land kept me anchored to my southern Colorado roots, I would not have challenged myself to make my passion my livelihood. My paternal grandparents Julia Crespin and Albert Montoya taught me to have a great love for my family's history and for southern Colorado. They made Pueblo, Colorado, home to me many years before I came here as a young professor. I wish that my maternal grandparents Melissa McGee and Fernando Herrera were still living—they would have been thrilled to put this book on their coffee table and share it with their friends over dirty martinis.

To Alysse McCanna for her assistance with footnotes and random summer e-mails. To Dawn DiPrince for her editing, insightful comments, and example of trying to balance home and work life. To my amazing students Stephanie Winchell and Ashley Martinez, who helped me with research, copies, footnotes, and sometimes just sat in the office so no one would come and bother me.

Finally, thanks to my partner, Patricio, who has embraced Colorado as his home and who doesn't wonder why I am up late at night working on the computer.

# Making an AMERICAN WORKFORCE

# Introduction

*Fawn-Amber Montoya*

Pueblo, Colorado, a dusty western high-prairie town at the foot of the Rocky Mountains, has a historic and symbolic attachment to the East Coast. To illustrate this connection, in May 1902, Pueblo opened its own Coney Island—Lake Minnequa—with a grand opening that included a band concert, balloon races, fireworks, an opera, fishing, and boat races. Sarah Bernhardt performed at Lake Minnequa, in 1906, and stated that this was the "only time in her career when she 'played' an amusement park." Pueblo's "Coney Island" included a ten-cent gate admission, a roller coaster, shooting gallery, hall of mirrors, roller-skating rink, boating, swimming, a theater and dancing on a pavilion built over the water. There were acres of lawns for games or picnics.

Pueblo residents gathered at Lake Minnequa and used it as a communal place to enjoy their leisure time. It was a place where lovers would meet and weddings would be celebrated. With its Coney Island-style, it represented the intermingling of happiness and industrialization, led in the region by the Colorado Fuel and Iron Company, whose corporate leadership centered on

DOI: 10.5876/9781607323105.c000

the East Coast. Lake Minnequa was the crown of the growing community of Bessemer, also home to the administrative offices of the Colorado Fuel and Iron Company (CF&I), and the Minnequa Steel Works.[1]

Despite the frivolity found at Lake Minnequa, industrial development around Pueblo, Colorado, had a darker side too. A dozen years after the fanfare of opening day at Pueblo's Coney Island, CF&I miners were embroiled in the Great Colorado Coalfield War, which began when striking miners were evicted from their company-owned homes in September 1913 and moved into tents on the Colorado plains—south of Pueblo. In the Ludlow tent colony on the morning of April 20, 1914, the day began with an exchange of gunfire between striking miners and the Colorado State militia and ended with the death of over twenty individuals, guardsmen, miners, and their families—including women and children.

*Making an American Workforce* examines the industrialization and development of communities in southern Colorado within this context of labor relations and East Coast company men and the impact on the families and immigrants who worked for the Colorado Fuel and Iron Company. This text relates the localized events, like Ludlow, and the local communities, like Bessemer, to broader themes of the industrial birth of the United States and the role of capitalism in the day-to-day lives of families.

## Labor Relations / Welfare Capitalism

The Colorado Fuel and Iron Company formed a sociological department headed by Richard W. Corwin and focused on improving the lives of the miners and their families through educational programs, healthcare, and a company periodical. Corwin saw the Sociological Department as a means to be able to educate and Americanize his labor force. The labor force included large populations of immigrant and migrant groups who came to the region to participate in the booming steel and coal economy. While CF&I saw the Sociological Department as a means of assisting with labor relations, the United Mine Workers, Industrial Workers of the World, and the Western Federation of Miners rallied the miners to join unions in which their rights would be represented. Corwin and later the Rockefellers saw their approach to managing employers as welfare capitalism, one in which they attempted to understand the employees and their needs and at the same time made sure that the employees provided an adequate supply of labor for the company. This approach to employee needs was part of a national dialogue throughout the United States centered on corporations' paternalistic behavior toward their employees. The approach used by CF&I to educating their workforce and constructing ideas of Americanization was not only a CF&I, a Colorado, or western Idea. After the Ludlow Massacre, John D. Rockefeller Jr. used the Employee Representation plan as a national and international model for employee relations.

The YMCA since the 1870s had engaged in dialogue about the "crisis of masculinity" that middle-class American men found themselves in. With the increase of immigration into the continent and working-class men being more physical fit, the YMCA, along with corporations, envisioned the creation of a system of welfare capitalism. Employers felt that they were rescuing their employees, and within this context they, the wage laborer, and management redefined new ideas of manhood. The YMCA felt that the best approach to this was to develop social relations modeled after a patriarchal household, one in which the employer was the patriarchal figure and the employees his children. Much of this dialogue among working-class communities emerged with the conflict that occurred between management and their employees. Rockefeller Jr. and CF&I felt that the YMCA would be able to assist in the unrest in southern Colorado.[2]

## Bessemer

The community of Bessemer grew up around the Colorado Coal and Iron Company's Steel Mill, which would later become the Minnequa Steel Works. The area west of the steel mill, by the 1880s, had garnered the name Bessemer after Sir Henry Bessemer, the inventor of a process that converted pig iron into steel. Before the building of Betsy—the first blast furnace of the CF&I mill—the new plant was reported to be on a "cactus-studded prairie two miles from 'downtown' Pueblo."[3] By 1883, Bessemer had a seventeen-piece brass band, was constructing a two-room school house, and had a population of between one and two thousand people who saw this community as home.[4]

In the spring of 1886, residents petitioned the Pueblo County court to incorporate Bessemer into a city.[5] In 1890, the city of Bessemer laid a main water line and allowed the Pueblo City railway to extend its horse-drawn cart service into Bessemer. At that time the governor of Colorado, John J. Routt, labeled Bessemer as a "second-class city," meaning that it was an up-and-coming community. In the same year, Bessemer garnered a hose cart for fire protection, established a one-man police department and, in 1889, the Pueblo Gas and Electric Light Company installed poles and wires for electric lights. During the national economic depression of 1893, Bessemer faced a looming crisis and its leadership decided that in the best interests of the community they should become part of the city of Pueblo. In 1894, the city of Pueblo annexed Bessemer.[6] The perceived potential for the community's growth was based on the influx of immigrants, the region, and the large number of jobs available at the Steel Works.

In the twentieth century, the Bessemer Neighborhood came to represent the Colorado Fuel and Iron Company because of the administration building and its growing immigrant and migrant communities who worked in the steel mill and came to live in the community. Bessemer, like other western communities located near an economically thriving environment, became transformed from an isolated location into a community where immigrants from all over the world and migrants from all over the United States would settle and make a life for themselves. In this region, like in other areas of the country, newcomers would bring their religions, language and traditions from their homelands; merge those with the traditions of others in the new region; and, within a few generations, complete the process of assimilating or acculturating to an American-style of life.

Lake Minnequa, Bessemer, and Pueblo together represent the spaces that were created with the growth of industry in the West. While CF&I employees and their families helped to form these communities, this region was deliberately developed by the dreams of East Coast entrepreneurs and businessmen who changed the landscape of this region and established communities where laborers would come to see themselves as part of a larger economy and labor force. Bessemer, Pueblo and other communities in southeastern Colorado came into existence due to the growth of the railroad industry and its increasing demand for coal, as the United States sought out new fuel resources. The administrators of this region adopted company policies that would structure the lives of their workforce ultimately making them what the company considered better employees and Americans.

## Roots of CF&I

As the community of Bessemer blossomed, two industrial men from the East Coast changed this geologically rich corner of Colorado. William Jackson Palmer brought about the foundation of a coal economy in the West, and John D. Rockefeller Jr. juggled the complex relationship between labor and company management. William Jackson Palmer entered Colorado with the dreams of building a railroad; he sought out mineral resources that would help with the efficiency of building a railroad. The coal within southern Colorado fueled Palmer's dreams and provided him with the means for a steelworks. According to Thomas Andrews,

> by exploiting the region's thick coal seams, Palmer believed, Colorado and New Mexico could escape the limitations of isolation and aridity under which they were laboring. He foretold a utopian future for the Rocky Mountain landscape, one powered by the same forces responsible for revolutionizing the British economy.[7]

The success of Palmer's railroad rested in its location near the coal fields, which provided the fuel for transportation to the region. The Denver and Rio Grande railroads opened the southern Colorado coal fields in Fremont county in 1872, fields further south in Huerfano by 1876, and in Las Animas county by 1878. At the same time, rival railroads like the Atchison, Topeka, and Santa Fe began building competing lines to these fields. With this competition, the coal fields, mainly represented by the Colorado Fuel and Iron Company and its subsidiaries, flourished. [8]

Like Palmer, the Rockefellers also invested (and profited) heavily in southern Colorado. At the turn of the twentieth century, the Rockefeller influence—while not direct—was consequential, as Rockefeller Jr. sat on the Board of Directors of CF&I. During the Rockefeller years at CF&I, communities throughout southern Colorado sprang to life. With the help of Dr. Richard Corwin, CF&I established the company's Sociological Department with the intent of assisting employees in becoming better workers and transforming them into "Americans." In addition to the Sociological Department, CF&I printed company publications that focused on the workings of the coal fields and the steel mill. Despite having a large investment in CF&I, the Rockefellers remained absent from the minefields and left the day-to-day operations in the hands of local management until the Ludlow Massacre of 1914.

In the fall of 1913, CF&I miners were embroiled in the Great Colorado Coalfield War, which began when striking miners were evicted from their company-owned homes and forced into a tent colony on the Colorado plains. In the Ludlow tent colony on the morning of April 20, 1914, the day began with an exchange of gunfire between striking miners and the Colorado State militia and ended with the death of over twenty individuals—guardsmen, miners, and their families. The shock over the deaths of women and children at the Ludlow tent colony thrust Rockefeller Sr. and Rockefeller Jr. into the media spotlight, and people throughout the United States demanded that the Rockefellers answer for the massacre. The Rockefellers had little direct connection to the Massacre, but their majority interest in the company was interpreted by union organizers as a sign that CF&I management may have ordered the strike. In response to hearings in Colorado and with the Federal Government, Rockefeller Jr., came to southern Colorado in 1915 and became more directly involved with the inner workings of the company. Through this work, he proposed an employee-relations plan that set up a structure not only for industrial-labor relations, but for the social betterment of the camps.[9]

Colorado Fuel and Iron Company, under the leadership of the Rockefeller family, was central to the creation of the workforce and the communities of this region. This text provides a look into how the Colorado Fuel and Iron Company deliberately built a workforce to meet its production needs and the impact of these practices and policies on the families and communities of southeastern Colorado. *Making An American Workforce* also addresses how CF&I ownership envisioned and implemented the formation of a company union—and how this idea of a company union is spread throughout the United States and even internationally. With scholarship from a diverse group of historians and a sociologist, this text expands the story of the Colorado Fuel and Iron Company and its influence on the American West; it enables the reader to contemplate the impact of CF&I on the lives of its employees and their families; and it demonstrates how the company's policies transcended southern Colorado, influencing the coal mines of Wyoming and the policy of company unions across the nation and the continent into the middle half of the twentieth century.

## Purpose of the Book

*Making an American Workforce* fills a void in regards to scholarship on the Colorado Fuel and Iron Company because it includes a strong focus on CF&I corporate policies after the Ludlow Massacre, specifically regarding the Employee Representation Plan and how the Employee Representation Plan was touted throughout the United States and the world. This work addresses the rise of compassionate capitalism with research specifically focusing on Richard Corwin and his creation of the Sociological Departments and his ideas about Americanization programs and Eugenics that endured into the late 1920s. Chapters address the role of the Ludlow Massacre in the changing nature of industrial relations in southern Colorado and in the United States. The text gives a strong review of the impact of the corporate response to Ludlow, including the implementation of John D. Rockefeller's Industrial Representation Plan as an answer to the criticism following the events at Ludlow; the far-reaching effect of this plan on CF&I-managed communities; and the impact of this corporate policy on ideas of corporate welfare spread on an international level. *Making an American Workforce* explores the impact of CF&I on the physical bodies of their employees, through leisure activities and physical competitions, with the implementation of Corwin's Sociological Department and the transformation in labor relations at Ludlow, while at the same time influencing national and international dialogue about labor relations. The takeover of field days by CF&I after the Ludlow Massacre illustrates that company managers felt that they were better at structuring the leisure spaces of its employees and that they could link leisure and recreation to the national dialogue about health and fitness through the YMCAs.[10] Themes for the text include the role of the body in the structuring of the labor force, both before and after the Ludlow Massacre; the national and international influence of the Colorado Fuel and Iron Company; and how CF&I's construction of an American workforce influenced its employees.

The bulk of the text focuses on the Ludlow Massacre and its impact on employees of CF&I in the establishment of a company union and how the ideas of the Employee Representation Plan were transmitted into the workforce of CF&I. In the first chapter, "Learning from Ludlow," Sarah Deutsch gives her perspective on the research that has been done on Ludlow in the past twenty-five years and the current state of the field. "The United Mine

Workers knew immediately that the events of their strike at Ludlow would form a key chapter in their history," she writes, "and to ensure its place they wrote that chapter in granite in 1918, when they dedicated a memorial to those killed at Ludlow on land the United Mine Workers of America (UMWA) purchased, encompassing the tent colony where the strikers had died." Deutsch illustrates that the relevance of Ludlow continues to live on through twenty-first-century scholarship.

In the second chapter, "Dr. Richard Corwin and Colorado's Changing Racial Divide," Brian Clason and Jonathan Rees argue that Richard W. Corwin, founder of the Sociological Department and a pioneer of medicine in Pueblo, Colorado, participated in the Eugenics movement in the 1910s. The Eugenics movement in the United States had its roots in the Progressive movement and its followers included Margaret Sanger. Scientists and medical practitioners of the time developed theories designed to illuminate which individuals were suitable to reproduce based upon principles of Social Darwinism and their ideal model of civilization. This chapter presents solid evidence that links Corwin to the American Eugenics Society and considers the idea that Pueblo's celebration of Corwin as the pioneer of medicine may obscure this lamentable yet significant aspect of his legacy. While Corwin may not have been a practitioner of eugenics, he kept up with the medical dialogue of his time. Further, this chapter gives the reader a better understanding of the organization of CF&I and how it became involved in the daily lives of its employees. The Americanization programs and the mentality of Corwin shaped the workers into thinking of themselves as a unit and gave them a better understanding of their connection to each other and their communities.

In chapter 3, "Governor Elias Ammons and the 1913–1914 Southern Colorado Coal Strike," Anthony R. DeStefanis addresses the centrality of Governor Ammon's role in the 1913–14 Colorado Coalfield Strike, as he held the power to summon the Colorado National Guard / State Militia. The National Guard made it possible to bring in strike breakers and assisted in establishing the power of the company in the labor strikes in Colorado. DeStefanis's chapter explains why Ammons called out the National Guard and how he funded it during the winter of 1913 and spring of 1914. This chapter also explains how the formerly union-friendly Ammons shifted sides to support the National Guard for his own political preservation within a larger Nativist dialogue that often pitted foreign-born union members against native-born guard members. DeStefanis includes the story of Roady Kenehan, the state auditor, who in defiance of Ammons refused to sign certificates indebting the Colorado state government to pay for the deployment of National Guard troops against the striking miners. Kenehan argued that coal mine operators needed to negotiate with the striking miners in order to reach a settlement. Despite Kenehan's refusal, the state, as explored in this chapter, funded the National Guard through the selling of Insurrectionary Bonds to individuals and businesses in Denver.

Chapter 4 takes a look at the effects of the Ludlow massacre, including the formation of John D. Rockefeller Jr.'s Employee Representation Plan in response to the Massacre and the impact of this plan on the national dialogue related to company unions. Historian Robin Henry, in her chapter, "In Order to Form a More Perfect Worker: John D. Rockefeller Jr. and Reform in Post-Ludlow Southern Colorado," addresses how John D. Rockefeller Jr. through the help of Ivy Lee, a public relations expert, became immersed in company policy and the day-to-day operations of CF&I. In response to this change in his leadership, Rockefeller Jr. not only implemented the Colorado Industrial Plan, an employee representation plan, but also theorized about the company's responsibility to its workers—both in the workplace and in their homes and personal life. Henry connects the reform work of Rockefeller Jr. in Colorado through the YMCA, with his reform work in New York and Illinois and other areas of the United States.

In chapter 5, "Field Days, YMCA, and Baseball: CF&I's Industrial Representation Plan and Gender Relations in Southern Colorado Coal-Mining Camps," Fawn-Amber Montoya addresses the embracing of recreation as part of Rockefeller's plan that focused on social betterment. She explores the rise of Field Days, which included contests such as the heaviest woman contest. Montoya examines the success of baseball as a means of Americanizing workers and their families for generations. Finally, she explores, through the lens of recreation, how CF&I management interpreted gender.

In chapter 6, "A Tale of Two Employee Representation Plans in the Steel Industry: Pueblo, Colorado, and Sydney, Nova Scotia," Greg Patmore examines and compares the history of two Employee Representation Plans (ERPs) during the interwar period. Patmore compares the plan at Pueblo, which was part of the ERP established by John D. Rockefeller Jr., at the Colorado

Fuel and Iron Company following the Ludlow massacre in 1914, with the introduction of an ERP in Canada. At the Sydney, Nova Scotia, steel plant of the British Empire Steel Corporation (BESCO), following the defeat of the unions in a major strike, management introduced an ERP in August 1923. Patmore argues that employee representatives at both steel plants exercised some degree of autonomy. Against a background of favorable labor legislation, both ERPs went into decline, although the ERP at Pueblo survived for longer against union organization. This comparative chapter enables the reader to see the impact of Rockefeller's work in an international context.

In chapter 7, "Putting the 'I' in CF&I: The Struggle over Representation, Labor, and Company Town Life on the Edge of *Aztlán* in a Wyoming Company Town," sociologist Ronald L. Mize looks at the role of Chicana/os as laborers in Sunrise, Wyoming. He addresses this group outside of the traditional perspective of Chicano scholars, who have tended to focus on the Chicana/o experience in the southwestern states of California, Texas, New Mexico, and Arizona. He illustrates how Sunrise became part of Pueblo's steelmaking industry.

While the text itself covers a variety of topics, it centers on the legacy of CF&I, engaging the reader in the variety of work surrounding the company's history. The interdisciplinary approach offers a textured analysis of the impact of CF&I and the Ludlow Massacre one hundred years after the event.

## Notes

1. Rawlings Library Newspaper Collection. Pueblo, Colorado *Pueblo Star Journal*, Sunday, December 8, 1974, 3c.

2. Thomas Winter, *Making Men, Making Class: The YMCA and Workingmen, 1877–1920* (Chicago: University of Chicago Press, 2002).

3. *Pueblo Chieftain*, October 16, 1952, 34.

4. Ibid., October 16, 1952.

5. Ibid., October 9, 1952, 2, and January 27, 1924, 6.

6. Ibid., January 27, 1924, 6.

7. Thomas G. Andrews, *Killing for Coal: America's Deadliest Labor War* (Cambridge, MA: Harvard University Press, 2008), 43.

8. Andrews, *Killing for Coal*, 53.

9. Jonathan H. Rees, *Representation and Rebellion: The Rockefeller Plan at the Colorado Fuel and Iron Company, 1914–1942* (Boulder: University Press of Colorado, 2010).

10. *Making an American Workforce* fits within the dialogue of Welfare Capitalism that is occurring throughout the United States in the twentieth century. Thomas Winter, in his work *Making Men and Making class*, addresses the role of the YMCA in constructing ideas of masculinity for the middle and working classes; that book has two chapters that specifically address the ideas of masculinity and its attachment to YMCA programs in the 1910s.

ONE

# Learning from Ludlow

*Sarah Deutsch*

In fall 2009 I was honored to participate in the conference that generated the papers for this volume. In this setting, where so much exciting new work was being presented, I was tasked with assessing the state of the field to date. The state of the field was buoyant. We were witnessing a sort of Ludlow Renaissance. That spring it seemed every time I turned on my computer, Amazon.com was inviting me to check out some new volume on Ludlow. And there is other work still in the pipeline, for example, Fawn Montoya's work on Rockefeller's disciplining of workers' bodies and not just their minds in order to form the ideal worker. Ludlow is now even a Bedford Books collection.[1] Bedford produces these books for college use. They are composed of firsthand sources and a bit of scholarly introduction. It is a series reserved for those iconic moments in American History that shape the arc of our national story.

What does it mean that Ludlow is now in that firmament? The arc of our national story perpetually changes. Nor is there necessarily consensus on the arc. The United Mine Workers knew immediately that the events of their

DOI: 10.5876/9781607323105.c001

strike at Ludlow would form a key chapter in their history, and to ensure its place they wrote that chapter in granite in 1918, when they dedicated a memorial to those killed at Ludlow on land the United Mine Workers of America (UMWA) purchased, encompassing the tent colony where the strikers had died. Yet, even those who would choose Ludlow as a central feature of the arc may not all use it to tell the same national—and increasingly transnational—story.

Thirty years ago, when I was first writing about Ludlow, there were few scholarly works to consult. There was a wonderful oral history project in progress. There was some trickiness in getting access to company records (I couldn't). And there was little general sense that this was somehow a Mexican American story. If people knew about Ludlow at all, they knew about the Greek strike leader, Louis Tikas, second in command at Ludlow's tent colony. Tikas was murdered by the Colorado National Guard on the day of the massacre, April 20, 1914, almost a hundred years ago, and he was the subject of a 1982 biography by Zeese Papanikolas.[2]

There was a small flurry of attention to Ludlow among scholars in the late 1980s, including my own book in 1987, Priscilla Long's 1989 volume on the US coal industry, and H. M. Gitelman's 1988 meticulous study of Ludlow's legacy.[3] Gitelman chronicled the relationship between Colorado Fuel and Iron Company (CF&I) head John D. Rockefeller Jr. and his confederate, Canadian reformer and later prime minister (1921–26, 1926–30, 1935–48) MacKenzie King, as they gave painful birth to an employee representation plan, better known as company unionism.[4] They hailed it, in the late 1910s, as the salvation of American capitalism from the violence of class discord. And then with the end of the 1980s, a decade of virtual silence about Ludlow followed. Finally, a twenty-first-century renaissance occurred, with Wolff's *Industrializing the Rockies*, Martelle's *Blood Passion*, Berman's *Radicalism in the Mountain West, 1890–1920*, and Andrews's *Killing for Coal*.

One of the tropes in the current crop of books is the neglect that preceded them. My favorite such story is the one about the family who take the exit from the highway to the Ludlow monument, and then are chagrinned to discover that the Ludlow Massacre did not involve Native Americans. Those misguided tourists, the implication is, were swept up in a different version of our national history, the one that poses the significance of the US West to the nation as lying in the contest for land between Euro-Americans and Indians, rather than in a history of conflict between capital and labor. This past neglect, in tandem with this other story of the US West, acts as a foil for the scholars' contentions of the dramatic significance of the events surrounding Ludlow in 1914, and for the necessity of recovering this past, particularly in this twenty-first-century moment, the necessity of shifting the arc of the national story to a different thread of contest.

In 2003, things came to a head in an unexpected way. In the same year that David Wolff's *Industrializing the Rockies: Growth, Competition, and Turmoil in the Coal Fields of Colorado and Wyoming, 1868–1914* came out, in the midst of a long labor struggle in the southern Colorado steel industry, the caretaker of the Ludlow memorial site arrived in May to prepare the site for an annual memorial gathering. To his horror, he found the male and female granite statues on the site decapitated and the woman's left arm sawn off. This desecration of what the *Denver Post* in a sympathetic editorial called Labor's sacred ground galvanized both labor unions and labor historians. Local unions raised reward money for information leading to the arrest of the perpetrators, and the annual memorial service garnered an audience of hundreds at this remote spot, instead of the usual handful. The event included among the speakers, with the assent of the UMWA, labor historian Julie Greene, then at the University of Colorado, representing the Labor and Working Class History Association (LAWCHA).[5]

In the aftermath, LAWCHA and the UMWA together launched a collaborative effort to have the site designated as a National Historic Landmark. Few sites nominated ever make it through the process, and a small portion indeed are labor history sites. As with the Bedford Books series, this was an attempt to stake a claim to a major place in the national narrative for labor history and labor wars.[6]

What about the early twenty-first century made it susceptible to this story? Or, put differently, what did the Ludlow story evoke? The twenty-first century dawned amidst an economic boom that saw an ever-widening gap between the rich and the working poor, that saw the rising power of transnational corporations, the evisceration of legislation protecting the right of workers to organize as well as other civil liberties, and increasing domestic anxiety about a global labor force manifested in what seemed daily controversy over immigration. Despite the fact that US guest worker programs historically have never reduced undocumented immigration, Congress repeatedly flirted with the possibility of new guest worker programs. Immigrants, documented and undocumented, demanded human rights. Scholars and nonscholars worried that the increasing presence of immigrants threatened our national identity. Politicians and the US government displayed a striking lack of consistency—on the one hand turning to Hispanic immigrants to fill spaces in the US Army left vacant by declining black enlistment, and on the other railing against immigrant labor.[7] No one seemed to argue that these great army jobs had to be reserved for citizens.

What has all this to do with the events in Southern Colorado nearly a century earlier? Then, too, citizens feared a runaway state, trampling civil liberties in cahoots with powerful corporations. They feared the loss of sovereignty, both national and individual. Then, too, though undocumented immigration referred only to Chinese, the popular press vacillated between pride at being the destination of an international world of dreamers and anxiety about how many of those dreamers spoke no English and might not be committed to the US form of government. Labor unions differed markedly in their inclusiveness, with the United Mine Workers in Southern Colorado being among the more inclusive. Employers displayed the same kind of schizophrenia regarding immigrant labor as now. While at Ludlow, the capital—both John Osgood's Victor American Mines and Rockefeller Jr.'s Colorado Fuel and Iron—was national rather than transnational, the labor force was unquestionably multinational. Roughly thirty-two nationalities who spoke twenty-seven different languages were represented among CF&I's workers, with roughly two-thirds non-US citizens. Lamont Montgomery Bowers, whom Rockefeller Sr. brought in to oversee Colorado Fuel and Iron in 1907, blamed mine accidents—according to the journalist Martelle in his 2007 volume *Blood Passion: The Ludlow Massacre and Class War in the American West*—on outside agitators and, though he employed them, disdained "these foreigners who do not intend to make America their home, and who live like rats in order to save money."[8] In Bowers's words, "[They] are over here for the purpose of selling their labor in the highest market in the world, and when they have a few hundred dollars to their credit in the banks of the countries from which they came, they will go back there to enjoy their bread and beer." In this paradigm, it is the immigrants rather than those who employ them for substandard wages who exploit the nation.

The pre-twenty-first-century history of Ludlow went something like the following: Driven by oppressive monopoly capitalists in the coal industry who attempted to control every aspect of the workers' lives in their new company towns, paying with company scrip only usable at company stores, the coal miners of southern Colorado, led by the United Mine Workers of America (UMWA) went out on strike in the autumn of 1913. They struck for better wages and conditions, and for union recognition. Since many lived in company towns, they were evicted and set up domestic life and union organization in tent colonies. The Colorado governor called out the National Guard to keep order, but the guard, like local politicians, was far from even-handed. Determined to allow strike breakers to reach the mines, and with guns trained on the tent colony at Ludlow, the National Guard murdered strike leader Louis Tikas and several others on April 20, 1914, and then set fire to the colony, smothering a group of women and children who had taken refuge from flying bullets beneath the floor boards of their tent. This was the Ludlow Massacre.

The twenty-first-century literature on Ludlow has its continuities and discontinuities with the earlier work. Both literatures emphasize the polyglot nature of the labor force, though the newer work on Ludlow tends to emphasize the immigrant over the roughly one-third of workforce and the strikers who were native born. The newer literature, like the old, emphasizes the reasonableness of the demands—though often posed by the press at the time as radical—presenting them as the ultimately American demands of self-determination and liberty in the face of an oppressive corporate regime that tried to control not only their labor but the intimate spaces of their daily lives. The images in these works—and this is one of the really great things about the new literature—had become so inexpensive to reproduce that, in distinction to the earlier works, they have lots of them! For example, pamphlets might show the company's propaganda, contrasting the house the worker could build—whether in the Italian village outside Starkville or a Mexican pueblo at Aguilar—with the house the company built; the company did not mention, of course, that adobe was much better insulated than frame. The propaganda shows the nice orderly company camps and set the photograph to make the workers' own housing look chaotic by comparison. The company does not—but the authors do—emphasize the origins of the company towns as a response to the 1894 coal miners' strike, and the creation of closed camps and various social services designed to prevent the resurgence of union identity.

But among the most significant of departures of the twenty-first-century literature is that it tends to emphasize not the battle at Ludlow and the victimization of the women and children, but the ten-day armed uprising of enraged strikers that followed, during which these polyglot strikers merged into a tornadolike force that took over and occupied a huge swathe of southern Colorado, destroying mine property and in some places killing company employees and state militiamen to the extent that reporters called it the beginning of a civil war and President Wilson finally called in the federal troops. Labor radicalism and violence in these works appears as the necessary pushback to the increased power and wealth of corporations and the state's willingness to operate as an arm of the corporation, in which the National Guard was inseparable, by the end of the strike, from the company mine guards it inducted.

Rather than focus on the victims at Ludlow, these works focus on the strikers' efficacy in defining their terms and defending their liberty as men, even as it means recognizing that the violence in southern Colorado was perpetrated by workers as well as employers. They present the workers as strategists and planners, as people who carefully leased land for tent colonies *before* the strike, placing the colonies as close as possible to the mines' entrances, rather than as suddenly evicted strikers scrambling for housing. They present strikers as understanding the larger economic world in which they struggled, making common cause despite the barriers of language, culture, and corporations; staking out their territory literally; and despite their relatively small numbers and meager financial backing, posing a significant threat to the status quo. In short, for these historians, Ludlow holds potential lessons for our own moment of corporate power, international migration, citizen apathy, and national anxiety.

This is not a trivial shifting of the frame. In some of these works it is an attempt to put Ludlow on a par with the uprising of 1877, when workers across the country determined to change the course of the nation from the road it seemed headed down after the Great Compromise of 1876 handed so much power to national corporations and the railroads. In 1877 those railroad workers seized control of entire cities and ran them with some efficacy. Many in the press and many business leaders feared it was the start of a communist revolution, only six years after the failed commune in Paris. This new literature on Ludlow enlarges the meaning of the place, calling attention to choices made about relations between labor, capital, politics, economics, and the land that had lasting significance in shaping the twentieth-century United States, and it presents the workers as active participants rather than passive victims in that discussion.

Within those broader commonalities, of course, the recent works differ in how they frame their story and where they see Ludlow as marking a critical turning point. I cannot within the constraints of this essay, do justice to the virtues of these various works, and I may not be comprehensive. Wolff, whose work I mentioned above as coming out in 2003, uses a larger framework of regional industrialization, and marks the strike as the culmination of the lesson that regional monopoly capitalism did not ensure economic stability. The higher wages in the Wyoming coal fields were well known in the monopolistically held Colorado fields, and workers wanted not just union recognition but the Wyoming wage scale. Yet despite the rapid expansion of coal production in Colorado in the first decade of the twentieth century, things did not look so rosy by 1913. In Wolff's work, production in the southern coal fields of Colorado by both of the major producers (Victor American and CF&I) had already gone flat years before the strike. With labor being among the few costs the corporations could control, coal companies opted for increasingly draconian labor relations: building closed company camps, hiring more company guards, letting wages lag behind the rising cost of living by 50 percent, and ignoring state laws forbidding pay in scrip and mandating an eight-hour day. In the face of the union-organizing drive in 1913, CF&I and Victor American raised wages, abolished scrip, and encouraged workers to select checkweighmen (who determined how much coal a worker had mined) but in the context of the holistic control companies now exercised over the lives of their workers, the workers held out for union recognition. These companies, with enormous war chests and a lack of competition within the state, settled back to outlast the strikers.[9]

They may have won the strike, but they lost the media war. Martelle, in *Blood Passion*, perhaps not surprisingly, sees Ludlow as a turning point in the manipulation of the media—"with each side using the media to turn public opinion its way."[10] His is the first work I've seen that details the venues of various documents on which historians heavily rely—explaining their authors' and newspapers' connections to one side of the strike or another. He takes apart the loaded terms of coverage—"massacre," for example—with its implication of intentional genocide, and he also meticulously follows the newspaper and local source trails to find that the miners killed nearly twice as many men as they lost in their battle with what he agrees was corporate feudalism. But the miners succeeded in dominating the media war. The prevailing image of the miners as victims of corporate violence, for which the women and children smothered in the flames at Ludlow stood as the symbol (though few would argue they were intentionally killed), virtually buried the ten days of miners' violence that followed. This image dominated the media and as a result has dominated the historical record; it was far more likely to garner sympathy for the labor movement and outrage against monopoly capital than would the image of roving bands of armed immigrant strikers.

With Berman's 2007 *Radicalism in the Mountain West, 1890–1920: Socialists, Populists, Miners and Wobblies*, this violence in southern Colorado falls into a larger context of political violence that, although this is a regional story, was hardly limited at this time to the Mountain West.[11] The events at Ludlow occurred in a period of widespread activity—with 1913 alone a year of free-speech fights, strikes, and contested elections in the region, all of which could be violent, when radicals of this region had some clout at the ballot box, held some governors in their sway, and found more acceptance for divergent views of what constituted true Americanism than would be the case four years, and even one hundred years, later. In this depiction, 1913 looks less like the early twenty-first century—indeed it looks like an almost unimaginable era of both ideological tolerance and unspeakable vigilantism.

This is an important corrective to our main story, because it embeds the workers' actions and ideas at Ludlow in a wider ideological dialogue; it allows the workers to go into the strike as political and not just labor actors, with these ideas already in mind, rather than having them emerge spontaneously from the strike. In this story, Ludlow does not stand out and is not a turning point—it is simply one significant battle among many. Even so, Ludlow seems to have stood in a class by itself. In my own research about New Mexico later in the 1910s, I have found constant reference to and fear of a spreading of what were termed the "labor wars" of southern Colorado.[12]

The power of the state looks more contested and less monolithic in this story—when Colorado's governor sees himself as indebted to the socialists, and, as Martelle also makes clear, the corporations greet with disgust the election of Woodrow Wilson in 1912 as president and, to them, worse still, his choice for the first ever secretary of labor in 1913, the year the strike at Ludlow began. Wilson chose a former United Mine Worker secretary-treasurer, William B. Wilson. It was this federal regime and its investigation of the strike, well before Ludlow, and then its hearings afterward, that helped shape public sympathy for the strikers and helped them win the media war, though by the time Wilson sent federal troops to Colorado, the strike was largely lost.

Andrews offers the most profound temporal context for the strike. His work draws on recent trends in history—including transnational approaches in his discussion of the immigrant workforce, and linking environmental history with labor history. In his well researched, elegantly and engagingly written, and prize-winning study, *Killing for Coal: America's Deadliest Labor War* (2008), Andrews reaches back to geologic time.[13] At the center of his narrative is the shift in the region from biopower to coal and the energy economy that swirls around it. In a dynamic that should sound familiar to us in our current oil economy, he finds that it was our increasingly insatiable demand for energy and our panicky willingness to go to great lengths, including trampling on various liberties, to avoid stoppages in energy supply that landed us on the contested ground of Ludlow and its aftermath.

In Andrews's version, the most comprehensive study to date, the lines drawn are blurrier. Even the seemingly parasitic company store comes in for revision. Colorado's company stores often offered lower prices than the local small shops, and a wider range of goods, which appealed to mining families. At the same time, those company stores failed to establish a monopoly, as peddlers continued to vend their wares in company towns. In the wake of virulent strikes in the 1890s, company control did reach into every aspect of miners' lives, but company housing and conditions did improve as well. The issue, however, was not simply wages and conditions. All the Americanization efforts, all the sociological programs, all the benefits did not outweigh what Andrews defines as the perpetual demands of the miners: "Safety, fellowship, a higher quality of life, autonomy dignity, and basic freedoms."[14]

In 2008, the same year as Andrews's book, came the culmination of the effort begun in 2003 to have the memorial at Ludlow named a National Historic Landmark. I return to that effort now, because in the process of making that case, the scholars involved not only drew on the relatively

FIGURE 1.1. Ludlow Monument (courtesy of Mary Kathleen Rose)

new field of history and memory, but traveled through a political process that led them to place a different set of actors in the foreground than has the recent literature outlined above. In an article on the process involved in the application for landmark status, Elizabeth Jameson and James Green, professors of history and members of the committee that undertook this work, wrote that "committee members' own interpretations of the Ludlow Massacre and their feelings about the importance of that history sometimes had to be reconciled with NHL [National Historic Landmark] significance criteria, and with the politics of achieving NHL designation."[15]

They worked with the National Park Service to understand what would constitute sufficient national significance and evidence supporting it. Like the other historians of the twenty-first century, "Some committee members felt strongly that the statement of significance should not be limited to a 'battles, dates, and outcomes' history of industrial conflict, but that social histories that included the processes of class formation, and the social organization of the tent colony should be included." And they further focused on "how it functioned as a multi-racial community that included women and families." The committee worked to translate their ideas about historical significance into a two-page statement that would be easily understood by nonhistorians. In parallel, they worked with an archaeologist to establish the archaeological significance of the site. In 2005, then US senator from Colorado Ken Salazar (later secretary of the interior) and his brother Congressman John Salazar, from the Pueblo district, promised to provide support in Washington. John Rodriguez, a senatorial aid, hoped that success with landmark status would open possibilities for government funding for enhancing the area "as an educational site devoted to the history of immigrants in western industrial development."[16]

The committee began with four major points of national historical significance: first, Ludlow "as the apex of a long series of western mining strikes that pitted employers, workers, and the state against one another." "The end of the strike," it continued, "which killed women and children, provided the context for checks on uses of state force, and from the perspective of employers and the state, for finding new ways to manage industrial relations and contain unions." The second point was the development of the company union model that emerged from the strike. The third point was the organizational strategy of the strike: leasing the land for the colonies and including the leadership and participation of all represented language groups and of women. The fourth point was the cultural significance of the strike and site "as a catalyst for memory and identification among contemporary workers

FIGURE 1.2. Names on the Ludlow Monument (courtesy of Mary Kathleen Rose)

and Mexican Americans in particular," as well as the national impact made by figures such as Upton Sinclair, who wrote two novels about the strike.[17]

Part of what is interesting to me about this list is the focus on two groups largely left out of the twenty-first century literature as significant actors in the strike: Mexican Americans and women. I want to end this essay by discussing first the one and then the other. Some of the recent works refer to the strikers as largely Italians and Greeks, though Greeks, despite their high profile and Louis Tikas's leadership, fell far behind American-born Anglos, Italians, and Austrians, and those labeled "Mexicans," who were almost entirely US citizens from Colorado and New Mexico. Despite the entire industrial enterprise coming onto a landscape that was predominantly Mexican American in the early twentieth century, none of the recent works foreground, and some don't even mention, the role of Mexican Americans in the strike, not just as the majority of the burned victims at Ludlow, but as numbered among the strike leaders as well. And while there is some mention of coethnics outside the mine in terms of Italians and others and their role in supplying miners, there is no mention of the crucial role played by Mexican Americans in this regard.[18] In the twenty-first-century literature on the strike, all immigrant groups are more or less on a par, and Mexican Americans are difficult to place, neither immigrant nor, somehow, belonging solidly in the nonimmigrant camp, much as they were seen by their corporate employers of the day.

In the foregrounding of some previously missing crucial elements of the history that have brought important new insights, other landscapes have receded. It behooves us to bring these aspects into dialogue with each other. These are not, after all, separate stories, and nothing better illustrates that than when on April 18, 2008, Senator Salazar submitted on behalf of himself and Senator Jay Rockefeller of West Virginia "A Bill to Designate the Ludlow Massacre National Historic Landmark in the State of Colorado." Salazar noted:

> The events that occurred during the Ludlow Massacre, and the site that memorializes the conflict, are central to our nation's story. The history is still significant to the Coloradans who live and work in the region. Residents of Las Animas, Huerfano and Pueblo counties, along with many people across America, rightly see the 1913–14 coal strike and the Ludlow Massacre as a defining moment in our shared history and integral to the region's identity. I am proud to introduce the bill in the Senate and will continue to work to ensure it is designated as a national landmark, so that we can better remember the struggles and sacrifices our nation endured on the path to safer and fairer labor conditions.[19]

FIGURE 1.3. Tent cellar at the Ludlow Monument (courtesy of Mary Kathleen Rose)

It is no accident that the bill's sponsors were Salazar and Rockefeller. By cosponsoring, Rockefeller acknowledged his family's part in that history, when John D. Rockefeller Sr. and Jr. controlled CF&I. And, most pertinent for my point here, Salazar's "family history traces the roots of many Ludlow miners."[20]

It is important, particularly at this moment, to bring back together the insights of these new twenty-first-century histories with the critical context of Mexican American history in the region. While Italian mine workers constructed Italian alpine villages in the area surrounding some of the coal camps, the Mexican pueblos in the area predated the coal extraction and starkly illustrate the impact of monopoly coal production on the land and as well as on the structure of social life. During the period of the strike, Las Animas County was still about one-quarter Mexican American. The mines were embedded in an increasingly economically marginalized pastoral hinterland dominated by Mexican Americans who sent family members to work in the mines and who, in times of strike, helped support them. The percentage of Mexican Americans was even higher in the county seat, Trinidad, where they ran two Spanish-language weekly newspapers, and their presence as voters, both women and men, loomed disproportionately large since many of the immigrant miners could not vote. As with other groups—Anglos, Italian immigrants, Japanese immigrants, and Mexican nationals—Mexican Americans showed up on both sides of the strike.[21]

Now, when Mexican immigration continues to be a hot-button issue, when proof of citizenship is far more likely to be demanded of Mexican Americans than of Irish Americans (despite the large undocumented Irish population in Boston), it is particularly important to integrate analytically and materially the complexity of the group of US citizens involved in the strike. It is equally important to emphasize not just a picture of polyglot immigrant strikers creating a new community in the mines (not at all the one the Rockefellers had in mind), but to emphasize the collaborations as well as tensions, as Ronald L. Mize's essay on CF&I's Wyoming Company town and Greg Patmore's essay on the steel industry in Colorado and Nova Scotia in this volume illuminate, that brought immigrant and nonimmigrant together in defense of their rights as workers.

Similarly, all these twenty-first-century authors recognize that had women and children not been killed at Ludlow, it might have had no larger profile

FIGURE 1.4. Statue of the Mother and Child at the Ludlow Monument (courtesy of Mary Kathleen Rose)

than any other violent strike. The ability to pose the women and children (who were seldom named lest the Italian and Mexican names interfere with compassion) as "innocent" victims of state- and corporate-sponsored violence was critical to the media war. Yet women, like the men of the strike, were everywhere, and not just under the tents. They were strategists, protesters, warriors, and marchers. They show up in these twenty-first-century books keeping house in the tent colonies, fighting strikebreakers, and marching on the governor's office and the National Guard. They show up as reporters covering Ludlow for the state and national press, as state legislative representatives, and as commissary managers.

Yet they are not yet analytically integrated in these books—at times they are simply there, too, and at times they are not. This is a pretty macho story in its twenty-first-century version. Except for their appearance as victims, their existence *as* women is not important in the works' explanation of the dynamics in southern Colorado. There are questions still to ask here, even beyond the household economy and regional diversity that were covered in some of the 1980s literature. When women did march as women, who directed them? The *New York Times* reported on May 14, 1914, on "The Wild Women of Colorado." Mrs. Alma V. Lafferty, ex-member of the Colorado legislature, it revealed, threatened to have five thousand suffragists march on the Colorado capital unless they received some answers and action on their report regarding Ludlow. The *Times* coverage was highly critical, seeing the threat as a good reason not to put women in politics, posing it as irrational, and asking who was looking after the kids. How integral was Lafferty's march to the larger set of strategies? How connected were these developments to the broader context of New Womanhood and woman suffrage battles beginning, again, to be won after the doldrums that ended in 1911. Did it matter that women in Colorado had been voting since 1896? Did it matter that Helen Ring Robinson represented them in the state legislature and that the protest leaders included ex-legislators? Did it matter what publics it allowed miners to mobilize? Did it matter to how they saw their own intervention? Did it create different possibilities of alliance?

In another episode, how did the working-class women who marched to liberate Mother Jones understand their intervention? We know that the men who opposed them placed the marchers on the governor's office in the context of wild women and suffragettes—they meant to pose them with the other radical dangers of the era. They were not necessarily wrong. It is crucial to remember that the radicalism of women's suffrage was not separate from the other radicalism of the era—the broader demand for an expansion and redefinition of democracy. Women Suffragists were deeply implicated in most radical and reform groups across a wide spectrum, and the reverse was also true, with critical alliances springing up between labor unions and women's rights activists across the US West. How did the union men with whom they were allied (sometimes in marriage) see them when they marched and when the women rushed out to obstruct the strikebreakers? And, finally, how crucial were the women in maintaining the sorts of networks on which striking miners would rely and build community and the resources to survive a prolonged strike? And what happened to these working-class women and their daughters afterward? No more than the men were they mired in some timeless construct of family and worker even while, as Robin C. Henry's and Fawn-Amber Montoya's chapters in this volume ably demonstrate, the coal companies may have wished it so. Moreover, they too had been mobilized into a particular energy economy, but perhaps their relation to it differed from that of the men. The work of gender in environmental studies is still in its infancy, and far more developed regarding masculinity and men than it is for women. There are exciting new avenues to be explored here.

The chapters in this volume focus on the employers' attempts to mold, as Henry puts it, "a more perfect worker" both before and after Ludlow with strategies ranging from eugenics to employee representation plans. In doing so, they place back in the frame of Ludlow's legacy both women as objects of manipulation, as mothers—eugenically good and bad—and as reformers; and Mexicans, both immigrant and citizen as objects of corporate managers who saw them outside the parameters of desirable citizens but useful

FIGURE 1.5. View of the Spanish Peaks from the Ludlow Monument (courtesy of Mary Kathleen Rose)

as antiunion devices, and as agents of their own destiny, as labor organizers, wounded workers, and allies in struggles for equity. In short, they have begun the work of bringing the strands of historiography together and demonstrate that the state of the field of research on Ludlow is exhilarating—fresh in its insights and generative of yet more questions.

## NOTES

1. Marilynn S. Johnson, ed., *Violence in the West: The Johnson County Range War and Ludlow Massacre* (Boston: Bedford / St. Martin's, 2008).

2. Zeese Papanikolas, *Buried Unsung: Louis Tikas and the Ludlow Massacre* (Salt Lake City: University of Utah Press, 1982). See also the 1991 University of Nebraska Press version with foreword by Wallace Stegner.

3. Sarah Deutsch, *No Separate Refuge: Culture, Class and Gender on an Anglo-Hispanic Frontier in the American Southwest, 1880–1940* (Oxford: Oxford University Press, 1987); Priscilla Long, *Where the Sun Never Shines: A History of America's Bloody Coal*

*Industry* (New York: Paragon House, 1989); Howard M. Gitelman, *The Legacy of the Ludlow Massacre: A Chapter in American Industrial Relations* (Philadelphia: University of Pennsylvania Press, 1988).

4. See Susan Monroe, http://canadaonline.about.com/cs/primeminister/p/pmking.htm, for more discussion of these favored social programs, including unemployment insurance, old age pensions, and family allowance, and also favored freer trade with the United States.

5. James Green and Elizabeth Jameson, "Marking Labor History on the National Landscape: The Restored Ludlow Memorial and Its Significance," *International Labor and Working Class History* 76 (Fall 2009): 6–25.

6. Ibid., 8.

7. See, for example, Lisette Alvarez, "Army Effort to Enlist Hispanics Draws Recruits and Criticism: Recruiting Latinos Has Become one of the Army's top Priorities," *New York Times*, February 9, 2006, 1, 22. On immigrants, see, for example, "We do want Immigrants—Legal Ones," *Raleigh News and Observer*, February 13, 2006. "Farmers Avoid Migrants Union Contract," *Raleigh News and Observer*, February 14, 2006, discussed farmers' seeking undocumented workers over the legal ones in the union.

8. Scott Martelle, *Blood Passion: The Ludlow Massacre and Class War in the American West* (New Brunswick, NJ: Rutgers University Press, 2008), 45.

9. David A. Wolff, *Industrializing the Rockies: Growth, Competition, and Turmoil in the Coalfields of Colorado and Wyoming, 1868–1914* (Boulder: University Press of Colorado, 2003).

10. Martelle, *Blood Passion*, 3.

11. David R. Berman, *Radicalism in the Mountain West, 1890–1920: Socialists, Populists, Miners and Wobblies* (Boulder: University Press of Colorado, 2007).

12. For examples, see *Albuquerque Morning Journal*, July 1917. Note, too, that at the conference Cecil Roberts, president of the United Mine Workers and Vice President, AFL-CIO, in his address reminded us of a similar battle in Matewan, West Virginia, in 1920.

13. Thomas G. Andrews, *Killing for Coal: America's Deadliest Labor War* (Cambridge, MA: Harvard University Press, 2008).

14. Ibid., 231.

15. Green and Jameson, "Marking Labor History on the National Landscape, 15."

16. Ibid., 15.

17. Ibid., 16.

18. For examples, see Deutsch, *No Separate Refuge*, 87–106.

19. Green and Jameson, "Marking Labor History on the National Landscape,"20.

20. Ibid.

21. Deutsch, *No Separate Refuge*, 87–106.Andrews, *Killing for Coal*, 188, discusses the erection of Hispano adobes on company land in the late nineteenth century; 206–7, the baleful consequences of mine expansion on local small farms, destroying the farm owners' land between 1900 and 1904; and 201–11, the destruction of "Mexican" housing in favor of company housing, but by the time he turns to Ludlow, these local "Mexicans" outside of the camps no longer seem to be part of the story.

TWO

# Dr. Richard Corwin and Colorado's Changing Racial Divide

*Brian Clason and Jonathan Rees*

The Pueblo Hall of Fame is housed in College Hall on the campus of Pueblo Community College. One of its inductees is Dr. Richard Warren Corwin, the former chief surgeon of Colorado Fuel and Iron Company (CF&I), the largest private employer in the state at the time he died in 1930. The plaque under Corwin's picture calls him "an ideal physician, an exemplary community advocate, and a marvelous combination of genius, energy, generosity and executive ability." A local middle school and the St. Mary–Corwin Regional Medical Center are named for him. "Many of his innovative concepts made a big impact on the care of Pueblo citizens," explains the plaque.[1] The preeminent historian of CF&I, H. Lee Scamehorn, has written that "Corwin's emphasis on community and social betterment reflected Progressive Era middle-class concerns for Americanizing recent immigrants, who constituted the majority of the workforce" at the company.[2] Besides his concern about Americanizing some recent immigrants, Corwin's belief in eugenics strongly demonstrated that he cared little for Americanizing others, especially the ones who were not white. By studying every aspect of Corwin's attitude

DOI: 10.5876/9781607323105.c002 

toward race, historians can better understand race relations in Colorado at a time when the Mexican and Mexican American population of the state was sharply increasing.

Francis Galton, a half-cousin of Charles Darwin, coined the term *eugenics* in 1883. It refers to a pseudoscientific philosophy that promotes an intelligent and healthy human race through the manipulation of heredity. Specific manipulations of heredity by eugenicists included forced sterilization, forced institutionalization, forced abortion, and euthanasia. Eugenics flourished during the early 1900s as a response to the influx of eastern and southern Europeans into America, since these immigrants were seen as a threat to the quality of the American gene pool. In an era named after the widespread hunt for continual progress, many believers in eugenics sought this goal through identifying the weak, the criminal, the feebleminded, and the sick. Once identified, they wanted either medical science or the state acting through medical science to prevent persons labeled in this manner from reproducing, or at least reproducing with the superior genetic stock of native-born Americans. Perhaps the most prominent practitioner of this ideology in Colorado during its heyday was Dr. Richard Warren Corwin.

Investigating Corwin's ideas about race is not an easy task. Race was an incredibly fluid concept during Corwin's lifetime. It not only referred to the color of a person's skin, but sometimes ethnicity or even a group of people's collective intelligence. While there is an archive at the hospital that now bears his name, there are no Corwin papers available for research. However, a gigantic archive of material related to the CF&I has opened for research in recent years. Archivists have found no specific Corwin papers there either, but clues to his beliefs do exist in those collections, particularly in the published records of the Sociological Department Corwin ran. Corwin's available eugenics-related statements suggest a broader effort at achieving white solidarity against a growing Mexican and Mexican American population that eugenic supporters saw as a threat. That perceived threat arose not from simple racism, but from couching those racist beliefs in the cover of a pseudoscience that strengthened greatly over the last two decades of Corwin's life. The purpose in describing Corwin's beliefs is not to deride the legacy of a man who did so many positive things for Puebloans of all races, but to illustrate the changing racial divide in southern Colorado from the early 1910s through the late 1920s.

## Life and Career

Richard Corwin was born in Binghamton, New York, to Walter Scott Corwin and the former Rhoda Little on May 24, 1852. While growing up, he had a deep interest in observing wildlife and enjoyed taxidermy as a hobby. Corwin's skill in taxidermy led him to Cornell University, where he received his formal education and was appointed taxidermist. In the years between 1874 and 1878, Corwin held the position of curator at the museum at Michigan University, where he taught anatomy, composition, and microscopy. During the same time, Corwin studied at the University of Michigan's Medical Department, from which he graduated in 1878. Following Corwin's stint at Michigan University, he interned for one year at Saint Luke's Hospital in Chicago, Illinois. In various years, Corwin studied overseas at European hospitals, becoming educated in hospital management and construction. Following his brief stint in Chicago, Corwin attempted to join a three-year expedition to South America as a physician and naturalist, but the expedition failed to depart.

Soon after the failed expedition to South America, the Colorado Coal and Iron Company (which would later be known as the Colorado Fuel and Iron Company) hired him to organize its medical department in Pueblo, Colorado. He arrived there in 1881 to find a workforce of about two thousand men in the steelworks and a severely inadequate medical facility. The only place that resembled a hospital was a "company house known as No. 8 Bessemer near the small iron furnace [that] was converted into a hospital."[3] The following year, 1882, revealed the true weakness of the No. 8 hospital conversion, when an increase of steel workers brought with them a typhoid epidemic. The epidemic prompted the Colorado Coal and Iron Company and the Denver and Rio Grande Railroad Company to build a hospital that could accommodate thirty patients at a time.

Corwin worked for CF&I from 1881 to 1928. While there, he embraced his position as chief surgeon of the Medical Department and Superintendent of the Sociological Department. In this capacity, Corwin managed the remarkable growth of CF&I's hospital while simultaneously improving its standard of care. When Corwin arrived in town, the Medical Department had only two physicians that cared for over two hundred workers and their families. With support from CF&I superintendent John Osgood, Corwin led CF&I

FIGURE 2.1 Richard W. Corwin and staff, 1902 (courtesy of the Bessemer Historical Society / CF&I Archives)

in a medical revolution, and by February 1902 the Medical Department had increased to "38 surgeons who cared for 60,000 persons—employees and their families—at the thirty-eight mines and mills in Colorado, Wyoming, and New Mexico."[4] With the influx of CF&I jobs and European immigrants, Corwin supervised the expansion of the Minnequa Hospital on the shores of Minnequa Lake in Pueblo. Minnequa Hospital replaced the old 1901 hospital located on the east end of Abriendo Avenue. Corwin maintained the latest and most technologically advanced surgical equipment. Many observers lauded his hospital for its superb examination tables, X-ray machines, steam sterilizers, and building architecture that allowed for maximum sunlight to enter, the movement of fresh air within the building, and handicap access points.

## The Pre–World War I Record

Colorado Coal and Iron created the Sociological Department in 1901 specifically to resolve racial and ethnic differences that had led to a strike at CF&I that same year. In its earlier years, the department stressed Americanization designed to bring people together, not racial differences designed to tear them apart.[5] According to Scamehorn, Corwin ran the department with concerns that went well beyond those of an ordinary company surgeon. "In numerous ways," Scamehorn writes, "the sociological department improved the quality of life in communities. It concentrated its efforts on education, domestic and industrial training, and leisure activities."[6] Corwin's interest in both the medical and social well-being of CF&I's employees made him a pioneering American practitioner of welfare capitalism. Welfare capitalism (called "welfare work" at the turn of the twentieth century) is the name historians give programs that companies instituted for their employees that are not necessary to attract and keep employees based on the demands of the labor market.

As Corwin's Medical and Sociological Departments flourished in the early 1900s, CF&I struggled with debt until John D. Rockefeller Jr. bought the company. Rockefeller Jr. was the son of the famous oil baron who oversaw the family's many far-flung investments after the elder Rockefeller retired, including CF&I. In response to an economic downturn in 1908, management cut the Sociological Department budget drastically because the department expenses were seen as unnecessary. These cuts in funding posed a serious threat to Corwin and his work trying to boost employee morale, motivation, and safety. However, with Rockefeller Jr. attempting to pull CF&I out of debt, the demand for productive and able-bodied workers created pressure upon Corwin to reduce worker injuries and maintain a healthy workforce that could turn out better production in the mines and mills. Rockefeller influenced industrial relations at CF&I in different ways too. Rockefeller Jr. spent at least one hundred million dollars on eugenics-related programs nationwide long before the popularity of this racist ideology peaked.[7] Some of that money went to improve the eugenics-related programs at CF&I's Sociological Department. This included money for eugenics, heredity, and Americanization lectures in CF&I-owned camps even after the cuts to the department's budget took place. This suggests the importance of eugenics to both Rockefeller and Corwin alike.

The CF&I Archives in Pueblo is not completely processed yet, and no Corwin-related papers have yet been found. However, Corwin left a published record that documents his belief in eugenics. One part of this record comes from his involvement with public education in Pueblo. In his 1913 *Report of the Joint Committee on Health Problems in Education*, Corwin shows great anger in response to a study that analyzed the sanitation of rural school districts throughout the United States. In the course of this discussion, he makes his position on eugenics crystal clear: "The average rural schoolhouse in relation to its purpose is not as well kept or as healthful as a good stable, dairy barn, pigpen, or chicken-house. But what more could be expected from a government that creates a cabinet department for animals but fails to recognize one for man; that appropriates millions for brute heredity and little or nothing for human eugenics?" As he continues, he describes the threat to the white race in more explicit terms:

> In our schools we find 2 percent of children known to be feeble-minded; in some schools, they average as high as 30 percent—and this does not include the morons, the higher class of defectives: . . . it is well known that the feeble-minded constitute the major portion of criminals, prostitutes, epileptics, drunkards, neurotics, paupers . . . found in and out of prisons; and that in a large number of our states the mentally defective are cared for when young but when reaching maturity and most dangerous are turned loose upon the community to become parents of a class, with each generation becoming more depraved. If for the next hundred years our schools would discontinue all higher and aesthetic education and devote their energy to improving the human stock; to feeding and breeding; to teaching that acquired traits die with the body, that inherited traits pass to the next generation, and that the laws of heredity are constant and are the same for bug and man . . . and to educating the people to know that environment is important but heredity more important, and eugenics most important, and that thru eugenics is the only hope of improving our race or saving our nation—if this were done, at the end of the century we should find the people not only 100 years older but 100 percent better, stronger, and wiser.[8]

The children of immigrants overwhelmingly dominated the schools Corwin dealt with at CF&I coal camps and in Pueblo. This response blames the poor sanitation conditions in these schools on the racial characteristics of the students. Mentioning eugenics is a logical response for someone who believes that the environment these children lived in is a direct result of their genes.

In other pronouncements, Corwin couched concern for the race in terms related to citizenship. This was a common tactic for eugenicists trying to alarm native-born whites about the threat of race mixing. In *The Administration of Health Departments—The Colorado Plan*, from 1913, Corwin notes that the child of today is the citizen of tomorrow and that it is the schools' responsibility to report on the physical, mental, and moral defectiveness of any and all children attending school:

> Many now know and understand but are lacking in the very mental qualifications that make for good and best; not until there is progress in moral mentality can there be racial improvement . . . we spend $32,000,000 annually upon the insane and encourage them to multiply their kind by giving them their liberty; we expend immense sums upon the feeble-minded, keep them under control when harmless, and turn them loose to reproduce more fools when of the age to become parents; in like manner we deal with the criminal, the epileptic, the alcoholic, and the prostitute, who are mental and moral defectives, permitting them to propagate their type . . . We teach environment and neglect heredity. We are a success at feeding but a failure at breeding.

For him, the solution to this problem was to teach eugenics in schools (presumably to white students since children who were threats to society would have been identified and isolated):

> The value of environment cannot be overestimated—it should be taught in every grade and by expert teachers, especially prepared; but of more importance is the teaching of the science of heredity. Heredity begins at the beginning; it is the foundation of existence; environment, the superstructure of life. We should teach better heredity—eugenics; every school and every grade should have instruction in heredity and eugenics. The cause of feeble-mindedness, criminality, epilepsy, alcoholism, pauperism, and prostitution should be known and the prevention understood. The cure cannot be brought about thru environment; *upon eugenics rests the salvation of the race*. (Emphasis added)[9]

Could he have been any more clear? Perhaps unrestrained from the need to keep even the most racially inferior workers happy and productive, Corwin let his true feelings show. Starting during the World War I period, the preserved record shows how Corwin's support for eugenics explicitly affected the policies of CF&I.

## Eugenics at CF&I

The other part of Corwin's published record that demonstrates his belief in eugenics comes from the reports he published as head of the Sociological Department and hospital at CF&I. During 1917 and 1918, CF&I experienced a reduction in laborers, nurses, and doctors as the United States entered World War I. That loss could not have come at a worse time. In 1918, a worldwide influenza epidemic that left many dead swept through CF&I towns and camps, overwhelming an understaffed medical department. Corwin's "Annual Report of Chief Surgeon" to CF&I President J.F. Welborn pushed for more efficiency within the Medical Department at CF&I during this tumultuous time. The recent influenza epidemic heightened Corwin's eugenics-influenced beliefs that sanitation and hygiene standards within the CF&I towns were not being upheld due to the unfit and feebleminded. In response to the lack of sanitation and hygiene that Corwin perceived at the hospital, he issued a three-tiered classification system that separated those who were willing and able from those who were feebleminded and unfit:

1. Those who know, have self-control, feel a moral responsibility, and exert every effort to protect themselves and others.
2. Those who know, but do not care, are indifferent, morally weak, shun responsibility, and protect neither self nor neighbor.
3. Those mentally feeble, unable to comprehend or reason, have no power of resistance, and are a constant source of annoyance and danger.

Corwin noted that the first class should be given every protection possible, the second class should be educated and reformed if possible, and the third class "should be guarded and protected. The state should care for the feeble-minded . . . those needing asylum . . . for life. The law cannot be too stringent for the benefit and protection of those who "can" for the benefit of the race."[10] Corwin's hospital saved thousands of Puebloans—including many who did not work for CF&I—during the epidemic, but they might have done even more if not for this kind of policy.

In 1922, Corwin announced the need for mental examinations to screen for the unfit among the applicants for employment at CF&I, referencing the army's use of mental tests, along with schools and juvenile courts that used them as well. A letter sent to Corwin from an unnamed court examiner states, "I am testing in the Juvenile Courts and Clinics of [name of city left out] and have not found one normal child mentally among those delinquents. With rare exception the cause of mental deficiency is hereditary."[11] Corwin questioned the whereabouts of the delinquent child's parents and where the parents were employed; implying that the parents were the cause of the child's delinquency due to poor genetics and poor nurturing. Corwin continued to imply that the parents also needed to take a mental examination and possibly be protected from society if found to be feebleminded and unfit. But Corwin's announcement of the need for mental testing was nothing new. As America emerged from the Civil War, Reconstruction efforts for the newly freed black slaves met opposition from southern states engaging in disfranchisement. Disfranchisement segregated blacks in the South and made voting impossible through the implementation of literacy tests. Mental exams at CF&I bore a striking resemblance to the literacy tests southern blacks faced, since both tests aimed at disempowering a class considered weak and inferior to the white elite.

In 1927, just as eugenics had passed its peak in popularity and shortly before Corwin's death, he accepted a nomination to be part of the Colorado Eugenics Committee.[12] The purpose of the Colorado Eugenics Committee was to create pro-eugenics propaganda and push eugenics legislation through the state of Colorado. The last of Corwin's eugenics-laden publications in the *Industrial Bulletin* and *Camp & Plant* would come in 1928. In the September 1928 edition of the *Industrial Bulletin*, Corwin spoke of eugenics by referencing Chicago-based Dr. William J. Hickson's assessment that "the criminal is a 'primitive'—he is a primitive man, underdeveloped in a part of his brain structure. This whole problem is a hereditary problem."[13] Corwin died in 1930. He did not live long enough to see the racial ground in Southern Colorado and the country's attitude toward eugenics shift.

## Colorado's Changing Racial Divide

As late as the 1890s, the majority of Colorado coal miners were native-born Americans or immigrants of English, Scottish, Welsh, or Irish descent. A severe labor shortage, as well as the threat of strikes, led mine owners to recruit immigrants from southern and eastern Europe and especially Mexico. They hoped that racial and ethnic divisions within the workforce would make it impossible for workers of all kinds to unite. Mexican immigration to the United States began to accelerate before World War I started, but grew into a huge influx during the 1920s. After a brief lull during the economic downturn of 1921, the number of Mexicans crossing into the United States accelerated again in 1923, quickly passing the wartime rate even though much of the immigration was now illegal.[14] Between 1920 and 1930, a time when the number of foreign migrants to Colorado dropped dramatically, the Mexican population of the state increased by 400 percent.[15] On August 1, 1918, approximately 20 percent of CF&I's miners were Mexican or Mexican American.[16] After strikes in 1919 and 1921, as many as 60 percent of the company's new hires in both the mines and the mill were people of Spanish/Mexican ancestry. Nationwide immigration restrictions on Europeans instituted by Congress in 1921 and 1924 assured that CF&I would have to employ a sizable number of these non-European immigrants for many years to come.

In the early twentieth century, Coloradoans generally divided the Hispanic population of the state into three groups: "Spanish," "Spanish Americans" and "Mexicans." As Paul S. Taylor explained in his comprehensive 1929 study of Mexican sugar beet workers in Colorado's Platte River Valley, "The term Spanish American as used among the laboring classes is confined almost entirely to the Spanish or Indo-Spanish descendants of the inhabitants of Southern Colorado and New Mexico prior to 1848 when they became part of the United States . . . Most Americans refer to them all as "Mexicans" quite indiscriminately."[17] In Colorado, these Mexican Americans made up 57.1 percent of the "Mexican" population in the 1930 census.[18] Miners and steelworkers, who dealt with this population at work every day, recognized this distinction more often than other Coloradoans. They generally referred to these more Americanized Mexicans as "Old Mexico Mexicans," meaning that they had been in this country so long that when their families first arrived, it was still Mexico. Taylor documented considerable tensions between Mexicans and Mexican Americans of both types during this era. Colorado Fuel and Iron Company, which had tracked the ethnic and racial background of its workers in this kind of detail for decades, had an interest in keeping all ethnic and racial tensions at a minimum so that their business could function properly. "No one can read the list of names of our employees without being impressed with the fact that many of them have come from other countries," declared the *Industrial Bulletin* in 1924. "Among all of these are many of the finest men one will meet in a lifetime."[19] The fact that they still felt the need to make such a declaration speaks to the intractability of this problem at both the mines and the mill. The tide of post–World War I Mexican immigration had upset the racial equilibrium that had existed before the conflict began.

If Corwin's status as a reformer and eugenics enthusiast seems contradictory, it is worth noting that it is entirely typical of many Progressives. The historian Daniel Bender has detailed the similar worldviews of Progressives and eugenicists, arguing that "eugenics inherited much from reform. Not only did numerous reformers move increasingly to eugenics by the late 1910s and 1920s but the same contingent of college-educated women who had once served as the backbone of reform had become the field-workers of eugenics." Frustration with new immigrants may be at the heart of this seeming contradiction as eugenics countered a once prevalent desire to help immigrants by placing "the blame for degeneracy squarely on the frail shoulders of workers and immigrants."[20] This seeming contradiction reflected frustration among reformers who came to see the immigrants they once wanted to assist as beyond help. Like his employer, Rockefeller Jr., Corwin was on the front lines of an unsuccessful labor reform effort at CF&I—the Industrial Representation Plan—better known as the Rockefeller Plan. Despite giving workers democratic rights, the coal miners there struck repeatedly during the 1910s and 1920s, while the steelworkers, struck only once but repeatedly protested the operation of Corwin's department.[21] Lowering his opinion of the workers he was supposed to help was a lot easier than developing labor reforms that all workers would fully accept.

While Corwin's belief in eugenics should not discount all of what he did for Pueblo, it is worth remembering that his reforms did more for some Puebloans than for others. As the economist Thomas C. Leonard writes of reformers like Corwin, "It is a temptation to regard progressive thought of a century ago as akin to contemporary progressivism, but Progressive Era progressives viewed the poor and disenfranchised with great ambivalence. Many clearly believed that defective heredity offered a basis for sorting the worthy poor from the unworthy poor and that uplift of the worthy poor required eugenic control of the unworthy poor."[22] In the late nineteenth century, race and ethnicity in America meant the same thing. Eugenicists—indeed, probably the majority of native-born Americans—assumed that the Polish, Italian, and Slavic workers who appeared on America's shores every day belonged to inferior races despite their white skin. As Corwin's workforce became increasingly Mexican, delineating the worthy from the unworthy poor became much easier as they could be separated by skin color.

## "Positive" vs. "Negative" Eugenics

Supreme Court Justice Oliver Wendell Holmes Jr., Senator Henry Cabot Lodge, President Woodrow Wilson—each believed in eugenics to some degree because this creed dominated sociological thinking during the later part of Corwin's lifetime. But not all these figures supported eugenics for the same reason, or recommended the same policies as a result of that support. Galton's original philosophy of eugenics came to be known as "Positive" Eugenics because it mostly involved improving the numbers and the quality of the babies produced by people belonging to races who eugenicists saw as superior. "Negative" Eugenics, on the other hand, proposed limiting or preventing the breeding of inferior races. The British physician C.W. Salleeby did not coin this second term until 1907, which suggests the darker direction eugenics took during the last two decades of Corwin's life.[23] Belief in Positive Eugenics has harmed but not destroyed the historical reputations of illustrious men. Discovering that a historical figure believed in Negative Eugenics suggests that his/her reputation may need serious revision.

People like Holmes and Lodge, for example, proscribed to Positive Eugenics. President Theodore Roosevelt, among them, wrote in 1902 that "It seems to me that it is a good thing from every standpoint that to let the colored man know that if he shows in marked degree the qualities of good citizenship—the qualities which in a white man we feel are entitled to reward—then he himself would not be cut off from all hope of further reward." While he also wrote that the "great majority of the negroes in the South are wholly unfit for suffrage," his famous dinner in the White House with Booker T. Washington is a testament to his belief that African Americans deserve some civil rights because they were capable of improving themselves.[24] In other words, Roosevelt's belief in eugenics was more paternalistic than hostile.

By the end of his life, Corwin subscribed to the kinds of Negative Eugenics beliefs that these other figures never did. For example, he believed that people from inferior races were incapable of improving themselves. Corwin's repeated use of the term *mentally defective*, a common eugenics theme during the mid-1920s, suggest that Corwin supported eugenics more strongly as time passed, even as these ideas increasingly fell out of favor with the public at large. While this insulting term does not have racial overtones today, it did during Corwin's lifetime. It suggests that Corwin feared that "mentally defective" people would harm the sustainability of the white race as a whole. Some of this view may be a function of Corwin's profession. After the passage of the Johnson-Reed Act in 1924, which set low quotas on the number of immigrants to the United States from what were deemed to be countries full of undesirables, anti-immigration reformers began to lobby for limits on immigration from Mexico and Latin America, which was not part of that law. As the historian Alexandra Minna Stern explains, proponents of further restriction often used eugenic terminology in order to make that case.[25]

Corwin's adherence to eugenics also fits well into a larger pattern in the rhetoric of eugenics proponents in general. In his book *Whiteness of a Different Color*, Matthew Frye Jacobson explains that "in general a pattern of racially based, Anglo-Saxon exclusivity dominated the years from 1840 to the 1920s, whereas a pattern of Caucasian unity gradually took its place in the 1920s and after."[26] In Pueblo and in CF&I's coal camps around Southern Colorado, the largely European immigrant workforce of the pre–World War I years quickly gave way to a workforce in which Mexican and Mexican Americans dominated the lowest-paid, most temporary jobs. Corwin's repeated statements about eugenics indirectly but clearly justified this situation, while simultaneously signaling to white ethnics that they too would have an opportunity to rise in the company's employ. After Corwin's death in 1930, the economic situation at CF&I turned so dire that management let go many, perhaps close to all, of their Mexicans and Mexican Americans employees.[27] Whatever hard feelings these workers had about the company's racial attitudes no longer mattered to their former employer.

The movement of African Americans out of the South during the war years and the movement of Mexicans into the Industrial West and Midwest helped separate race and ethnicity in America forever. Second-generation white immigrants, who spoke English without accents, had lived in America long enough to "pass." Miners and millworkers of Mexican descent, whether newly arrived in the United States or whether from families who had lived in Colorado for decades, faced a different situation. Instead of making detailed distinctions between Spanish Americans and recent arrivals, the white population of Colorado, including CF&I (the state's largest private employer) increasingly lumped all people of Mexican descent together into one race, one that many people thought inferior whether they believed in eugenics or not.[28] The rise of the Nazis in Germany did more than anything else to discredit eugenics in the United States, but racism still persists.

The racial makeup of southern Colorado, like our society in general, is changing today just as it was in Corwin's time. The social and economic costs and benefits of immigration are just as hotly contested now as they were then. Corwin's persistent belief in eugenics should remind us that racism persists even as racial classification systems change. More important, it demonstrates how racist philosophy can be continually adapted to fit changing demographic circumstances. Corwin's name remains throughout the Pueblo cityscape because of what he built and as a memory to his medical legacy. His racial legacy, while much more controversial, is still worthy of consideration because of what it can still tell us about race relations in Colorado today. The dynamics underlying immigration and employment in Corwin's day fostered extremist ideologies and disturbing solutions, just like they do now.

## Notes

1. "Dr. Richard Corwin," Pueblo Hall of Fame, inducted March 14, 1992, http://www.pueblocc.edu/AboutUs/Foundation/AnnualFundraiser/1992_Inductees.htm, accessed April 25, 2008.

2. H. Lee Scamehorn, *Mill & Mine: The CF&I in the Twentieth Century* (Lincoln: University of Nebraska Press, 1992), 15.

3. Dr. William Senger, *Colorado and Its People*, vol. 4 (New York: Lewis Historical Publishing Co., 1948). Originally written by Senger sometime before 1948.

4. *Camp & Plant*, Vol. 1, no. 8, p. 105 (digitized copy from the Bessemer Historical Society and CF&I Archives).

5. Sarah Deutsch, *No Separate Refuge: Culture, Class and Gender on an Anglo-Hispanic Frontier in the American Southwest, 1880–1940* (New York: Oxford University Press, 1987), 95–96.

6. H. Lee Scamehorn, *Mill & Mine: The CF&I in the Twentieth Century* (Lincoln: University of Nebraska Press, 1992), 84.

7. Edwin Black, *The War against the Weak: Eugenics and America's Campaign to Create a Master Race* (New York: Four Walls Eight Windows, 2003), 93.

8. R. W. Corwin, "Report of the Joint Committee on Health Problems in Education, National Education Association" (1913): 418–20.

9. R. W. Corwin, "The Administration of Health Departments—The Colorado Plan, National Education Association" (1913): 659–62.

10. R. W. Corwin, "Annual Report of Chief Surgeon," *Industrial Bulletin*, 1918.

11. Ibid., "Chief Surgeons 41st Annual Report," *Industrial Bulletin*, August 15, 1922.

12. Dr. Richard Warren Corwin to American Eugenics Society Secretary, April 17, 1927, Simon Flexner Papers, American Philosophical Society, Philadelphia.

13. R. W. Corwin, Chief Surgeon's 47th Annual Report, vol. 13, no. 6, *Industrial Bulletin*, September 1928.

14. Deutsch, *No Separate Refuge*, 120, 125.

15. Eric Margolis, "Western Coal Mining as a Way of Life," *Journal of the West* 24 (July 1985): 22.

16. Colorado Fuel and Iron Company, "Statement of Nationality of Employees at Coal Mines and Coke Ovens," August 1, 1918, Company Correspondence, Bessemer Historical Society and CF&I Archives.

17. Paul S. Taylor, *Mexican Labor in the United States*, vol. 1 (1930), 212.

18. Ibid., vol. 2 (1933), 49.

19. *Colorado Fuel and Iron Company Industrial Bulletin* 9 (February 15, 1924): 25–26.

20. Daniel E. Bender, *American Abyss: Savagery and Civilization in the Age of Industry* (Ithaca, NY: Cornell University Press, 2009), 10–11.

21. Jonathan Rees, *Representation and Rebellion: The Rockefeller Plan at the Colorado Fuel and Iron Company, 1914–1942* (Boulder: University Press of Colorado, 2010); see esp. chap. 3.

22. Thomas C. Leonard, "Eugenics and Economics in the Progressive Era," *Journal of Economic Perspectives* 19 (Autumn 2005): 218.

23. Ruth Clifford Engs, *The Eugenics Movement: An Encyclopedia* (Westport, CT: Greenwood Press, 2005), 160–61, 182–83.

24. Thomas G. Dyer, *Theodore Roosevelt and the Idea of Race* (Baton Rouge: Louisiana State University Press, 1980), 108–9.

25. Alexandra Minna Stern, *Eugenic Nation: Faults and Frontiers of Better Breeding in Modern America* (Berkeley: University of California Press, 2005), 68.

26. Matthew Frye Jacobson, *Whiteness of a Different Color: European Immigrants and the Alchemy of Race* (Cambridge: Harvard University Press, 1998), 91.

27. Rees, 177.

28. Rees, 89–97.

THREE

# Governor Elias Ammons and the 1913–1914 Southern Colorado Coal Strike

*Anthony R. DeStefanis*

On November 7, 1913, Roady Kenehan, the state auditor of Colorado, left Denver on a train bound for Seattle where the American Federation of Labor (AFL) was holding its annual convention. Kenehan went to the convention as a labor supporter, but getting out of town served another purpose. Kenehan was trying to stymie efforts to raise the funds needed to pay the expenses of the Colorado National Guard. Ten days earlier, Governor Elias Ammons had called the Guard to police a strike by approximately nine thousand coal miners in southern Colorado. The state, however, did not have the money to pay the expenses of a National Guard call out. To solve this problem, Governor Ammons and southern Colorado's coal mine operators, led by Colorado Fuel and Iron Company (CF&I), reached an agreement with several Denver-based banks to make a loan to the state. Roady Kenehan was the monkey wrench in this plan. As state auditor, Kenehan had to authorize dispersal of the loan money and otherwise administer the Guard's expenses. Kenehan skipped town because he thought this financing plan was illegal, but also because, as a union supporter, he strongly suspected that the Guard would

DOI: 10.5876/9781607323105.c003

try to break the coal miners' strike. Indeed, the National Guards were established during the late nineteenth century for the explicit purpose of having an effective strikebreaking force on hand, and they collectively played a crucial role in breaking hundreds of strikes between the end of the Civil War and World War II. In Colorado, the state militia was formed in 1879 and over the next fifty years, the Colorado National Guard was called out on duty twenty-three times. Seventeen of those call-outs brought the Guard into a strike situation, where it almost always acted to break the strike. Kenehan's stunt left Governor Ammons and the mine operators with no choice but to wait for him to return and then haul him into court, where they hoped a judge would force the rebellious state auditor to do his job.[1]

Roady Kenehan's efforts to stop the coal mine operators from using their alliance with Denver's bankers to fund National Guard strike duty highlights the influence that the mining industry enjoyed over Colorado state government by 1913. As we will see, Kenehan's efforts to check this influence failed because he did not, as state auditor, have sufficient authority to stop the mine operators from carrying out their plan to finance the National Guard. Governor Ammons, however, had the sole authority in the state to call out the Guard, and only he could approve the mine operators' financing plan. The Guard, furthermore, acted effectively to break the strike. Thus Ammons is the single most important figure for understanding both why the Colorado National Guard ended up on strike duty and why the 1913–14 southern Colorado coal strike ended in defeat for the miners.

Ammons's actions are also important for understanding why this strike became one of the most violent labor conflicts in US history.[2] At least seventy-five people were killed during this strike and by helping the mine operators break the strike, Guardsmen made themselves the sworn enemies of the striking miners. The Guard's alliance with the mine operators poisoned the relationship between the striking miners and the Guard and led to the Ludlow Massacre, in which fourteen women and children and six striking miners and union officials were killed during a day-long battle between the Colorado National Guard and residents of a tent colony near the Ludlow, Colorado, railroad depot.[3]

Governor Ammons clearly had a tremendous impact on charting the course of this strike. Previous scholarship on the 1913–14 coal strike has portrayed Ammons as hapless and weak, and thus an easy mark for the coal mine operators, who were unrelenting in their determination to break the strike. In essence, these scholars have said that Ammons, who like Roady Kenehan was a Democrat and a supporter of organized labor in Colorado, had the authority to resist the operators that Kenehan lacked, but that the governor lacked the strength of mind and strength of spine that Kenehan displayed in his efforts to stop the National Guard call out.[4]

This critique of Ammons is certainly valid. The governor was indecisive, and he did succumb to the unrelenting pressure from the mine operators to call out the National Guard. This chapter, however, seeks to complicate our understanding of Ammons by exploring two related issues. First, I will explain why Governor Ammons called out the National Guard and then helped perform the financial gymnastics necessary to pay for the Guard's strike duty. This section will indeed show that Ammons was no match for the mine operators, but it will also show the extent to which the mine operators and their allies acted as a class to protect their interests. Placed in this context, it's not at all surprising that the operators were able to compel Ammons to do their bidding.

Second, I will explain why the governor likely abandoned the striking miners and threw his support behind the National Guard once the troops were in the field. Previous scholars of this strike have not addressed this question, but it is an important one because Ammons's support gave the Guard's officers the latitude they needed to help the mine operators break the strike. This question is all the more important because it is surprising that Ammons, a Democrat who was elected in 1912 with labor's support, became an avid defender of the National Guard.[5] One might argue that Ammons's support for the Guard stemmed from the same weaknesses that made him an easy target for the mine operators as they pressured him to call out the National Guard. The record, however, suggests that Ammons decided to back the Guard not because of pressure from the mine operators, but because he thought it was what was best for his political future and because he was not comfortable backing the striking miners, many of whom were recent immigrants, in a showdown with a National Guard that was entirely white, mostly native born, and commanded by an officer corps that was middle and upper class. The governor's discomfort with the immigrant working-class miners, furthermore, also demonstrates that labor was not a helpless victim of his decision to call out the National Guard. Ironically, the labor movement likely played a role in forming the governor's perception of the immigrant miners who suffered from his decision to call out the National Guard and throw his support behind his soldiers once they were on strike duty.

---

That the Colorado National Guard would be able to break the 1913–14 southern Colorado coal strike was by no means a given. Lack of state funding was a chronic problem that only intensified when the Guard was on active duty. In his history of the Colorado National Guard, longtime Guard officer John Nankivell wrote that during the 1913–14 coal strike, the Guard had to cover "an uninviting country larger than the state of Rhode Island . . . All of this vast territory had to be occupied by the military forces . . . to protect the numerous small mining properties and their inhabitants, to maintain the lines of communication, and to checkmate the movements of the roving bands of belligerent strikers."[6] Nankivell served in the National Guard during the 1913–14 coal strike and his biases are obvious, but he was right that the Guard faced a significant challenge in Las Animas and Huerfano Counties, where the strike was centered. Meeting that challenge would require a significant cash outlay to pay, feed, clothe, house, arm, and otherwise equip the Guard. The state of Colorado, however, was in no position to provide this funding in the fall of 1913. According to Governor Ammons, only twenty million of Colorado's sixty-six million acres were on the tax rolls, and just one-eleventh of this territory generated almost all of Colorado's tax revenue. This low level of taxation was, in part, a result of the many sweetheart deals that state officials had cut with industrialists like southern Colorado's coal mine operators. These deals meant that mine operators paid little or no taxes on the land they owned or leased from the state. During the strike, Governor Ammons observed that as a young state—Colorado achieved statehood in 1876—it had "many necessary institutions to build within a brief period of time." "Our burdens of taxation are therefore," he continued, "necessarily great, especially under the policy adopted by my predecessors of withdrawing and withholding lands and resources from . . . taxation." Indeed, the state received only $12,378.67 in yearly taxes from the almost fifty-nine thousand acres of land the state leased to coal mine operators.[7]

Governor Ammons was well aware that the state did not have the between $4,000 and $5,000 per day it would take to support the National Guard on strike duty. There were, however, ways of raising money to fund the Guard. Colorado had floated $900,000 in debt to finance a National Guard call out during strikes by the Western Federation of Miners and the United Mine Workers of America (UMWA) in 1903 and 1904. The state also received financial help from the mining companies involved in those strikes. Colorado Fuel and Iron, several other mining companies, and the pro-business Citizens' Alliances that cropped up during these strikes contributed $200,000 for maintaining the National Guard during the 1903–14 strikes.[8]

Following a familiar path in fall 1913, the mine operators persuaded a group of Denver-based banks known as the Denver Clearing House Association to advance the state an initial $150,000 at 6 percent interest to pay the Guard's expenses. It is likely that the mine operators were able to convince the Clearing House Association to participate in their plan because of the connections Denver's banks had to the mining industry. The First National Bank of Denver, which had deep roots in Colorado's gold-mining industry, was one of the Clearing House's most important members. Eben Smith and David Moffat were major executives at the First National in the 1860s and 1870s, before their Smith-Moffat mining syndicate became a major concern. Moffat eventually served as president of the bank from 1880 to 1911.[9]

By 1913, Lamont Bowers, chairman of CF&I, had also developed close business relationships with the board of directors of several Denver banks. He had good reason for doing so. In late 1912, John D. Rockefeller Jr., whose family owned CF&I, asked Bowers why the company's money was deposited exclusively in Colorado banks when more attractive interest rates were available elsewhere in the country. Bowers told his boss that labor's influence in the Colorado legislature meant laws were introduced there that he claimed "would hamper and cripple our operations and reduce profits to zero." To fight passage of such legislation, CF&I needed the support of Denver's bank directors, who he assured Rockefeller Jr. "play a mighty important part in this state in dictating its laws." Bowers also told Rockefeller, Jr. that he could bribe lawmakers and other important officials for their support, but he found the more effective way of gaining political influence was to simply keep CF&I's money in Denver's banks. "Without our direct solicitation," Bowers informed Rockefeller Jr., "we are able to secure the cordial cooperation of the wealthy officers and stockholders of several influential banks who, for self-interest or for the common good, or both, will give us their support."

Colorado Fuel & Iron's money "is a very important matter to them," Bowers added, "and they will go to great lengths to prevent assaults upon us."[10]

After securing the cooperation of the Denver banks, the mine operators turned to convincing Governor Ammons to accept their financing plan and call out the National Guard. In this mission, the operators had help. Before the strike began, the mine operators had hired the Baldwin-Felts Detective Agency to guard their property and incite violence aimed at forcing Governor Ammons to send in the National Guard to restore order. Because the mining industry dominated political life in Las Animas and Huerfano Counties, Baldwin-Felts had the cooperation of James Grisham and Jefferson Farr, the sheriffs in these two counties, who deputized Baldwin Felts detectives and the mine guards they hired. Baldwin-Felts did its job well. Intense fighting between the striking coal miners on one side, and deputy sheriffs, mine guards, and Baldwin-Felts detectives on the other, broke out shortly after the strike began in late September 1913 and continued into October.[11]

Ending the violence in Las Animas and Huerfano Counties was a constant concern for Ammons. On October 15, the Clearing House Association bankers met with Ammons to formally offer a loan at 6 percent interest and urge the governor to call out the troops.[12] Ammons resisted, but his resistance only brought more pressure from the operators and their banker allies. As this persuasion campaign continued, Bowers told Rockefeller Jr.:

> We have been able to secure the cooperation of all the bankers of the city [Denver], who have had three or four interviews with our little cowboy governor, agreeing to back the State and lend it all the funds necessary to maintain the militia and afford ample protection so that our miners could return to work, or give protection to men who are anxious to come here from Texas, New Mexico, and Kansas, together with some from States farther East. Besides the bankers, the chamber of commerce, the real estate exchange, together with a great many of the best business men, have been urging the Governor to take steps to drive these vicious agitators out of the State.[13]

After the October 15 meeting with the Clearing Association and the mine operators, Ammons told Edward Doyle, Secretary Treasurer of the UMWA's District Fifteen, that if the violence did not stop, he would have no choice but to send in the Guard. Clearly moving in that direction, Ammons met again with the Clearing House Association bankers on October 20 and signed off on their financing plan if he decided to send the Guard to southern Colorado. That option, however, still did not bring the governor any peace, in part, because State Auditor Roady Kenehan had begun publically signaling his opposition to the Clearing House Association's plan for funding a Guard call out. The only decision Ammons could make was that it was time to see for himself what all the fuss was about in the southern part of his state.[14]

Predictably, the violence stopped once Ammons arrived in southern Colorado on October 21, 1913. Indeed, if Ammons had simply moved the state capitol from Denver to Trinidad, the largest town in Las Animas County, he might have permanently quashed the operators' plan for getting him to call out the Guard. Upon his arrival, Ammons encountered a rally of four thousand miners and their supporters. The miners carried signs designed to tell Ammons who was instigating the violence and what they expected from their governor: "We Are Not Afraid of Gatling Guns, We Have to Die Anyway; "You Cannot Whip Us into Citizenship with Sheriffs and Gatling Guns"; and, suggestively, "The Democratic Party is on Trial."[15]

As Ammons toured the coal camps and tent colonies, Frank Hayes, vice president of the UMWA, excoriated the operators and Baldwin-Felts for bringing machine guns into southern Colorado. "I consider the use of machine guns the most outrageous [*sic*] in the history of America," he declared. "The officials of the coal companies ought to instruct their representatives to take them away." In perhaps the biggest understatement of the strike, Hayes asserted that "the appearance of a machine gun is a source of aggravation to the strikers and is not conducive to peace and good order."[16]

On his return to Denver, Ammons said he was glad he had made the trip, but that he had "talked with no one who had offered . . . a satisfactory solution of the difficulty." Perhaps to indicate that he was still undecided about what to do, Ammons also said that "the strike is no Sunday school picnic, but conditions aren't as bad as I had been led to believe."[17]

As soon as Ammons left southern Colorado, however, the violence began again in earnest. Within a week, southern Colorado had become a battlefield.[18] As the violence raged, Ammons called representatives of the three largest coal-mining companies involved in the strike—John C. Osgood of the Victor American Fuel Company, Jesse F. Welborn of CF&I, and David W. Brown of the Rocky Mountain Fuel Company—to the State House along with UMWA President John White and Vice-President Hayes. Ammons hoped he could get the two sides to meet, and he called in former US. Senator Thomas Patterson to help mediate negotiations between the union and the operators. Patterson was the publisher of the *Rocky Mountain News*, a newspaper that remained neutral in its strike reporting, but he was also known as a friend of labor in Denver. Patterson first met with the UMWA's White and Hayes, and White agreed to abandon the union's request for recognition—the issue that in the operators' collective mind was completely unacceptable—in exchange for a meeting with the operators.[19]

Patterson left the State House office White and Hayes occupied, and went to the adjoining office, where the operators cooled their heels. All three representatives of the mining companies got angry when they heard the union's proposal. They asserted that they would never meet with the union and, according to Paterson, argued that the union officials "were merely interlopers, intermeddlers" who "had no business here" because they "did not live in the state." The operators went on to use "bitter names" to describe White and Hayes and "placed responsibility for the violence in the southern coal fields squarely on their shoulders." They also held to their contention that any meeting with union officials could be interpreted as recognition of the union. Patterson rejected this characterization of the situation, told the operators that they were being unreasonable, and pointed out that only a brick wall separated Osgood, Welborn, and Brown from the union officials who wished to meet with them. The operators declared that they would leave the room if White and Hayes stepped over the threshold. Seeing no hope for a resolution to the strike and with the death toll in southern Colorado mounting, Ammons called out the National Guard in the early morning hours of October 28. It had taken a month, but the mine operators' strategy of pressuring the governor while fomenting violence in the coal fields had worked.[20]

As the Guard made its way south from Denver, Ammons had to figure out how he was going to overcome Roady Kenehan's opposition to the financing plan he had approved.[21] As state auditor, it was Kenehan's job to issue and administer the certificates of indebtedness that the state would distribute to the National Guard as payment for their service. Merchants would also receive these certificates as payment for supplies they furnished the Guard. Merchants and Guardsmen would then take these certificates to a bank and cash them, drawing on the money that the Clearing House Association had loaned the state.[22]

Because Kenehan had to sign and authorize the certificates of indebtedness and do the paperwork necessary to distribute them, his opposition meant something. The state auditor claimed that interest payments coupled with the widespread abuse of similar certificates meant that the Guard's service in the 1903–4 strikes would eventually cost the state $6 million dollars. Kenehan was appalled by this figure, charging that the Guard spent "thousands of dollars for balls, parties, and other entertainments . . . to which questionable women were invited and hundreds of dollars for carriages to take these women to the land of the forbidden."[23] Kenehan also argued that 4 percent was the highest interest rate Colorado law allowed (the Clearing House Association had asked for 6 percent interest) and that the coal strike did not meet the legal conditions necessary for issuing certificates of indebtedness.[24]

The state auditor had other reasons for refusing to administer these certificates. As a resident of Colorado and union supporter, he suspected that the National Guard would try to break the miners' strike. Kenehan dug in and refused to participate, declaring that "the coal mine owners should be required to negotiate with their employees concerning a settlement of the strike" and that only a court order could compel him to go to work.[25] By refusing to administer the certificates, Kenehan essentially called a strike of his own, and like so many workers who chose to strike, he dared the judiciary to issue an injunction against him. But instead of hanging around and waiting for the courts to act, Kenehan skipped town to attend the AFL's convention in Seattle.[26]

Kenehan was not the only member of Ammons's administration who resisted the mine operators and the Clearing House Association. Democratic Secretary of State and State Labor Commissioner James B. Pearce publicly declared his support for the miners early in the strike.[27] In a private letter to Ammons, Pearce also pointed out that the mining companies in Las Animas and Huerfano Counties leased land from the state and that the money collected from those leases went into the state's permanent school fund. Pearce recommended that the governor take over the operation of the mines because, as he put it, the mine operators acted in the interest of "their excessive gain" and because "they are in constant quarrel with their employes, [sic] they keep the state in turmoil, they are arrogant and oppressive to the public and paralyzing to general business." This arrangement, Pearce argued, would allow the state to collect the profits of coal production, which, in turn, would place more money into the state's school fund.[28]

Given his hesitancy to call out the Guard and his concern that doing so would alienate his labor allies, Ammons might have used Kenehan's obstinacy and Pearce's opposition as justification to further delay calling out the Guard. Here, Ammons, as previous scholars of this strike have argued, appeared weak. He clearly had the support of fellow Democrats in his administration, but instead of building a united front with his political allies, Ammons chose to follow the path the mine operators had laid out for him. At the same time, Ammons's concern about the violence in southern Colorado was legitimate and he knew that he had little power to stop the violence without calling out the National Guard. Thus once he did so, the governor acted to make sure his troops had all they needed despite his own misgivings and the objections of those within his administration.

Ammons now needed to supply the Guard while the legal effort to compel Kenehan to administer the certificates of indebtedness moved forward. He managed to neutralize his striking state auditor by striking a deal with five clothing and supply companies—several of which were the mine operators' company stores—for $2,000 in food and other supplies. Ammons also brought in uniforms and other supplies from the federal War Department. Finally, the governor received an offer from a group of Pueblo businessmen to underwrite $50,000 in military expenses, though there is no evidence that Ammons accepted this money.[29]

Having temporarily solved the Guard's food and supply problems, Ammons still needed the certificates of indebtedness to pay the troops. On Thanksgiving Day 1913, Guardsmen camped at the adjutant general's headquarters in the strike zone burned Roady Kenehan in effigy because by this time, they had not been paid for almost a full month of strike duty.[30] The Colorado Supreme Court's decision came within a few days. The court treated Kenehan like any other striking worker: they ruled against his claims and ordered him to produce the certificates of indebtedness at 4 percent interest. Colorado issued these certificates through the fall 1914, and eventually spent $673,000 on the National Guard payroll, supplies, and other expenses. The roll of certificate recipients kept by the state treasurers' office lists hotels and restaurants where Guard officers stayed and dined. The list also includes many private individuals and businesses, including coal companies involved in the strike. Three of the coal companies struck by the UMW—CF&I, the Victor American Fuel Company, and Sunnyside Mining Company—received a total of $4,300 in certificates of indebtedness. The Guard most likely bought coal from these companies to heat their living quarters during a strike that stretched through a cold Colorado winter.[31] Jesse Welborn, president of CF&I, also testified after the strike that his company's stores held between $75,000 and $80,000 in certificates of indebtedness for other goods supplied to the National Guard during the strike.[32]

After agreeing to the $150,000 loan from the Denver Clearing House Association, Governor Ammons also raised another $100,000 from the bank clearinghouses in Colorado Springs and Pueblo. After this $250,000 in cash ran out, Guardsmen were issued additional certificates of indebtedness for pay and the Guard used these certificates to acquire supplies and settle other bills. These certificates, however, were IOUs—there was no cash available to pay them off—and by spring 1914, Guardsmen, merchants, and other businesses held $423,000 in unpaid certificates of indebtedness. Ammons now had to find a way to pay back the initial $250,000 in cash that the banks had put up at 4 percent interest along with the $423,000 in unpaid certificates of indebtedness.[33]

Toward those ends, Ammons called a special legislative session in May 1914 and asked for a $1 million bond issue. The governor estimated that the state's total bill was $650,000, but he asked for $1 million because he thought it might be necessary to call out the Guard again.[34] The special legislative session quickly authorized the bond issue, and the state immediately released these bonds for sale. The Colorado state treasurers' biannual report for 1913–14 showed 125 buyers of these Insurrectionary Bonds—which is what the state legislature chose to call them—totaling $672,359.[35]

Examining who bought these bonds gives us a glimpse of how class worked during the 1913–14 coal strike. The buyers of these bonds were Colorado banks that had well-established ties to Colorado's mining industry. Other buyers included National Guard officers, private citizens, brokerage houses, and businesses. Colorado Fuel & Iron and Sunnyside Coal Mining bought these bonds, as did the Colorado Supply Company, which was CF&I's company store. The Denver & Rio Grande Railroad, which established the mining outfit that eventually became CF&I, purchased bonds and so did the stores that had given the Guard $2,000 in supplies at Governor Ammons's request. Even the Smith-Brooks Printing Company, who published the official documents for the state of Colorado and the Colorado National Guard, pitched in and bought $1,500 in bonds.[36]

The vast majority of these bond buyers lived and worked in Denver. They also lived down the street and around the block from each other in the same two city neighborhoods, and worked, down the street and around the corner from each other, in the city's business and banking district. It's not much of a stretch to say that Insurrectionary Bond buyers knew each other and were fairly representative of Denver's upper class.[37]

Banks often buy state bonds whatever their purpose and business owners, National Guard officers, and private citizens undoubtedly bought their Insurrectionary Bonds as a safe investment for themselves, their families, and their businesses. Most, however, also had an obvious interest in supporting the Guard's efforts to break the coal strike. They also did not purchase their bonds during a time of industrial peace in Colorado. Instead, they bought them after the Guard had been on strike duty for months and after the destruction of the Ludlow tent colony and the killings that came with it. Moreover, the strike had not yet ended when the state offered these bonds for sale in May 1914. Given the National Guard's obvious bias in favor of the mine operators during the strike, buying bonds earmarked to pay the Guard's expenses has to be seen as an expression of support for the Guard's actions. These bond buyers clearly acted as a class. That is, they sought to protect the interests of men like themselves against an adversary—the UMWA and the striking miners—that they undoubtedly saw as a threat to the political, economic, and social order they had established in Colorado.

It is telling, however, that most of those who became literally invested in breaking the miners' strike lived in Denver, and not in the towns around Las Animas and Huerfano County's coal camps two hundred miles away. While it is difficult to exaggerate the level of social, economic, and political control that the CF&I held over their workers, the company was unable to prevent them from organizing with the UMWA or from going on strike. Successful union organizing was no small feat in a place so thoroughly dominated by companies whose anti-unionism bordered on the pathological.[38] Such control also did not prevent the Democratic mayor of Trinidad, the largest town in Las Animas County, from publicly refuting the mine operators' contention that troops were needed in the strike zone. The Trinidad Trades Assembly also met early in the strike to declare that the Guard was not needed in southern Colorado, and three thousand Trinidad residents signed a petition asking the governor not to send troops.[39]

By appealing for state intervention through the National Guard, the mine operators tacitly acknowledged that they had not achieved hegemony in Las Animas and Huerfano Counties; their domination there was based in coercion, not in consent, and thus they had to rely on the state's coercive power to keep their workers in line. Unable to gain consent for their domination of these two counties, these mining companies instead concentrated where they believed their influence was greatest.[40] Many of the top executives of the coal companies involved in the 1913–14 strike lived in Denver, and when the strike began they spent a good deal of their time at home lobbying the state's governor and the National Guard, with help from Denver's bankers, with whom the mining industry had close business relationships; the Denver Clearing House Association; the Chamber of Commerce; the real estate exchange; the city's prominent business people; and sympathetic members of their hometown's upper class.[41]

It is clear, then, that the National Guard was central to the mine operators' ability to successfully organize against the strike would have been in far more doubt if they had been unable to convince Governor Ammons to first call out the National Guard and then acted to make certain that the Guard had the money and supplies it needed to remain on strike duty. Ammons's decision to give the operators what they wanted meant that the mine managers and superintendents in southern Colorado would have the Guard's help with importing strikebreakers from out of state and making sure that these nonunion men could work without interference from the strikers. The Guard, then, was crucial in turning the 1913–14 strike into a defeat for the striking miners, and thus Ammons's decision to call out the Guard is crucial for understanding why the operators triumphed.

Explaining Ammons's decision concerning the National Guard, though, is more complicated because Ammons really made two decisions. The first was to call out the Guard, ensure that the state could fund the Guard on strike duty for an extended period of time, and force State Auditor Roady Kenehan to sign and administer the certificates of indebtedness. Pressure from the mine operators certainly helped drive these decisions. That the mine operators and their banker allies were able to box Governor Ammons into this particular corner revealed the extent to which the deck was stacked against him because though Ammons was the head of the state of Colorado, he lacked the ability to control other crucial government officials. More important, the state was not independent of the mine operators' influence. Ammons tried to act as a mediator between the UMWA and the mine operators, but the operators were able to undermine and ignore Ammons's efforts to negotiate an end to the strike because they had found other state actors who were more than willing to help carry out their strikebreaking plan. Sheriffs Jefferson Farr and James Grisham wore the uniform of government authority in Las Animas and Huerfano Counties, but they placed their deputy sheriffs under the command of the Baldwin-Felts detectives, whom the mine operators had hired to help break the strike. Thus Sheriffs Grisham and Farr worked to promote and protect the interests of the mine operators, and they did everything they could to carry out the operators' strikebreaking plan. The mine operators were convinced, moreover, that the Colorado National Guard would act to break the strike if only they could get Ammons to put the Guard in the field. Again, the mine operators believed that the Guard would work for them, and not for their commander-in-chief, the governor of the state of Colorado.[42]

Ammons's second decision—to throw his support behind the National Guard and to abandon the striking miners once the Guard was in the field—is more difficult to explain. Late in the strike, Ammons stated that he "never did anything with as much regret in my life as I felt when I called out the National Guard."[43] Why, then, did he suddenly become the National Guard's advocate once the troops were in the field? The answer to this question lies in assessing how the governor likely understood Colorado politics and how committed he was to the striking miners. Colorado's labor unions had supported Ammons as a candidate in the 1912 election, but the governor's support for the largely immigrant miners who went on strike in 1913 did not, as it turned out, run that deep. Ammons's nativist predilections also likely pushed him away from the miners and toward the overwhelmingly white and native-born National Guardsmen he had called out on strike duty.

Once the National Guard was in the field, the governor paid little attention to Adjutant General John Chase's efforts to break the strike and expressed little support for the striking miners. At the same time, he made sure to publicly and privately support his troops. This shift toward the National Guard probably reflected how the political calculus changed for Ammons once the

Guard was on duty. In the context of the 1913–14 coal strike, Ammons likely saw shifting away from his labor supporters as politically necessary because he was up for reelection in less than a year. Ammons had won in 1912 largely because of the split between the Republicans and the Progressives that was embodied nationally by Theodore Roosevelt's run for the White House as a Progressive. This split allowed Democrat Woodrow Wilson to win the White House and Democrat Ammons to win the Colorado governor's office.[44] As the strike turned violent and Ammons called out the Guard, he probably could not see getting reelected in 1914 as a sitting governor who had championed the cause of a group of impoverished, mostly immigrant workers in a remote corner of the state.

Soon after calling out the Guard, Ammons criticized State Auditor Kenehan and declared that "those boys down there are endangering their lives and are undergoing many hardships in behalf of the state." Referring specifically to Kenehan's efforts to hold up the funds necessary to pay the Guard, Ammons vowed: "I intend that they shall have their pay and all of it. They get little enough as it is." The governor frequently expressed similar sentiments once the Guard was on strike duty and went out of his way to intercede with employers in Denver who threatened to fire employees absent from their jobs because of their service in the Guard. These words and actions indicated that the governor was indeed labor's defender, but his concern had become primarily for the state workers who made up the Colorado National Guard.[45]

Guardsmen played a role in helping their governor express solidarity with them. Ammons received many letters from soldiers describing the hardship strike duty caused them during the month it took Ammons to force Roady Kenehan to administer the certificates of indebtedness that would pay Guardsmen for their service. Some of these letter writers asked for leaves of absence while others mounted a petition campaign that collected hundreds of signatures. This petition demanded that Ammons pay his troops for strike duty, but also pulled at the governor's heartstrings by pointing out that many Guardsmen had families to support. "Unless the men receive the pay which is due them for their services to the State of Colorado," one letter writer claimed, "Their families will actually suffer from poverty, if not suffering at the present time."[46] By acquiring the money to pay and supply the troops and by letting the Guard's officers do as they pleased to break the strike—a strategy that would end the strike sooner rather than later—Ammons acted in the interests of the mine operators, but he also acted as a politician seeking to protect a constituency that worked for the state of Colorado.

Comparing the workers who served in the Colorado National Guard to the workers who went on strike in southern Colorado's coalfields also helps explain why Governor Ammons acted as he did. During the strike, Ammons said that the Guard was made up of "farmers, tradesmen, mechanics, and artisans, with an unusually large proportion of professional men."[47] He was largely correct. The Guard's officer class in 1913 was made up almost entirely of middle- and upper-class men. Most officers were business owners and professionals in civilian life—attorney, physician, and engineer were common occupations—or they held jobs as clerks, bookkeepers, accountants, business managers, or civil servants. More than half hailed from Denver, and many were prominent citizens in that city who had political influence. The enlisted ranks were more working class. Enlisted men were primarily clerks, laborers, farmers, and skilled tradesmen, but all National Guardsmen were white and most were native born.[48] They and their families and friends, therefore, were citizens who were quite capable of expressing their dissatisfaction with Ammons in the upcoming election. Portraying himself as a defender of the National Guard would curry favor with these voters and with the many Anglo-Coloradans who no doubt looked askance at a strike of largely immigrant working-class coal miners that had turned violent.

Thus, Ammons praised the Guard whenever he had the chance. In an article he authored in July 1914, just four months before the November election, Ammons defended his Guardsmen, contending that "these men have served their state with a truly commendable devotion, to the sacrifice of their own personal interests, risking their lives in a quarrel not of their making and in which they had no interest . . . If ever patriotism found its expression, it is in the unrecompensed and unselfish services of the soldiers of the state."[49]

At the same time, Ammons knew that coal company domination of political life in Las Animas and Huerfano Counties produced Republican majorities on Election Day. The coal company camps in Huerfano County, for instance, were individual precincts where Sheriff Farr counted the vote before reporting the totals to county election officials. Mine superintendents also marked the ballots of illiterate miners for the preferred Republican candidates, and the mining companies distributed cards on election day that specified their preferred candidates for the literate and illiterate alike. The coal operators' creation of a one-party state in these two counties likely also worked to push Democrat Ammons away from the striking miners and toward his National Guardsmen. Why would the governor go out of the way to help immigrant working-class miners who, if they had become citizens and were eligible to vote, faced immense pressure to cast their ballots for his party's opponents?[50] Ammons might have seen a successful strike as an opportunity to break the coal operators'—and the Republican Party's—hold on Las Animas and Huerfano Counties. Indeed, it was the UMWA's intention to bring political as well as industrial democracy to southern Colorado.[51] For Ammons, however, throwing all in with the striking miners and their union with the intention of strengthening the Democratic Party's position in Las Animas and Huerfano Counties was a risky proposition. It was clearly more prudent for the governor to seek the votes of citizens who were already free to vote as they pleased and who voted in places where elections were not rigged.

In the months immediately after calling out the Guard, the governor also began portraying himself as a man who was not on the coal operators' side or the striking miners' side. Instead, the governor claimed, he was on the side of law and order. Ammons took this stance as he faced increasing criticism from the UMWA and Colorado's State Federation of Labor for allowing Guardsmen to help import strikebreakers into southern Colorado.[52] After a constituent wrote Ammons several antiunion letters, Ammons responded: "The strike leaders certainly occupy untenable ground when they attempt to hold me responsible for every little indiscretion of the militia men . . . The only duty I know in this matter or shall know will be the restoration of order and the reinstatement and enforcement of law."[53] Around the same time, Ammons echoed this theme in a letter to fellow Democrat and Colorado Congressman George Kindel. Ammons wrote: "I intend, of course, to follow a policy of enforcement of law and order regardless of consequences but sincerely hope that the people of Colorado . . . will stand by me in that policy."[54]

The governor's commitment to law and order, however, did not extend to the actions of the National Guard. In December 1913, Colorado's State Federation of Labor (CSFL) held its annual convention in Denver and took this opportunity to highlight the abuse and intimidation that National Guard troops had heaped on the striking miners and their families since their arrival in southern Colorado two months earlier. It was clear that Guardsmen were acting aggressively to break the strike and, in doing so, were certainly stretching the bounds of what was legally permissible. Ammons, however, ignored the CFSL's and the UMWA's complaints about the Guard and refused to acknowledge that Guardsmen were physically abusing and otherwise mistreating striking miners and their families. He went as far as offering $100 for proof that the Guard had robbed any miner. The State Federation of Labor was so incensed that they launched a recall of the governor and convened a committee to collect evidence of the Guard's abuses.[55] In hearings held in late December 1913 and early January 1914, the CSFL's investigating committee collected 760 pages of testimony from 163 striking miners, members of their families, and other residents of southern Colorado about the abuse they had experienced at the hands of National Guardsmen.[56]

Ammons was unmoved, and he continued to champion the cause of law and order. It is clear, too, that this emphasis was part of his thinking about political strategy in the upcoming election. In July 1914, after the destruction of the Ludlow tent colony, the governor responded to a letter from a Democratic constituent who had written to express his support. Ammons condemned the violence that the striking miners had perpetrated after the killings at Ludlow and shared his views on how the party should position itself in the election that was just a few months away: "I do not believe the Democratic Party . . . can possibly win except upon a basis of law enforcement, and I would regret more than anything what can happen politically to see our party take a stand in defense of lawlessness no matter of what nature."[57] By emphasizing "law and order" while ignoring the role of the National Guard, Baldwin-Felts, the mining companies, and the sheriff's offices in Las Animas and Huerfano Counties in creating lawlessness and disorder, Ammons placed blame for the strike's violence squarely on the shoulders of the striking miners. This interpretation certainly conjured stereotypes of "new immigrants" as "unruly," "hotheaded," and "savage" that were common among the native born and suggests that Ammons was trying to separate himself from a constituency that many native-born Coloradans viewed with suspicion.[58]

Ammons continued to express similar sentiments even after the strike had ended. In his biennial address delivered on January 8, 1915, the governor conveyed support and sympathy for the National Guard and called for new laws "defining and providing sufficient penalties for treason, sedition, and armed resistance to the militia and civil officers of the state."[59] While testifying publicly before the US Senate's Commission on Industrial Relations the previous month, Ammons answered a question about the importation of strikebreakers by stating that "the only thing I could do was to assume an impartial attitude and enforce the law." Later, while relating a conversation that he had with UMWA leaders before the strike began, Ammons said: "I spoke to them urging them that they should allow me the opportunity of trying to enforce the laws of the State before they called a strike. They said that the law had never cut any figure down in this southern field [southern Colorado]. I told them that I didn't know anything about that."[60]

It is telling that Ammons pled ignorance concerning the coal industry's political domination of Las Animas and Huerfano Counties. This claim strains credulity because Ammons had been active in Colorado politics since 1890 and had been speaker of the state's House of Representatives.[61] Given his history, it would have been difficult not to know that the coal operators controlled politics in these two counties and thus controlled how the law was applied and to whose benefit. Indeed, the Colorado Democratic Party's platform in 1912 asserted that "the domination of the counties of Huerfano and Las Animas by a great industrial corporation through its alliance with and control of the county governments has been a long continued and intolerable condition" and called for "legislation empowering the governor, the attorney general, and the courts to destroy these conditions and restore the people of these counties their right of self-government."[62] If Ammons was unwilling to talk publically about the political realities in southern Colorado and the contents of his own party's platform, then he clearly was not willing to challenge the political dominance that the coal operators' enjoyed.

Political considerations and fear of being punished at the polls for championing the miners' cause, however, were not the only likely reasons Governor Ammons chose to stand behind his state workers in the National Guard. Ammons's own perception of the immigrant miners who struck in southern Colorado also played a role. Ammons was not a strident nativist, and he didn't use overt anti-immigrant sentiment to gain support from Anglo-Coloradans, but he did display a definite discomfort with the many immigrants who mined coal in southern Colorado. It is likely, therefore, that Ammons also chose to back his National Guardsmen over the striking miners and their union because he was more comfortable culturally with the overwhelmingly white and native-born National Guardsmen he had called out on strike duty.

Ammons revealed his nativism several times during the strike. For example, in August 1914, when the coal strike was in its eleventh month and the First World War was just beginning in Europe, Governor Ammons told Colorado's Democratic US Senator Charles Thomas that he had noticed how the European belligerent governments were asking their citizens in the United States to come home and join the military. This development made Ammons wonder if something could "be done to call these same subjects out of Colorado." "If we could get some one to two thousands of the men belonging to these same nationalities out of Colorado our strike situation would almost be settled . . . If press reports are correct the same class of men are being called for from other portions of the country and I see no reason why they should overlook Colorado."[63] Senator Thomas agreed with Ammons in his reply, but told the governor that such a solution would not happen immediately. Thomas wrote: "Unfortunately for our state, those you would like to see removed are largely the subjects of Southern European countries who are now at peace." Still, Thomas was optimistic: "The possibilities are, however, that they will be involved sooner or later and then if we can get a move on the situation, so to speak, I shall be glad to cooperate to the best of my ability."[64] Ammons drew hope from Thomas's letter and told the senator that he was watching how the war might "affect our undesirable population and if anything of the kind happens, I am very glad indeed to know that the matter will be looked after."[65]

Ammons's desire to empty Colorado of "undesirables" is telling because it shows the governor engaging in a fantasy. Shipping one or two thousand southern and eastern European immigrants out of southern Colorado would have drastically reduced the state's coal supply and would have done significant damage to the coal-mining industry, but Ammons was not thinking about that in his exchange with Senator Thomas. Instead, he was thinking about how undesirable these immigrants were and how he might get rid of them. This exchange also shows that the governor blamed the 1913–14 coal strike and the violence that came with it solely on the immigrant miners. Of course, Ammons's fantasy erased the horrible and dangerous conditions under which these immigrant workers labored; the mining industry's social, economic, and political domination of Las Animas and Huerfano Counties; and the violence and intimidation, culminating in the Ludlow Massacre, that the coal mine operators, Baldwin-Felts, and the Colorado National Guard had carried out during the strike.

Ammons's nativism was also on display at the joint conference he arranged between striking miners and the coal mine operators two months into the 1913–14 strike. The mine operators involved in the strike had steadfastly refused to meet with any union members or leaders because they worried that any such meeting could be interpreted as recognition of the union. Still, Ammons was able to convince representatives of the three largest coal-mining companies in southern Colorado to come to the conference table in late November 1913. John C. Osgood, Jesse Welborn, and David W. Brown made clear that, as Brown put it, the meeting was to discuss the complaints of the men "as men only, not as labor representatives in any way." Archie Allison and T. X. Evans, who worked for the CF&I, and David Hamman, who mined coal for Victor American were the workers' representatives at this meeting. All three were native born or had immigrated from Great Britain, and it's likely that these men were chosen because English was their native language. That they were not new immigrants from southern and eastern Europe or Mexico helped shape the conversation at this meeting.[66]

Late in the meeting, this exchange about the quality of the men who worked the mines occurred:

John Osgood (Victor American Fuel Company): The men who help us to get men are men working in the mines. They write back to their friends or relatives, perhaps Italy or Austria, telling what the conditions are.

Archie Allison (miner): or else to Greece? (laughter)

Osgood: Yes, to Greece. I wish they did not write there (laughter). The best employment agency we have is the men working in our mines.

David Hamman (miner): You are speaking about the Greeks. We are getting in worse men than the Greeks ever were.

D. W. Brown (Rocky Mountain Fuel Company): Who are they?

Hamman: They are those Old Mexico Mexicans. They are not to be trusted.

Osgood: They won't stay longer than four or five days in a place, will they?

Hamman: They came with these big, high hats; they came to Trinidad with their dinner pails and blankets and had never seen a coal mine.

Osgood: Who is supporting them?

Governor Ammons: Why, the relief fund.[67]

The mine operators were clearly following the divide-and-conquer strategy that so many employers used at the turn of the twentieth century to drive a wedge between the native born and old-stock immigrants from northwestern Europe and new immigrants from southern and eastern Europe and, in this case, Mexico, when they struck in the same workplace or industry. Evans, Allison, and Hamman must have been quite uncomfortable sitting across the table from some of the most powerful men in Colorado and they certainly followed their employers' lead in this conversation. Still, Allison and Hamman initiated a discussion of how some of their fellow strikers—Greeks and Mexicans, in particular—were undesirable workers. Ammons, furthermore, who did his best during this meeting to act as a mediator between the workers and their employers, could not help but agree that these new Mexican migrants were suspect and likely to become public burdens.[68]

Ammons's exchange with Senator Thomas and the comments he made at the joint conference were private, but the governor also publically expressed his discomfort with the striking immigrant miners. In an article the governor penned for the *North American Review* in July 1914, he wrote that "the coal-mining population of Colorado is composed very largely of South-European immigrants who speak practically no English and have yet little understanding of the American form of government." He also described the miners as "ignorant and, I am afraid, disposed to lawlessness" and blamed the battle between striking miners and the National Guard that led to the Ludlow Massacre on the "stored up wrath of this alien population." Later, in his public testimony before the Commission on Industrial Relations, Ammons said he warned the UMWA's leadership that "they had a population down there of people of a great many nationalities who spoke different languages, who understood little of our laws and customs, and that if a strike was started, they would be hard to control."[69]

Governor Ammons was not alone in his concern about "undesirable" immigrants. Nativism was widespread at the turn of the twentieth century, and the immigrant status of the striking miners was crucial to how mine operators and supervisors, National Guardsmen, newspaper reporters, and the native-born citizenry of Colorado viewed them. Anti-immigrant sentiment was also a powerful force in the American labor movement. The AFL, the largest labor organization in the United States at the turn of the twentieth century, supported the exclusion of Chinese immigrants, sought legislation to restrict or ban immigration from southern and eastern Europe, and balked at organizing unskilled, "new" immigrants. Employer use of these immigrants as strikebreakers in the years after the Civil War, and labor union defeats in these strikes, pushed the AFL and many native-born workers to see immigration as part of the larger employer arsenal for opposing unionization that included spies, private detectives like Baldwin-Felts, police, and National Guard troops.[70]

Because many AFL union members were themselves immigrants or the descendants of immigrants from the British Isles and northwestern Europe, however, unions could not oppose all immigration. Still, as Gwendolyn Mink has observed, "New immigrants were visibly different; they moved into industry at lower levels and for lower wages, spoke unfamiliar languages, and carried different cultural baggage." These differences left the AFL room to encourage their members and political supporters like Governor Ammons to see old-stock immigrants as racially different from and superior to new immigrants.[71]

The UMWA was exceptional within the AFL because the union tried to organize new immigrants at the turn of the twentieth century. The UMWA's native-born and old-stock immigrant officials, organizers, and union members in southern Colorado, however, were conflicted about organizing immigrant workers. Archie Allison and David Hamman made this ambivalence clear in their comments at the joint conference with the mine operators and Governor Ammons. Edward L. Doyle, secretary-treasurer of the UMWA's District Fifteen and a central figure in the strike, was also of two minds when it came to new immigrants. Doyle was born in Spring Valley, Illinois, to a family that was likely of Irish or English descent and he saw a clear difference between "his people" and more recent immigrants. In his testimony before the Commission on Industrial Relations, Doyle said: "Well, all of those immigrants, remembering that this country is free—it ought to be remembered that those people that come here should not be allowed to intermarry, the southern European races and the yellow races and so forth." Doyle also argued that "the immigrant coming over should be made to take an oath that he will not work for less wages and longer hours, or do anything to draw back the progress that has been made. In other words, that if they are going to be made citizens, that they shall recognize a standard in life and that they should have an opportunity to develop and make better men and women and not permit them to be brought into this country and be used as tools to bring down the standard to the level of the county from which they came." At the same time, Doyle approved of the UMW's inclusiveness, declaring that "in our organization we have no objection to any creed, color, or nationality. We do not say to the Pole, the Frenchmen, or the Russian, 'You get out of here,' but we say, 'Come in;' ours is a humanitarian movement, and we will help you out of that rut you have been traveling in."[72]

The Western Federation of Miners (WFM), moreover, which had nothing but scorn for the AFL's craft unionism and the UMWA's official rejection of socialism and which for a decade at the turn of the twentieth century was Colorado's most powerful union, prohibited Asian, Mexican, and southern and eastern European immigrants from living and working in Cripple Creek, Colorado, and showed little interest in organizing these workers when they entered Colorado's mining industry. Taking the WFM's nativist position on immigration also gained votes for Democratic, Socialist, and, for a time during the 1890s, Populists candidates in the metal-mining districts of Colorado where the WFM held sway and most miners were native-born or old-stock immigrants from the British Isles and northwestern Europe. Nativism was not the only reason these miners voted for the Democratic, Socialists, and Populist Parties. They correctly viewed the Republican Party, which also generally resisted immigration restriction in Colorado and elsewhere, as the party of capital. Thus, class consciousness and nativism worked hand-in-hand to build support for the Democratic, Socialist, and Populist tickets.[73]

Clearly, the nativism that Governor Ammons expressed was not inconsistent with the labor movement's view of immigrant workers. Seen from this perspective, it is not surprising that Ammons, although he was a pro-labor Democrat, was uncomfortable championing the cause of immigrant working-class miners and chose to support and defend the state workers in the Colorado National Guard. He was their boss, but Guardsmen in the enlisted ranks, in particular, were "his people" in a more important way: they were white and native born or of older immigrant stock and held "respectable" positions as clerks, farmers, and skilled tradesmen. These National Guardsmen, furthermore, fit the description of the segment of the working class that the labor movement in Colorado and in the country at large had asked politicians like Governor Ammons to support. The immigrant strikers, on the other hand, were largely unskilled, alien "undesirables" whom much of the labor movement viewed with suspicion and contempt. Thus, Ammons defended the workers that labor wanted him to, but these workers also fit the general description of those who regularly joined the enlisted ranks of the labor movement's sworn enemy in Colorado: the Colorado National Guard.

---

How Elias Ammons came to call out the Colorado National Guard and guarantee its financial viability reveals how powerful southern Colorado's mine operators had become by the early twentieth century. Governor Ammons was not a tool of the mine operators, and he managed to resist for a month their calls for troops. The operators, however, were just as effective at organizing themselves as the UMWA had been at organizing southern Colorado's coal miners. The operators, furthermore, organized a wide range of allies. As the CF&I's Lamont Bowers told John D. Rockefeller Jr. early in the strike, the operators had organized support from Denver's bankers, the chamber of commerce, the real estate exchange, and many of the city's most prominent businessmen. The operators' position in the strike was also backed by the sheriffs in Las Animas and Huerfano Counties, a National Guard that was willing to break the coal strike, and a sympathetic Colorado Supreme Court that sanctioned the operators' National Guard financing plan by forcing Roady Kenehan to administer the certificates of indebtedness. Finally, the mine operators had developed relationships with labor agents across the country who would send them nonunion workers—mostly immigrants who had just entered the country—without telling them that the job they had accepted was to act as strikebreaker. The UMWA, on the other hand, organized a group of some of the most marginalized and least powerful people in Colorado.[74]

The wide-ranging power and influence that the mine operators enjoyed made all the more important Governor Ammons's willingness and ability to defend the UMWA and the striking miners. Ammons was not able to stand up to the mine operators, but his failure to do so is not surprising given the amount of pressure that the mine operators were able to place on him. That, however, isn't the only reason the mine operators were able to induce Ammons to do their bidding. He was also ambivalent about throwing himself wholeheartedly behind the striking miners. He was likely concerned about his political future and how unequivocal support for the striking miners might damage his chances for reelection. Mixed with those political concerns was the governor's cultural discomfort with the immigrant strikers along with his outright nativism. By trying hard to organize southern Colorado, the UMWA attempted to erase the line dividing new immigrants from the native-born and old-stock immigrants that the AFL, WFM, and the Democratic Party had helped draw through the American working class. Ammons, however, was not interested in that project. While he was not a strident nativist, he clearly did not hold Colorado's new immigrant population in very high regard and was not going to stake his administration and chances for reelection on defending these immigrant strikers. In effect, Ammons's support for labor only went as far as the labor movement had asked Democratic politicians to go. The UMWA and the striking miners, however, had pinned their hopes on Ammons to either keep the Guard out of southern Colorado or ensure that the Guard would not break the strike once in the field. The governor disappointed these labor constituents, but Ammons's decision to back the Guard and allow General Chase and his troops to break the 1913–14 coal strike also suggests that labor's defeat was not exclusively the consequence of the mine operators' enormous power to create an unholy alliance with the state. Defeating an opponent as formidable as the operators clearly required a united labor movement that was clear and consistent in what it wanted—and expected—from elected officials. That such a labor movement did not yet exist helped turn this strike into a defeat for the miners.

## Notes

1. *Executive Orders*, Papers of Governor Elias Ammons, Colorado State Archives, Denver (hereafter, Papers of Elias Ammons), box 8849C, vol. 21; *Rocky Mountain News* (hereafter, *RMN*), October 21, October 27, November, 7, November 9, November 13, 1913. The exact number of miners who struck is impossible to determine. George P. West, in his report for the US Senate's Commission on Industrial Relations, estimated that there were nine thousand strikers in southern Colorado. See Commission on Industrial Relations, *Report on the Colorado Strike*, 64th Cong., 1st sess., 1915, S. Rept. 415, 5. This figure is also in line with other contemporary estimates. William H. Riker, *Soldiers of the State: The Role of the National Guard in American Democracy* (Washington, DC: Public Affairs Press, 1957), 47–55; *A Report on Labor Disturbances in the State of Colorado from 1880 to 1904, Inclusive with Correspondence*

*Relating Thereto*, prepared under the direction of Carroll D. Wright, Commissioner of Labor, 58th Congress, 3rd sess., 1905, S. Doc. 122, 360 (hereafter, as *A Report on Labor Disturbances in the State of Colorado from 1880 to 1904*); Colorado State Department of Military Affairs, Colorado State Department of Military Affairs Collection, Colorado State Archives, Denver (hereafter, Colorado State Department of Military Affairs Collection), "Active Duty-Colorado Military Forces." The organized Colorado military was referred to as the "state militia" until 1897, when the Colorado legislature renamed it the "National Guard of Colorado." Geoffrey R. Hunt, *Colorado's Volunteer Infantry in the Philippine Wars, 1898–1899* (Albuquerque: University of New Mexico Press, 2006), 30.

2. The literature on the 1913–14 southern Colorado coal strike begins with George S. McGovern's "The Colorado Coal Strike, 1913–14" (Ph.D. diss., Northwestern University, 1953). He published this study with Leonard F. Guttridge as *The Great Coalfield War* (Boston: Houghton Mifflin Company, 1972). Also see Barron B. Beshoar, *Out of the Depths: The Story of John R. Lawson, A Labor Leader* (Denver, Colorado: Golden Bell Press, 1958); Zeese Papanikolas, *Buried Unsung: Louis Tikas and the Ludlow Massacre* (Salt Lake City: University of Utah Press, 1982); Manfred F. Boemeke, "The Wilson Administration, Organized Labor, and the Colorado Coal Strike, 1913–14" (Ph.D. diss., Princeton University, 1983); Priscilla Long, "The Women of the Colorado Fuel and Iron Strike, 1913–14," *Women, Work, and Protest: A Century of US Women's Labor History*, ed. Ruth Milkman (Boston: Routledge & Kegan Paul, 1985); Long, *Where the Sun Never Shines: A History of America's Bloody Coal Industry* (New York: Paragon House, 1989), chap. 12–14; Anthony R. DeStefanis, "Guarding Capital: Soldier Strikebreakers on the Long Road to the Ludlow Massacre" (Ph.D. diss., College of William and Mary, 2004); DeStefanis, "Violence and the Colorado National Guard: Masculinity, Race, Class, and Identity in the 1913–14 Southern Colorado Coal Strike," in *Mining Women: Gender in the Development of a Global Industry, 1670–2005*, ed. Jaclyn Gier Viskovatoff and Laurie Mercier (New York: Palgrave/MacMillan, 2006), 195–212; Scott Martelle, *Blood Passion: The Ludlow Massacre and Class War in the American West* (New Brunswick, N.J.: Rutgers University Press, 2007); Thomas G. Andrews, *Killing for Coal: America's Deadliest Labor War* (Cambridge, MA: Harvard University Press, 2008); DeStefanis, "The Road to Ludlow: Breaking the 1913–14 Southern Colorado Coal Strike," *Journal of the Historical Society* 12, no. 2 (September 2012): 341–90.

3. "Those Killed in the Colorado Strike," Papers of Edward L. Doyle, box 1, ff 47, Western History Collection, Denver Public Library, Denver, Colorado; Martelle, *Blood Passion*, 222–23.

4. Andrews, *Killing for Coal*, 253–57; Martelle, *Blood Passion*, 86–87, 98–100, 120–22, 137–38; McGovern and Guttridge, *The Great Coalfield War*, 76, 87–88, 99, 122–23, 134, 138, 145–46, 150–52, 155–56, 168–70. McGovern is more critical of Ammons in his

dissertation. See McGovern, "The Colorado Coal Strike, 1913–14," 182–85, 195–204, 207–9, 219–20, 239–52, esp. 252.

5. The coal operators also supported Ammons in 1912, but that support was not heartfelt. They saw that the split between the Progressives and the Republicans in 1912 was going to lead to a Democratic victory and they wanted to be on the winning side. See Martelle, *Blood Passion*, 86, and Beshoar, *Out of the Depths*, 43.

6. John H. Nankivell, *History of the Military Organizations of the State of Colorado, 1860–1935* (Denver: W. H. Kistler Stationary Company, 1935), 189.

7. Governor Elias Ammons to President Woodrow Wilson, May 25, 1914, and Ammons to Wilson, August 25, 1914, Papers of Elias Ammons, box 26750, file folder 1; Testimony of Elias Ammons, US Senate, Commission on Industrial Relations, *The Colorado Coal Miners' Strike*, 64th Cong., 1st sess., 1916, S. Doc. 415, vol. 7, 6415 (hereafter, *CIR Testimony*); *RMN*, October 29 and November 9 and 13, 1913; United Mine Workers of America, "Militarism: What It Cost the Taxpayers," Papers of Josephine Roche, box 6, folder 9, 3, Norlin Library, University of Colorado, Boulder.

8. *A Report on Labor Disturbances in the State of Colorado from 1880 to 1904*, 350. On the 1903–4 Colorado mining strikes, see Melvyn Dubofsky, *We Shall Be All: A History of the Industrial Workers of the World* (Chicago: Quadrangle, 1969), 47–55; George H. Suggs, *Colorado's War on Militant Unionism: James H. Peabody and the Western Federation of Miner* (Detroit: Wayne State University Press, 1972); Elizabeth Jameson, *All That Glitters: Class, Conflict, and Community in Cripple Creek* (Urbana: University of Illinois Press, 1997), chap. 8, 9; J. Anthony Lukas, *Big Trouble: A Murder in a Small Town Sets off a Struggle for the Soul of America* (New York: Simon & Schuster, 1997), 224–31; George G. Suggs Jr., "The Colorado Coal Miners' Strike, 1903–04: A Prelude to Ludlow?" *Journal of the West* 12 (January 1973): 36–52.

9. Lamont Bowers to John D. Rockefeller Jr., November 18, 1913, "Rockefeller, Jr., Exhibit No. 2," *CIR Testimony*, vol. 9, 8421; Jameson, *All That Glitters*, 44–45; Joseph E. King, *A Mine to Make a Mine: Financing the Colorado Mining Industry, 1859–1902* (College Station: Texas A&M University Press, 1977), 167.

10. Bowers quoted in McGovern and Guttridge, *The Great Coalfield War*, 78–79.

11. On Baldwin-Felts's role in this strike, see Martelle, *Blood Passion*, 12–14, 52–57; McGovern and Guttridge, *The Great Coalfield War*, 76, 87–88, 99, 122–23, 130–32. For a different analysis, see DeStefanis, "Guarding Capital," 140–43, 164–79.

12. *RMN*, October 16, 1913.

13. Lamont Bowers to John D. Rockefeller Jr., November 18, 1913, "Rockefeller, Jr., Exhibit No. 2," *CIR Testimony*, vol. 9, 8421–22.

14. "Minutes from the Meetings of the UMW Policy Committee, August 4, 1913–November 5, 1914," Papers of Edward L. Doyle, box 1, ff 53; *RMN*, October 21, 1913.

15. *United Mine Workers Journal*, October 30, 1913.

16. *RMN*, October 21 and 23, 1913.

17. Ibid., October 23, 1913.

18. DeStefanis, "Guarding Capital," 181–89.

19. Testimony of Thomas Patterson, *CIR Testimony*, vol. 7, 6480, 6483; *RMN*, October 28, 1913.

20. *CIR Testimony*, 6480–81, and the testimony of Elias Ammons, ibid., vol. 7, 6413.

21. *RMN*, October 21 and 27, 1913.

22. *RMN*, November 16, 1913.

23. *RMN*, November 30, 1913.

24. *RMN*, October 27 and November 16, 1913.

25. *RMN*, October 27, 1913.

26. Ibid., November 7 and 9, 1913.

27. Ibid., October 9, 1913.

28. Secretary of State James B. Pearce to Ammons, October 13, 1913, Papers of Elias Ammons, box 26751, file folder 6; *RMN*, October 14, 1913.

29. *RMN*, November 15, 1913.

30. Testimony of Professor James H. Brewster, *CIR Testimony*, vol. 7, 6660.

31. Records of the Treasurer of Colorado, "Debt Register," vol. A, 1878–1914, Colorado State Archives, Denver. Maintaining the guard on strike duty cost the state $673,000. This figure, however, does not include the 4 percent interest that the bank clearinghouses charged on the money they loaned the state.

32. Testimony of Jesse Welborn, *CIR Testimony*, vol. 7, 6707.

33. *RMN*, May 5, 1914; Ammons to M. D. Foster, March 7, 1914, Papers of Elias Ammons, box 26751, file folder 7; Testimony of Elias Ammons, *CIR Testimony*, vol. 7, 6415; Testimony of Captain Philip Van Cise, ibid., vol. 7, 6820.

34. *RMN*, May 6, 1914. This special legislative session convened immediately after the Ludlow Massacre, the ten-day war that followed, and the arrival of the US Army in southern Colorado. President Wilson, however, wanted to pull the troops out as soon as possible because he had also just sent US troops to Mexico and was reluctant to burden his relatively small military with two commitments. Wilson's desire to relieve the army of peacekeeping duty in southern Colorado was what made Ammons think another National Guard call out might be necessary.

35. See the reporting on the special legislative session in *RMN*, May 5, 1914 to May 16, 1914; *Biennial Report of the Treasurer of the State of Colorado, 1913–1914*, Records of the Treasurer, State Treasurer's Office, Denver, 57–62.

36. *Biennial Report of the Treasurer of the State of Colorado, 1913–1914*, Records of the Treasurer, 57–62.

37. Ibid. I took the names of bond buyers listed in the *Biennial Report of the Treasurer of the State of Colorado, 1913–1914* and found their home and business addresses

in the 1914 Denver city directory. I then consulted a 1911 Denver street map to determine where the bond buyers lived and worked.

38. On the CF&I's domination of southern Colorado, see McGovern and Guttridge, *The Great Coalfield War*, 27–35; DeStefanis, "Guarding Capital," 53–125.

39. *RMN*, October 1, 21, 23, 1913; McGovern, "The Colorado Coal Strike, 1913–14," 183–86; Long, *Where the Sun Never Shines*, 279; Andrews, *Killing for Coal*, 254.

40. Quintin Hoare and Geoffrey Nowell Smith, eds., *Selections from the Prison Notebooks of Antonio Gramsci*, (New York: International Publishers, 1971), 12–13, 195, 239, 262–263; Marcus E. Green, "Gramsci Cannot Speak: Presentations and Interpretations of Gramsci's Concept of the Subaltern," in *Rethinking Gramsci*, ed. Marcus E. Green (New York: Routledge, 2011), 73.

41. Herbert Gutman made a similar point about how industrialists were often strangers in the cities and towns where their factories, mills, and mines were located and thus had to appeal upward for help from state officials. See Gutman, "The Braidwood Lockout of 1874," *Journal of the Illinois State Historical Society* 53 (1959): 5–28; Gutman, "Class, Status, and Community Power in Nineteenth-Century American Industrial Cities, Paterson, New Jersey: A Case Study," *Work, Culture, and Society in Industrializing America: Essays in American Working-Class and Social History* (New York: Random House, 1977), 234–60; Ira Berlin's introduction to Gutman's work in *Power and Culture: Essays on the American Working Class*, ed. Ira Berlin (New York: New Press, 1987), 14.

42. Grisham wrote his first letter to Governor Ammons asking for state troops just two days after the strike began. See Sheriff James Grisham to Elias Ammons, September 25, 1913, and October 10, 1913, Papers of Elias Ammons, box 26751, file folder 6. Sheriff Farr wrote to Ammons less than a week into the strike. See Sheriff Jefferson Farr to Ammons, September 29, 1913, ibid., box 26751, file folder 6; McGovern and Guttridge, *The Great Coalfield War*, 30–35; DeStefanis, "Guarding Capital," 109–20.

43. Testimony of Elias Ammons, *CIR Testimony*, vol. 8, 7170.

44. James Chace, *1912: Wilson, Roosevelt, Taft & Debs—The Election that Changed the Country* (New York: Simon & Schuster, 2004).

45. *RMN*, November 15, 1913; Elias M. Ammons, "The Colorado Strike," *North American Review* (July 1914): 38.

46. The files of correspondence in the Papers of Governor Elias Ammons contain many such letters. See the Papers of Elias Ammons, box 26747, file folder 1. Also see Ammons to Adjutant General John Chase, November 12, 1913, box 26751, file folder 6, for Ammons's attempts to intervene on behalf of Guardsmen whose jobs were threatened because they were on strike duty. The petition Guardsmen circulated appears is in box 26751, file folder 7

47. Ammons, "The Colorado Strike," 38.

48. "The Rosters of the Colorado National Guard, 1912–15," Colorado State Department of Military Affairs Collection; "Official List and Directory: The National Guard of Colorado, October 6, 1912, Office of the Adjutant General," the Papers of Captain Hildreth Frost, Western History Collection, box 1, envelope 2, DPL, Denver; DeStefanis, "Guarding Capital," 252, 291–93.

49. Ammons, "The Colorado Strike," 38.

50. McGovern and Guttridge, *The Great Coalfield War*, 30–35; Martelle, *Blood Passion*, 32–33; DeStefanis, "Guarding Capital," 104–23.

51. DeStefanis, "Guarding Capital," 124–25.

52. *RMN*, December 18, 1913.

53. Ammons to William P. Daniels, December 26, 1913, Papers of Elias Ammons, box 26745, file folder 3.

54. Ammons to George Kindel, December 27, 1913, Papers of Elias Ammons, box 26747, file folder 1.

55. *RMN*, December 18, 1913.

56. *RMN*, December 13, 1913; McGovern and Guttridge, *The Great Coalfield War*, 168; Papanikolas, *Buried Unsung*, 146, 150–53; Martelle, *Blood Passion*, 155.

57. Ammons to E. A. Whittlesey, July 13, 1914, Papers of Elias Ammons, box 26750, file folder 1. Ammons echoed these sentiments when he testified publicly before the US Senate's Commission on Industrial Relations.

58. "New immigrants" was a term that emerged in the 1880s to refer to immigrants from southern and eastern Europe who began coming to the United States in large numbers during that decade. The term became a way of distinguishing these immigrants from "old" or "old stock" immigrants who came to the United States from the British Isles and northwestern Europe. The term also strong implied that these "new" immigrants were inferior to earlier, "old stock" immigrants.

59. Biennial Message of Governor Elias Ammons, January 8, 1915, Papers of Elias Ammons, box 8850A, vol. 22.

60. Testimony of Elias Ammons, *CIR Testimony*, vol. 7, 6417.

61. Stone, *A History of Colorado*, vol. 2, 32–38

62. Democratic Party of Colorado, *Democratic State Platform: Progress in Every Plank* (Denver: Democratic State Central Committee 1912), 9.

63. Ammons to Senator Charles S. Thomas, August 3, 1914, Papers of Elias Ammons, Box 26749, file folder 5.

64. Charles Thomas to Elias Ammons, August 11, 1914, Papers of Elias Ammons, box 26749, file folder 5.

65. Ammons to Thomas, August 17, 1914, Papers of Elias Ammons, box 26749, file folder 5.

66. "Proceedings of Joint Conference, State Capitol (Denver), November 26, 1913," and "Business Interests," Papers of the Colorado Fuel and Iron Company, RG 2, box 24, Rockefeller Archives Center, Sleepy Hollow, New York.

67. Ibid., 181.

68. The solidarity across ethnic and racial lines that southern Colorado's coal miners developed before and during the 1913–14 coal strike was remarkable and should be kept in mind when thinking about these miners' comments. See, for instance, Andrews, *Killing for Coal*, 257–66, for his analysis of the conference between the coal mine operators and the three striking miners.

69. Ammons, "The Colorado Strike," 34, 39, 40; testimony of Elias Ammons, *CIR Testimony*, vol. 7, 6417.

70. DeStefanis, "Guarding Capital," 204–79; Gwendolyn Mink, *Old Labor and New Immigrants in American Political Development: Union, Party, and State, 1875–1920* (Ithaca, NY: Cornell University Press, 1986), 45–68.

71. Mink, *Old Labor and New Immigrants in American Political Development*, 52, 68. In Colorado, Secretary of State and State Labor Commissioner James B. Pearce echoed the AFL's position on immigration as the coal strike began. Pearce, who, like Governor Ammons, was a Democrat, contended that when he was a boy in Ohio the miners there "were made up of the best class of skilled laborers who were all American-born or Scotch, Irish, Welsh, and English." The miners in southern Colorado, however, were "a conglomerate mass of Italians, natives of the Slavonic countries, and Greeks." After revealing that a mine operator had told him that if the strike continued, he would bring in strikebreakers from Mexico, Pearce observed that "such a class of labor would simply be one shade lower than that which is now . . . in the field." Pearce went on to say that the "best conditions of workers in countries where the miners came from are not as good as the worst conditions in the US" and that the immigrant miners "might be hoarding their savings to send them back to their home countries. If that was true, the workmen were of no benefit to America." Pearce made these comments as he declared his *support* for the coal strike and the union. Pearce's comments appear in the *RMN*, October 9, 1913.

72. Testimony of Edward L. Doyle, *CIR Testimony*, vol. 8, 7017–18.

73. Mink, *Old Labor and New Immigrants in American Political Development*, 113–57; Jameson, *All That Glitters*, 140–96.

74. Lamont Bowers to John D. Rockefeller Jr., November 18, 1913, and "Rockefeller, Jr., Exhibit No. 2," *CIR Testimony*, vol. 9, 8421–22.

FOUR

# In Order to Form a More Perfect Worker

## John D. Rockefeller Jr. and Reform in Post-Ludlow Southern Colorado

*Robin C. Henry*

The tumultuous events of the winter and early spring of 1913–14 transformed the coalfields and company towns of southern Colorado and marked a new episode in relations between labor and management. In the aftermath of the largest and deadliest strike in US history, no one could know the changes that lay ahead for all parties involved. As the shock of the events wore away, tears turned to anger and miners' families, as well as many Americans, wondered how a mining strike could result in the death of thirty-three men, women, and children. For those Americans who had never felt particularly sympathetic toward labor unions, the deaths of women and children tipped the balance, if not in favor of labor unions, at least away from the owners and managers of Colorado Fuel and Iron Company (CF&I). At the center of this firestorm lay John D. Rockefeller Sr. As the director and chief stockholder of CF&I in southern Colorado, as well as a nationally recognizable businessman and philanthropist, Rockefeller appeared to be a natural focus for all the anger, rage, grief, and emotion that swirled around what the *Rocky Mountain News* called the Ludlow Massacre. When workers and labor activists learned

DOI: 10.5876/9781607323105.c004

that Rockefeller had transferred stock and controlling shareholder status to his son, John D. Rockefeller Jr., their anger shifted to Junior as well.

This chapter examines the ways in which Rockefeller Jr. used the crisis of Ludlow and the soft power of reform not only to revolutionize the workplace but also to remove the last vestiges of frontier living and make southern Colorado more hospitable to social reform and antivice movements. Though Rockefeller himself did not play an active role in statewide reform or politics, his financial backing and support helped create, support, and sustain an environment willing to demonize, clamp down on, and regulate vice. As an adherent to the Progressive Era principles of welfare capitalism, the gospel of efficiency, and muscular Christianity, Junior used organizations, such as the Young Men's Christian Association (YMCA), longitudinal statistical studies on vice, the new pseudoscience of eugenics, and eventually the law to reshape his workers, providing the necessary tools to turn the workers into docile company men. While Rockefeller relied on his national experiences in reform and antivice organizations to guide his decision at CF&I, the work that Rockefeller funded in Colorado also influenced and affected national and international social betterment work throughout the twentieth century. Thus, in his desire to meet his managerial needs at CF&I, Rockefeller helped bolster a fledgling social reform agenda within Colorado and connect it into the larger national and international reform movements that would continue to make an impact on social betterment throughout the world during the twentieth century.

Even in the aftermath of the strike and violence, Rockefeller blamed outside pressures—the United Mine Workers of America (UMWA) and labor activists, such as Mother Jones—for attempting to force his workers to unionize. Throughout, he remained steadfast in his belief that he and his board had made the correct decisions to protect their company and the welfare of the stockholders. Initially, Junior's business philosophy mirrored his father's. Testifying in front of the US House Subcommittee of the Committee on Mines and Mining in March 1914, he praised his father and the CF&I executive board, finding no fault in the business structure that established Rockefeller Sr. as an absentee owner that delegated authority to the CF&I executive board, and monitored the company's performance remotely by pouring over statistics. It was a model that had worked at Standard Oil, so why change?

Junior's testimony helped support his father and CF&I, but only as a close observer; when he testified, Junior held no stock in CF&I. To reward his son's loyalty, however, Senior transferred ten thousand shares—a 40 percent controlling interest—to his son, increasing his share and risk in the company.[1] Within a month, this reward would begin to feel more like a curse as the news of dead women and children reverberated across the nation. Outspoken and defiant, Junior initially blamed the miners for the death of their families, claiming that "while this loss of life is profoundly to be regretted, it is unjust in the extreme to lay it at the door of the defenders of law and property, who were in no slightest way responsible for it."[2] The public criticism he and his family received, however, made him question his father's business practices, seeing them, for the first time, as antiquated. Recognizing that he had been inadequately informed about the situation at CF&I, Junior slowly realized that he needed to repair his family's public image and restore the public's trust in him as both a businessman and philanthropist. With the help of Ivy Lee, an early founder of the field of public relations, Rockefeller Jr. began the process of reconstructing his image and relationship with the American public.

From day one, Rockefeller turned over every aspect of his life and business entirely to Lee, who suggested a multifaceted approach to correcting the public's perception of Rockefeller as a corporate monster. Lee's goal was to make everything Rockefeller did explicit and transparent, declaring, "The days of the rear door philosophy [are] over. Mr. Rockefeller will have to enter through the same door as everyone else."[3] Lee believed that making him more knowledgeable of and active in every facet of CF&I would help change public perception. Lee's involvement in Rockefeller's, and thus CF&I's, future marked a turning point in the relationship between Rockefeller and the miners throughout his holdings in southern Colorado.

Lee helped guide Rockefeller through the tumultuous first year after the strike. He prepared him for his testimony given again before the House Subcommittee on Mines and Mining in April 1914 and for his January 1915 testimony in front of the US Commission on Industrial Relations. After his congressional appearances, Lee encouraged Rockefeller to take a goodwill tour of the CF&I mines and company towns later that summer. But these were only short-term actions. In order to make a longer lasting and more meaningful impact on his mines and miners, Lee persuaded Rockefeller

FIGURE 4.1 John D. Rockefeller Jr. (seated front and center) with employee representatives outside of the CF&I Administration Building, 1915 (courtesy of the Bessemer Historical Society / CF&I Archives)

to reject the mantel of the absentee owner, and instead convinced him to become more involved in the daily business practices and structure of his company. With Lee's guidance, Rockefeller helped create, develop, and implement the Colorado Industrial Plan. Better known as the Rockefeller Plan, this employment improvement plan reconfigured the managerial structure of CF&I and marked what historians David Montgomery and Jonathan Rees have identified as a dynamic shift in labor-management relations in the United States, and eventually throughout the world. Though the creation of a company union did not satisfy workers' demands for collectivization, for managers it marked a middle ground and remained a standard form of company-run organization until the Wagner Act of 1937.[4] Throughout 1914 and 1915, Rockefeller spoke at universities, corporate boardrooms, and worksites to promote his industrial plan and to mark what he believed to be a new day in industrial management. Equally important, he hoped that by providing a company union through which the miners could participate and articulate their ideas and concerns, he would restore his reputation with miners while maintaining the respect of his fellow businessmen.

Though the Rockefeller Plan helped to transform labor-management relations throughout the twentieth century, it represented only half of his plan to reconstruct his labor force. For Rockefeller, restructuring the relationship between labor and management left the reconstruction process incomplete and thus vulnerable to future crises. Therefore, Rockefeller believed it was necessary to not only reconfigure the work environment, but to reconstruct the miner. Though this was Rockefeller's first social experiment to reconstruct his miners' home, work, and personal life, he drew on both hard and soft reform measures, creations of decades of work in reform movements in New York and Chicago, sociological research, and the work of CF&I's Sociological Department (SD) and its highly regarded physician Dr. Richard W. Corwin.[5] Like many men of his age and class, Rockefeller was involved in Progressive Era reform and involved himself with organizations, such as the YMCA, as well as local organizations that supported efforts to clean up cities and do away with vice. Rockefeller, however, had assets beyond those of the average reformer. His financial and personal connections allowed him to delve deeper into vice reform and help fund research projects, support the passage of legislation, and expand organizations that made a significant impact in local and national reform throughout the twentieth century.

Rockefeller's reform interests in southern Colorado were two pronged. First, he saw CF&I as a place to implement some of his and others' best ideas—ideas borne of local, regional, and national efforts to reform American cities—that emphasized a sense of community, and the importance of Protestant, middle-class values in order to transform his miners into more perfect workers. Rockefeller's attempts at reconstructing his miners' behavior did not stop in the workplace. He tightened control of personal behavior, including efforts to change men's leisure activities—drinking, swearing, church attendance, participation in social and political clubs, and sexual behavior. Second, he used his reform efforts in southern Colorado to advance other national reform and antivice projects that served as the foundations for Rockefeller-sponsored organizations, such as the Bureau of Social Hygiene, the Rockefeller Institute for Medical Research (RIMR), and the Rockefeller Foundation, which had a larger national and international impact throughout the twentieth century. Thus, the

Ludlow Massacre remains a pivotal moment not only in labor relations but also in the history of the Rockefellers and reform in the twentieth century.

Rockefeller first turned to the YMCA to help reform miners. Junior had grown up with an appreciation of the YMCA and its potential to act as a liaison for young men between the modern world of corporate capitalism and the traditional morals of their youths.[6] The secretaries of the YMCA—all white, middle-class men—were filled with what Robert Wiebe identifies as "an earnest desire to remake the world upon their private models"[7] and worked to instill the philosophy of the Protestant, white, middle class at YMCAs throughout the nation. This phenomenon led to a homogenous YMCA leadership in the 1910s and 1920s and perpetuated negative stereotypes of immigrants, African Americans, and the working class. Though never a YMCA secretary, Rockefeller easily fell into this categorization, and thus felt comfortable with the YMCA as an organization at CF&I.

Following in the footsteps of his father, Rockefeller began contributing to the YMCA in 1902. By 1914, Rockefeller was a longtime supporter of the YMCA ethos and significant financial contributor. His fiscal support of the YMCA's evangelism demonstrated his belief that "the time [was] ripe for an aggressive and comprehensive campaign among the North American Associations for the preaching of the gospel to young men, for the promotion of Bible Study and enlisting these young men in definite Christian services."[8] Through games, conversations, lectures, Bible studies, and civic classes, Rockefeller believed that the YMCA could serve, in historian Thomas Winter's assessment, as a "key to a revolution in identity" by building a community between men of all classes in the image of the middle class.[9]

This long-standing relationship between Rockefeller and the YMCA was exactly the type of philanthropic endeavor that Ivy Lee wanted to exploit on behalf of his fallen client in spring 1914. Lee took Rockefeller's years of fiscal contributions and personal involvement in the YMCA and used them to bolster Rockefeller's image as a Christian man. By 1914 Rockefeller's overall contributions amounted to $22,500, or roughly 5 percent of the YMCA's annual budget. As in earlier years, he continued to earmark his donations, focusing on Bible study, student outreach, and a growing and important department for Rockefeller, the Industrial Department (ID).[10]

As one of the largest YMCA departments, the Industrial Department was something Rockefeller relied on to provide necessary tools for his workers and teaching a work ethic and sense of manhood that reflected the middle-class values of welfare capitalism. Not only was it the distinct purpose of the ID to mold foreigners into citizens, with Rockefeller's influence, it also established programs to attempt to "promote right relationships between management and labor."[11] By 1913, on the eve of the Colorado strike, it had enrolled over 23,000 immigrants in classes to study English and American citizenship. Teachers and volunteers from the Industrial Department would identify ports of entry, such as Ellis Island, and important railroad destinations, such as Chicago, where immigrants traveled, and meet them when they disembarked. The members of the ID wanted to let the newly arrived immigrants know of the assimilation and instruction tools available to them immediately, before too many other influences could take hold. Industrial Department secretary W. S. Richardson stated:

> The importance of this work can hardly be over-estimated when we realize the necessity of training the multitude of immigrants, which are constantly coming to this country. What the Christian Church may not do for obvious reasons, the YMCA can readily do, both in leading to an understanding of the English language and of our political and civic life.[12]

Though Lee focused on the YMCA overall, Rockefeller believed the ID held the key to solving his real problem, his ill-formed workers.

The YMCA's language on manhood and character development also intrigued Rockefeller. Winter points out that the secretaries designed the language about manhood to express their middle-class ideas about the ideal relationship between managers and laborers, a language that would increase the loyalty of the worker to the company and decrease what Rockefeller believed was "a natural impetus to social and labor unrest."[13] In several editions of the YMCA publication *Railroad Men and Industrial Magazine*, workers could read articles entitled "Where a Man Spends His Money and His Leisure, Determines His Efficiency" and "An Industrial Worker's Efficiency Depends upon His Living, Working, and Recreative Conditions."[14] True men, according to the YMCA philosophy, not only showed their loyalty to their company through declining to participate in activities that could lead to social or labor unrest but they also were efficient workers, with living and working conditions that conformed to middle-class models.

This final message was as much for the employers, such as Rockefeller, as it was for the employees. Though the employees had a responsibility to choose a path toward workplace democracy, they had a responsibility to create environments that reinforced ideas about manhood and cordial relationships between themselves and their workers. Through managers' diligent attentions, the YMCA professed, socialist agitators would have less of a change to recruit naive newcomers and corrupt them. This philosophy was very much in line with Rockefeller's own desires for reconstructing the men in his mines. He fully supported programs both at the YMCA and independently at CF&I that taught principles of democracy and a Protestant, middle-class work ethic, such as baseball teams, Bible and English classes, home and beautification contests, and citizenship lectures.

Supporting and improving upon the YMCA in southern Colorado was a popular idea with CF&I executives, as well as with Lee and Rockefeller. Lee advised Rockefeller to not only continue his contributions to the YMCA, but to increase them with a special caveat that the additional contributions go directly to building YMCA programs and facilities in Denver, Pueblo, and in the mining communities surrounding the CF&I mines in southern Colorado. After Ludlow, Rockefeller's YMCA contributions did increase by a substantial amount, from $22,500 in 1914 to $40,000 by 1918.[15] By increasing his contributions, Rockefeller helped the YMCA of Colorado target the needs of his miners and support a message of welfare capitalism in three new ways. First, the YMCA organized a new Mining Department to address specific needs in the mines and mining towns.[16] Second, Rockefeller helped found a new YMCA branch at Minnequa, built "for the benefit of its employees at the Minnequa Steel Works in Pueblo" at a total expense of $225,000 jointly born by Rockefeller father and son.[17] It consisted of a state-of-the-art "modern, well equipped Association building adjacent to the Steel Works . . . with one or two small buildings to be added later."[18] Third, Rockefeller helped fund the erection of six new YMCA camps near the Morley, Sopris, Segundo, Primero, Rouse, and Lester Mines. In a letter to Starr J. Murphy, W. S. Richardson emphasized that Rockefeller's donation would be allocated to fund programs that underscored "the Americanization of foreigners, with an emphasis on religious work."[19]

Richardson understood Rockefeller's desire to use the YMCA programs to help reconstruct the character of the miners with the hopes that they would shed their previous "socialistic views" and adopt American ideals that would align more closely with Rockefeller's own, and allowed the mines to operate without threat of agitation. For the most part, the YMCA's mission and work replicated the philosophy and reform efforts already conducted at CF&I by the internal Sociological Department, founded in 1901 by J. C. Osgood to address decade-long labor problems and to mitigate future industrial warfare.[20] Because it appeared more independent than the Sociological Department, however, Lee believed that the YMCA might prove to be a safer, neutral ground to continue teaching the principles of welfare capitalism in the post-Ludlow period. Thus Rockefeller hired Clarence J. Hicks from the YMCA to conduct CF&I's industrial relation programs, slowly turning the Sociological Department programs over to the YMCA.

With increased funds, came increased membership. Not only did the YMCA boast of a nearly 12,000-man membership at its Denver branch, but it also averaged about 5,000 men at its southern Colorado coalfield facilities.[21] To emphasize a connection between the presence of the YMCA and a flourishing sense of workplace democracy, Hicks noted a decline in worker unrest and agitation "of the kind we knew in '14" that he attributed to the "remarkably improved conditions in the mining camps through the positive influence of the YMCA."[22] Particular to the YMCAs in CF&I communities, each YMCA had classes and discussion groups to talk about the Rockefeller Industrial Plan. Therefore not only were miners exposed to the general ideology of the YMCA, but also to the specifics of the Rockefeller Plan. By incorporating the social and industrial, Rockefeller used the YMCAs as one part of his larger strategy to control the environment of CF&I and turn his workers into "a big family."[23]

Rockefeller's "big family" may have incorporated new YMCA programs that specifically targeted what he identified as the key components of labor unrest, but he also built on the foundation of nearly fifteen years of social betterment, hygiene, and Americanization programs in and around CF&I company towns. In a 1902 edition of the in-house publication, *Camp and Plant*, the author touted the commitment the company had to "social betterment in the Rocky Mountains," writing,

> For years the Colorado Fuel and Iron Company has done much for the betterment of its employes [*sic*]. It has aided schools, supported churches, estab-

> lished kindergarten, and maintained hospitals. It is now spending thousands of dollars to improve the conditions of men and their families. It may be of interest to our readers to know that it is spending a quarter of a million of dollars on a hospital plant exclusively for its employes [*sic*].

Although the author emphasizes the size and breadth of commitment the company had to its employees,[24] the use of words such as *exclusively* and phrases like "it may be of interest to our readers" draws attention to the fact that not only was the company funding the programs, but it also wanted the employees and other external readers to know of its actions. Additional articles approached the subject of "social betterment" in different ways and speak more to the employees. Instead of touting the good deeds of the company, these articles remind readers to enter contests for the best lawn and gardens in the Minnequa mining camp, as well as to provide up-to-date statistics from the YMCA baseball league.[25] Other articles encouraged the miners' wives "to take their children to the YMCA buildings for bathing facilities"; reminding them that not only is regular bathing the first step to reduce epidemics in the camps, but that the YMCA is vigilantly looking for the first signs of contagion.[26] Still other titles, such as "From Poor Cooking to Drunkenness" and "Hygienic Conditions of the Mines," give a sense of the full-court press that the YMCA gave on the subject of hygiene and social betterment. These constant reminders—both large and small—show the ever-present social hygiene and betterment message miners and their families received on a consistent basis. Miners could not overlook the YMCA philosophies on cleanliness, hygiene, order, efficiency, beauty, and health; they pervaded every edition of the in-house magazine. Taking a cue from the SD, the YMCA and Junior used these principles to assimilate his workers and decrease worker agitation.

Rockefeller took ideas from his work with national and international reform organizations to transform his workers. It was through this work, in part, that Junior found his passion for reform. Both father and son Rockefeller supported medical, educational, and social reforms—giving generous sums to reform movements, such as the Anti-Saloon League and establishing the Rockefeller Institute for Medical Research, the General Education Board, and the Bureau of Social Hygiene. But historians often cite Rockefeller's service as foreman of the New York City Grand Jury investigating the trafficking of white women and children in 1909–10 as the nexus of his personal involvement and investment of time and energy in social hygiene and sexual reform movements.[27] Like many men of the Progressive Era, Rockefeller believed that education, science, and money could be combined to alleviate, if not completely eliminate, social problems and labor unrest that challenged the stability of the capitalist system. Early in 1911, Rockefeller became interested in the pseudoscience of eugenics. Like many people the world over, he believed that genetic markers, ethnicity in particular, served as important indicators of personality, talents, and moral weaknesses. In February 1911, Junior began contributing to the Committee on Eugenics to support this research in the hopes of improving relations between labor and management. This organization promised to bring the Eugenics movement to the United States and work with government officials and reform-minded citizens and philanthropists to gather more information about the "reasons of inherited qualities, defective, criminal, or susceptible to disease through the three-pronged methodology of 'investigation, education, and legislation.'"[28] Starr J. Murphy, Rockefeller's lawyer, believed that these three principles of the Committee on Eugenics mirror Rockefeller's own approach to solving problems. In March, he wrote again to Rockefeller, stating,

> I have become greatly interested in this subject of Eugenics, and believe it is to be one of those fundamental things which underlie all our problems of education, of crime, and of charity. When these laws are fully worked out they cannot fail to profoundly affect our theories of education, our whole attitude toward the question of crime and its prevention and treatment, and the effect of knowledge on these subjects in the minds of the public generally, and will certainly have an effect on the perpetuation of defective strains.[29]

Murphy suggested that Rockefeller invest $5,400 in a new doctor, Dr. Davenport, who was just beginning his work in eugenics, with a focus on crime prevention. Between 1911 and 1915, Rockefeller maintained his financial commitment with Davenport, but continually pushed him to partner with more prestigious and well-funded and better-equipped institutions, such as the Rockefeller Institute for Medical Research, which had been founded in 1901 to support "medical research with special reference to the prevention and treatment of disease,"[30] or the Johns Hopkins Medical School to complete his research. By 1913, Davenport maintained his independence, but had created a Board of Scientific Directors, including Alexander Graham Bell, and members from Yale, Johns Hopkins, and Harvard Medical Schools. Two years later, however, Davenport's research, which had promised to transform law enforcement, had only managed to apply the principles of eugenics to the marriage law of one state, Pennsylvania; the law stated, "no marriage could be performed in the State without a certificate showing that both parties were free from communicable disease."[31] With such small returns on his investments, Rockefeller discontinued his support for Davenport in 1915, but continued to fund similar eugenics studies conducted by Dr. Richard W. Corwin, physician at CF&I in Pueblo through 1920.

Corwin serves as an example of Colorado's influence on the national discussion of eugenics and reform. Rockefeller identified Corwin's work in Pueblo as instrumental in developing the trust of local workers while promoting a strong Protestant work ethic in his mines and a strong model of corporate welfare. As CF&I physician, Corwin believed that the southern and central European immigrants flooding Colorado were "drawn from the lower classes of foreign immigrants" and that they expressed "primitive ideas of living and ignorance of hygienic laws."[32] To combat these problems, Corwin believed that immigrants needed special help and guidance to become Americanized.

To provide this help, Corwin used Rockefeller money to establish programs that he believed strengthened the worker and his family. Corwin supervised a small medical and research team that provided both general medical care and social betterment programs for the miners and their families. Like the YMCA, he sponsored classes in American cooking and English language, set up baseball leagues, and held gardening and home decoration competitions, as well as provided temperance dining rooms for the miners and their families. Though Corwin was centered in Pueblo, he had traveled to all the CF&I camps, to provide general healthcare and to observe the miners' general behavior. By 1914, Corwin also provided Colorado's public schools with a uniform curriculum, steeped in Protestant, middle-class ethics, so that when families moved among the mines, the children's education remained consistent.

During the post-Ludlow years, Corwin experienced a financial windfall when Rockefeller and the CF&I management increased their funding and supported facility upgrades and expansions. In fact, Murphy wrote to Corwin shortly after his visit with Rockefeller to Colorado in the summer of 1915 and expressed how impressed he and Rockefeller were with Corwin's work and clinic.[33] Corwin also maintained a cordial correspondence with Rockefeller, sending him notes of congratulations on speeches given and papers delivered that mentioned his work, as well as the CF&I-YMCA. Never wanting to appear on the frontier of the medical community, Corwin, however, was always quick to point out the ways in which his clinical work relied on and connected to larger research projects and grants around the country, such as the distribution of influenza and pneumonia vaccines to the company employees and their families.[34] By 1918, however, Corwin was competing with the Rockefeller Institute for Medical Research for Rockefeller's attention and money. Though Rockefeller never fully abandoned Corwin and his work, by 1920 he and his management had encouraged Corwin to apply to the RIMR and not to Rockefeller directly for clinic funding and research monies.

In addition to Corwin's work, Rockefeller supported national studies to investigate vice and sexual behavior. Though he partnered with the Committee of Fifteen in Chicago and financially supported studies throughout New York, Rockefeller realized that if reformers were ever going to make headway in tackling these problems, they needed to conduct studies outside of the two largest American cities. Cities in the West held particular interest for Rockefeller, not only because they remained understudied but also because if he were ever to reconstruct his southern Colorado miners, he needed to eliminate vice and prostitution. Therefore, in 1917 Rockefeller commissioned the Bessemer Historical Society (BHS) to conduct two multicity investigations of prostitution and vice. For the first study, the Bureau sent Dr. H. B. Woolston to cities throughout the United States. Covering all regions and sizes of cities, Woolston investigated how the nation's cities dealt with vice.[35] Comprehensive in its focus, Rockefeller intended this study not only to pinpoint regional and local problems that each city addressed, but also to identify how local legal and law enforcement communities dealt with vice outside of New York and Chicago. The second study focused specifically on how western cities dealt with prostitution and vice. Under the direction of Raymond Fosdick, the bureau sent Joseph R. Mayer to visit cities in the West, including Oakland, Portland, Vancouver, Seattle, Butte, Salt Lake City, and Denver. These studies' findings would help Junior in developing his plans for the miners.

Though the new Mining Department, YMCA branches, and YMCA camps represented a new, more focused commitment on Rockefeller's behalf to mold his miners, it was still more of the same. Despite the difficulty in gauging the miners' sense of wanting to be taught to be Americans, it is clear that Rockefeller believed that the YMCA, Dr. Corwin's work in eugenics, and national organizational research were all vehicles to make these changes. Rockefeller, however, believed that soft reform and sociological data only went so far in aiding industrialists; he also supported passage of reform legislation, such as state- and nationally sponsored prohibition amendments. Longtime holders of the belief that alcohol fueled vice and unrest among workers, both Rockefellers had for many years been supporters of the Anti-Saloon League, a national organization, donating over $350,00 to the parent organization and to the Ohio and New York State organizations between 1900 and 1919.[36] Since the founding of its first temperance society in Aurora in 1858, Colorado prohibition efforts had experienced a mixed, level of support. While in 1866 the prohibition fraternity the Independent Order of Good Templars, boasted to have over 1,000 members, saloons continued to increase, reaching over 300 in Denver alone by 1880. In Colorado Springs, Pueblo, and the southern Colorado CF&I company towns attempts to ban saloons and alcohol met with mixed results. Even the state chapter of the Anti-Saloon League, founded in 1898, struggled to make a positive impact, and both the 1908 and 1910 prohibition amendments failed.[37] Beginning in 1912, the Rockefellers began contributing to the Colorado Anti-Saloon League, a financial commitment the family kept until 1926. In the wake of the Ludlow crisis, however, Junior took it upon himself to increase his contribution to the Colorado State branch, to support dry politicians and judges, and to throw financial backing behind the state prohibition amendment, which finally became law in 1916. Like many reformers, Rockefeller believed that prohibition would transform the reputations of Denver and Colorado as rough-and-tumble frontier towns, into one of a modern city. On a more personal level, Junior also believed that prohibition would play a key role in creating an environment more amenable to law and order, while decreasing labor unrest. Though Rockefeller was by no means alone in his commitment to prohibition, or his enthusiasm to legislate behavior, his support and distribution of monies throughout the state for dry issues, candidates, and reforms went a long way in solidifying its passage.

Once again, Rockefeller turned to the YMCA as a transformative location for his miners and as an alternative to saloons. Reassuring his workers, he wrote to them, "[You do not need to think that] the closing of the saloon will deprive you of a place of amusement, or drive you to leave your camp and seek some illegal "dive."[38] Instead, Rockefeller urged employees to make use of new or updated buildings and recreation rooms at the camps, where they could find "soda fountains, with also a good assortment of bottled soft drinks and ice cream, tobaccos, candy, piano Grafonola, pool tables, small games, a very complete list of magazines and papers and writing facilities, minstrel shows, tournaments, educational clubs, Bible classes, and other varied activities being promoted by aggressive leaders of the respective interests."[39] All difficult comparisons between soda fountains and beer halls aside, Rockefeller truly saw these new activities as a way to shape, mold, and supervise the leisure time of his workers. Through the YMCA, he was able to build recreation halls that, in his eyes, would provide a bevy of suitable activities, which in turn he hoped would show his workers the way to a more harmonious relationship with management. What is most striking, though, is the heavy-handed approach and pressure surrounding leisure. For Rockefeller leisure was serious business and needed "aggressive leaders" to help his workforce recreate appropriately.

These changes were noted by Albert W. Stone, a writer for the YMCA publication, *Association Men*, in a 1924 article commemorating the decade of change since the Ludlow strike. He observed that the men no longer talked about socialism, grievances, or strikes. Instead, the "talk turned of 'dividends,' 'common stock,' and such matters among the fifty-four nationalities of the company's family."[40] Though his claim does not take into consideration workers' views or the continued strikes and disagreements between management and labor, Stone believed Rockefeller's transplantation of the YMCA to his southern mines had aided in reconstructing the miners and, thereby, decreasing the unrest. Nevertheless, subsequent strikes and demands to unionize clearly show that not *all* talk had transitioned to corporate capitalist chitchat.

Rockefeller's miner reconstruction plan did change the physical appearance and daily habits of his mining communities, however. According to Dr. Peter Robert's report to the YMCA, by 1919 the Pueblo area had more churches with higher levels of attendance, more schools with a greater percentage of men completing the eighth grade, and more men participating in industrial

FIGURE 4.2 "Patriotic Rally of Walsen Miners" at the YMCA Club House; hundreds of miners and their families of European Descent "enthusiastically attended the rally," 1917 (courtesy of the Bessemer Historical Society / CF&I Archives)

democracy programs at the YMCA, than before the strike. The internalization of the YMCA and Rockefeller's message remain less clear, however, than new buildings and programs. As Colorado moved into the 1920s, the economic unrest of 1914 appeared to be dampened, but not entirely over. Miners still grieved and went on strike for higher wages, more control of their work environment, and the ability to unionize, but never to such a devastating pitch of 1914. Rockefeller believed that his Industrial Representation Plan contributed to this decline in worker violence, but he also wrote of the "overwhelming achievement of remaking the miners in our image." He continued, "They were only yearning to be taught how to be Americans."[41] Though it is difficult to gauge the miners' sense of wanting to be taught to be Americans, it is clear that Rockefeller's ideas on masculinity, social improvement, and the trust he placed in the YMCA helped to change the parameters of acceptable behavior in southern Colorado in the early twentieth century.

Though the Rockefeller and the YMCA-CF&I held similar goals for inculcating into the workers a middle-class philosophy, the workers had mixed

FIGURE 4.3 Girls of several nationalities in educational class, 1920 (courtesy of the Bessemer Historical Society / CF&I Archives)

feelings about the changes. Many did not participate in the programs; baseball teams formed, Bible groups held discussions, English classes took place, but behind the scenes, some miners did not feel that their needs were met by either CF&I's new Industrial Plan or the YMCA's socialization programs. According to the Robert's report, the pressure to shop at the company store decreased after the IP took effect in 1915. The miners, however, continued to voice their discontent with the company store's monopoly, claiming that the only alternative was a monthly visit from a single, poorly stocked peddler. The same complaints arose about company housing. Though never as violent, strikes occurred regularly after 1914, showing that there remained unresolved issued between CF&I and the miners. Roberts also found miners resistant to the social activities, finding that instead of enthusiastically clamoring to join the company baseball teams, workers instead felt pressured to participate in the program after work, and to give up their lunch hours to weekly, and in some cases twice-a-week, Bible classes. The heavy-handed implementation of these socialization programs reflected Rockefeller's belief that measures needed to be taken to reconstruct the miner himself. Though they did not change the conditions in his Colorado mines to completely conform to his image, they did reflect a more active presence of control from Rockefeller and his management team at CF&I.

In later years, Rockefeller's influence on social issues and sexual behavior reached beyond CF&I and Colorado, to affect public policy in the United States and around the globe. Rees argues that Rockefeller's IP "held considerable influence in Canada, and it effects can still be seen in industrial relations practiced in the United Kingdom, Japan, Germany, Australia."[42] But in the post-Ludlow years, Rockefeller maintained his interest in the Progressive Era project of perfecting humanity through expanding his work with the BHS and the Rockefeller Foundation. The BHS's mission to combat early twentieth-century cities' epidemics of social disease and crime took Rockefeller's ideals about masculinity, sexuality, behavior, and democracy to broader American and global audiences, thus contributing to what historian Daniel Rodgers identified as the transnational chatter of Progressive reform.[43] For example, the BHS helped develop programs to combat sexually transmitted diseases during World War I—a policy that remained intact though not administered by the BHS during World War II—as well as addressing more general issues of sexuality, promiscuity, and prostitution.[44]

Though the bureau's main battleground was New York City, its policies toward sexuality and sexual behavior had long-lasting effects on social policy throughout the nation, most notably by increasing the reliance on the state to regulate sexual behavior. Through the creation and implementation of the Rockefeller Plan, Montgomery argues, we can see the relationship between the state and the workplace transforming, but I suggest that the same principle applies to the relationship among the state, nonstate organizations, and the worker overapplying Protestant, middle-class values in order to form a more perfect worker.[45] What may be one of the most interesting results of Rockefeller's attempts to change the character of his Colorado workers remains the depths and lengths to which he involved himself, his family, and eventually the Rockefeller philanthropies in the ongoing conversations about masculinity, sexuality, class, and culture throughout the twentieth century and beyond.

## Notes

1. Ron Chernow, *Titan: The Life of John D. Rockefeller, Sr.* (New York: Random House, 1998), 572–74; Raymond B. Fosdick, *John D. Rockefeller, Jr.: A Portrait* (New York: Harper and Brothers, Co., 1956), 143–45.

2. Rockefeller Family Papers, RG2, series BI, subseries CF&I, box 13, folder 105, Rockefeller Archives Center (hereafter cited as RAC).

3. Ray Eldon Hiebert, *Courtier to the Crowd: The Story of Ivy Lee and the Development of Public Relations* (Ames: Iowa State University, 1966), 104.

4. David Montgomery, *The Fall of the House of Labor: The Workplace, the State, and American Labor Activism, 1865–1925* (New York: Cambridge University Press, 1987), 348–50, 355; Jonathan H. Rees, *Representation and Rebellion: The Rockefeller Plan at the Colorado Fuel and Iron Company, 1914–1942* (Boulder: University of Colorado Press, 2010), 29–52; Ruth Hutchison Crocker, *Social Work and Social Order: The Settlement Movement in Two Industrial Cities, 1889–1930* (Chicago: University of Illinois Press, 1992), 95–110; H. Lee Scamehorn, *Mill & Mine: The CF&I in the Twentieth Century* (Lincoln: University of Nebraska Press, 1992), 120–40; Daniel Nelson, "The Company Union Movement: 1900–1937: A Reexamination," *Business History Review* 56, no. 3 (Autumn 1982): 340–42; Thomas G. Andrews, *Killing for Coal: America's Deadliest Labor War* (Cambridge, MA: Harvard University Press, 2010), 286–91.

5. Frank J. Weed, "The Sociological Department at the Colorado Fuel and Iron Company, 1901–1907: Scientific Paternalism and Industrial Control," *Journal of the History of Behavioral Sciences* 41 (Summer 2005): 269–70.

6. Helen Lefkowitz Horowitz, *Rereading Sex: Battles over Sexual Knowledge and Suppression in Nineteenth-Century America* (Amherst: University of Massachusetts Press, 2002), 278–90; Thomas Winter, *Making Men, Making Class: The YMCA and Workingmen, 1877–1920* (Chicago: University of Chicago Press, 2002), 56–62; Fosdick, *John D. Rockefeller, Jr.*, 344.

7. Robert H. Wiebe, *The Search for Order, 1877–1920* (New York: Hill and Wang, 1967), 23.

8. Letter from Cannon to Rockefeller Jr., RG2, series BI, subseries CF&I, box 13, folder 105, 3, RAC.

9. Winter, *Making Men, Making Class*, 85.

10. Letter from W. S. Richardson to Starr J. Murphy, March 30, 1914, Rockefeller Family Papers, III2R, Welfare Interests-Youth, box 24, folder 246, 6, RAC.

11. Letter from W. S. Richardson to Starr J. Murphy, April 3, 1917, ibid.

12. Letter from W. S. Richardson to Starr J. Murphy March 30, 1914, ibid.

13. Winter, *Making Men, Making Class*, 14.

14. YMCA publications, Kautz Family Archives, Minneapolis; Winter, *Making Men, Making Class*, 35.

15. Letter from W. S. Richardson to Starr J. Murphy, March 30, 1914, Rockefeller Family Papers, III2R, Welfare Interests-Youth, box 24, folder 246, 6, RAC.

16. "Expert Aid for CF&I Clubs," *Industrial Bulletin*, vol. 2, no. 4, 10, CF&I papers, Bessemer Historical Society (hereafter BHS) and CF&I Archives.

17. "YMCA at Minnequa Steel Works," *Industrial Bulletin*, vol. 2, no. 4, 4, CF&I papers, BHS and CF&I Archives.

18. Ibid.

19. Ibid.

20. Weed, "The Sociological Department at the Colorado Fuel and Iron Company, 1901–1907," 271–73.

21. Hicks, "Relation of the YMCA," 12, folder 156, box 18, series BI, RG2, Rockefeller Family Papers, RAC; YMCAs were built and improved in the mining communities connected with CF&I in southern Colorado in Minnequa, Morley, Sopris, Segundo, Primero, Rouse, and Lester.

22. Hicks, "Relation of the YMCA," 12.

23. Albert W. Stone, "Since the Days of Ludlow," *Association Men*, February 4, 1924, 246, folder 117, box 14, series BI, RG2, Rockefeller Family Papers, RAC.

24. "Social Betterment in the Rocky Mountains," *Camp and Plant*, vol. 1, Saturday, March 1, 1902, number 12, BHS and CF&I Archives.

25. "How the CF&I Company aids in beautifying homes," *Industrial Bulletin*, vol. 1, no. 6, 7, CF&I papers, BHS and CF&I Archives.

26. *Camp and Plant*, vol. 1, no. 8, 6, CF&I papers, BHS and CF&I Archives.

27. Brian Donovan, *White Slave Crusades: Race, Gender, and Anti-Vice Activism, 1887–1917* (Chicago: University of Illinois Press, 2006), 121; David J. Langum, *Crossing over the Line: Legislating Morality and the Mann Act* (Chicago: University of Chicago Press, 1994), 24–37; David J. Pivar, *Purity and Hygiene: Women, Prostitution, and the "American Plan," 1900–1930* (Westport, CT: Greenwood Press, 2002), 83, 120–27.

28. Letter from Starr J. Murphy to Rockefeller, February 9, 1911, Rockefeller Family, RG 2.2, series Economic Interests, box 1, folder 2, RAC.

29. Letter from Murphy to Rockefeller, March 17, 1911, RF, RG 2.2, series EI, box 1, folder 2, RAC.

30. *The Philanthropic Boards Established by John D. Rockefeller*, New York: 1916, 6, RAC.

31. Letter from Murphy to Rockefeller, June 27, 1913, RF, RG 2.2, series EI, box 1, folder 2, RAC.

32. R. W. Corwin, "Advances in Medical Department Services," *Colorado Fuel and Iron Company Industrial Bulletin* 4 (January 15, 1919): 7; Montgomery, *Fall of the House*

*of Labor*, 237; Jonathan Rees, *Representation and Rebellion: The Rockefeller Plan at the Colorado Fuel and Iron Company, 1914–1942* (Boulder: University Press of Colorado, 2010); Tolman, *Social Engineering*, 55; Scamehorn, *Mine & Mill*, 85–88; Weed, "The Sociological Department at the Colorado Fuel and Iron Company, 1901–1907," 274–78.

33. Murphy to R. W. Corwin, July 20, 1915, box, 14, series BI, RG2, RFP, RAC.

34. Corwin to Rockefeller, December 5, 1918, box 14, series BI, RG2, RFP, RAC.

35. "Vice Conditions Visited by Dr. H. B. Woolston" June 1917, BHS, series 3.2, box 9, folder 194, RAC.

36. Fosdick, *John D. Rockefeller, Jr.*, 249.

37. Letter from Rockefeller Jr. to Emmet D. Boyle, April 30, 1918, RAC; Elliot West, "Cleansing the Queen City: Prohibition and Urban Reform in Denver," *Arizona and the West*, vol. 14, no. 4 (Winter 1972): 338–43; Robin C. Henry, "Criminalizing Sex, Defining Sexuality: Sodomy, Law, and Manhood in Nineteenth-Century Colorado" (PhD diss., Indiana University, 2006), 74–76.

38. "The End of the Saloon at CF&I Properties," *Industrial Bulletin*, vol. 1, no. 2, December 22, 1915, 9, CF&I papers, BHS and CF&I Archives.

39. "The YMCA in CF&I Camps," *Industrial Bulletin*, vol. 1, no. 5, 8, CF&I papers, BHS.

40. Ibid.

41. Letter from Rockefeller Jr. to Welborn, July 13, 1923, folder 127, box 15, series BI, RG2, Rockefeller Family Papers, RAC.

42. Rees, *Representation and Rebellion*, 3.

43. Daniel T. Rodgers, *Atlantic Crossings: Social Politics in a Progressive Age* (Cambridge: Belknap Harvard University, 2000), 290, 420, 460.

44. Donovan, *White Slave Crusades*, 112–24.

45. Montgomery, *The Fall of the House of Labor*, 3.

FIVE

# Field Days, YMCA, and Baseball

## CF&I's Industrial Representation Plan of 1914 and Gender Relations in Southern Colorado Coal-Mining Camps

*Fawn-Amber Montoya*

On a spring morning in April 1914, Colorado National Guard troops and striking coal miners in Ludlow, a small community in southeastern Colorado, engaged in gunfire that left strikers, strikers' wives, strikers' children, and troops dead. This massacre and the Coalfield War in southern Colorado from 1913 to 1914 left a mark on labor relations in southern Colorado and in the United States; in the aftermath, relationships were characterized by the belief that East Coast corporate management would willingly harm its employees to stop strikes. The Ludlow Massacre gained public attention when the local and national media emphasized the fact that the loss on this day was the deaths of women and children who, when the camp caught fire, suffocated in cellars underneath the tents.

The Colorado Fuel and Iron Company (CF&I), John D. Rockefeller, and his associates bought the majority of company stock a little over a decade before the massacre at Ludlow. While the Rockefeller family owned the company, they left the day-to-day affairs in the hands of their management team located in Denver. Colorado Fuel and Iron Company attracted large groups

DOI: 10.5876/9781607323105.c005

of immigrant laborers and migratory workers to the area. This diverse workforce brought along with them ideas that enabled them to ask for higher wages and safer working conditions. In 1914 and 1915, the United States federal and Colorado state governments inquired into the incident at Ludlow. The Rockefellers responded to the negative attention with a visit to the affected areas of southern Colorado by John D. Rockefeller Jr., son of the tycoon John D. Rockefeller. During his visit in fall 1915, Rockefeller Jr. introduced his ideas for a company-run union. The Industrial Relations Plan emphasized the need to improve life in the coal-mining communities of southern Colorado.[1] At the same time that Rockefeller Jr. introduced this plan, the Rockefellers allowed the Young Men's Christian Association (YMCA) to document the camps and prepare a report that allowed for the social and physical betterment of CF&I employees, their families, and overall camp life. The YMCA document, the Towson Report, illustrated that employees needed to have more access to recreational activities in order to live a more enriching lifestyle that would bring less dissatisfaction with the company and reduce the threat of strikes.[2] The report called for the establishment of YMCA buildings throughout the camps and encouraged miners to participate in athletic activities such as baseball.

The Rockefeller family's response to the massacre created an environment in southern Colorado ripe for the creation of gender roles for coal camp employees and their families through the publication of the *Industrial Bulletin*, encouragement of athletic competition and recreational activities, and the establishment of the YMCA in the coal camps. These new ideals established gendered spaces in which men and women learned how to fulfill company-approved ideas of gender. According to CF&I, men needed to be physically fit miners and the expectation for women was to be less fit than the men, the producers of children, and the caretakers of the home.

After the Ludlow Massacre of 1914, national public opinion toward The Colorado Fuel and Iron Company, the state of Colorado, and the Rockefeller family centered on the idea that these capitalistic entities were unconcerned with the living or working conditions of their employees. In 1915, John D. Rockefeller Jr. traveled to Southern Colorado to survey the physical and psychological damage of the Ludlow Massacre and to present CF&I's new Industrial Representation Plan. Rather than focusing on the company's ideas about labor, company officials began to evaluate and introduce the concept of employee/employer participation. Before Rockefeller Jr.'s visit, CF&I's managerial style did little to focus on the social or economic needs of the employee. Rockefeller's appeal to employees came across in speeches and in print. As he toured the southern Colorado coal camps and the Pueblo, Colorado, steelworks, he surveyed the damage that the strikes of 1913 and 1914 and massacre of 1914 had on employee morale. He spoke out about the need for support from all areas of the company and emphasized that the company required each of the legs of a "Square Table" to stand successfully and serve the purposes and desires of all who participated in company relations. His speech emphasized the contributions of stockholders, directors, officers, and employees to the overall success of the company.[3] The repetition and imagery of this analogy gave a tangible picture to employees of how Rockefeller Jr. perceived employee relations. He stated that each group contributed in their own unique way, either through monetary investment, bureaucratic organization, or productive labor. This idealized version of equality among all participants in the company and its affairs actually favored the bureaucratic structure and its investors.

The new plan for industrial representation called upon employee and company representatives to meet regularly to address the numerous needs of employees both in the workplace and within their respective communities. The publication and distribution of CF&I's *Industrial Bulletin* gave employees insight into company news and reports. Rockefeller's visit represented the company's public image that its stockholders tried to express to CF&I employees and the nation's media. This appeal centered on the reality that employees were central to the company and that their participation and voice in company activities would be welcomed and respected, as long as their involvement remained within the framework of the company-mandated hierarchy.

The *Industrial Bulletin* became a mouthpiece for the company to articulate ideas about gender to its employees, their families, and their communities. Company recreational activities depicted in its publication encouraged displays of femininity and masculinity through the behavior and abilities of the physical body by describing appropriate behavior for women, men, girls, and boys. The Young Men's Christian Association on the national level engaged in this dialogue and envisioned the organization as making men and subsequently defined middle-class standards of masculinity. After the 1870s these ideas of masculinity turned from middle-class to working-class men.[4]

Beyond these periodicals and letters to company employees, CF&I arranged the construction of numerous buildings for the national YMCA, and the establishment of YMCA publications as a means of meeting the social and recreational needs of CF&I employees. The introduction of the YMCA into southern Colorado brought the physical health and athletic abilities of employees and their families to the forefront of the company.

Rockefeller Jr.'s visit to southern Colorado included a speech in October 1915. He appealed to the employees as a "common stockholder" concerned with the success of the company and willing to sacrifice monetary wealth for the benefit of the employees. After this appeal, Rockefeller introduced his Plan of Representation in four parts: representation, division of CF&I into representative districts, a method for prevention and adjustment of industrial disputes, and, finally, social and industrial betterment.[5] As part of Rockefeller's social and industrial betterment, he proposed that a company representative and the president's executive assistant supervise the practices of advisory boards, hospitals and doctors, and the employees' representatives.[6]

Through the process of approving this industrial plan, company and employee representatives met between October 1915 and January 1918 to discuss a consensus for Rockefeller proposed plan. They established policies and methods for improving employees' living conditions by establishing bathhouses and social centers.[7] This contribution and concern for employees altered the environment of the southern Colorado coal camps, because the stockholders and company directors realized that in order to please their employees, they had to guarantee that they represented their interests beyond the workplace. This also established a company plan that focused on the physical health of employees.

Colorado Fuel and Iron's belief in the contribution of rural employees to the national success of a company affected the class and gender status of the workers. Attempts by CF&I to define or articulate ideals of masculinity were a characteristic of the United States at the turn of the twentieth century. On a national level, Theodore Roosevelt reinvented or established himself as masculine through his western adventures, military service, clothing, and physical appearance. Roosevelt embraced ideas that masculinity was about uplifting others, "the White man's burden. This epitome of manhood—characterized by physical strength and adventure—emerged as the dominant ideal, one who with the closing of the frontier would still be able to find a

FIGURE 5.1 Winner of the first prize in the Sociological Lawn and Garden Contest at the Frederick Mine, 1924 (courtesy of the Bessemer Historical Society / CF&I Archives)

space for himself in the United States. During World War I there was, with the push for conscription, a crisis of masculinity with the clear realization that there were men unfit for combat and that civilization had distanced men too far from their primitive masculinity. The national dialogue around a renewed interest in masculinity was a response to women's quest for greater participation in the public sphere during the Progressive Era.[8]

The beginnings of the publication of the *Industrial Bulletin* revealed a close relationship between CF&I management and the YMCA. Numerous articles emphasized the YMCA and the inclusion of its membership dues and an encouragement to join the YMCA. These publications, with their heavy backing from the YMCA, either through advertisements or the association's editorial board, further established the YMCA as a pivotal player in the development of physical bodies and employee morale.[9] Competition and athletic experiences tested and tried the body in a public setting approved by the CF&I. At the same time this public interaction and the prizes awarded for being the ideal man or woman held a symbolic meaning for YMCA

FIGURE 5.2 Steelworks YMCA educational class on automobile mechanics, 1919 (courtesy of the Bessemer Historical Society / CF&I Archives)

participants. The YMCA established a pattern by which women were valued for their reproduction and that men's knowledge of their labor and strength signified a standard for masculinity. In southern Colorado, we see this model of manhood through the rise of the YMCA.

The YMCA entrenched itself in southern Colorado and in the lives of mine workers through its organization, buildings, and ideology. In 1915 the YMCA created its own mining department in the state of Colorado. The state and international committees of the YMCA appointed a special committee to work in the camps of CF&I.[10] As the YMCA approved and erected new buildings, CF&I—through monetary donations, the inclusion of YMCA activities in company publications, and the presence of CF&I management at YMCA functions—supported these endeavors. The association became an integral part of social life in southern Colorado. The senior secretary of the YMCA, Charles Towson, verified that

> the Association has taken the initiative in this matter, the Company merely granting it permission for the study and report. No effort was made by the

company to enlist the Association, and no suggestion was imposed as to policy or program.[11]

In a series of oral interviews collected by California State University, Fullerton, in the 1970s, Alfred Montoya referenced the connection that he saw between the company and the YMCA: "They had company stores, that's where they paid yeah. They had a Y, a YMCA, you had the pool halls . . . CF and I was better, that was a better company to work for because they would take care of the camps and then they were concerned about the men too."[12] From Towson's perspective, CF&I and the YMCA remained separate entities, but for Montoya there was a direct relationship between his employment at CF&I and the YMCA. According to the Towson Report and Alfred Montoya's oral interview, the relationship between the two illustrated that physical locations and sporting events created a happier and stronger employee.

This relationship between the YMCA and CF&I, while there was apparently a distinct line between them in official commentary from executive boards, became fluid as the YMCA established new social centers in CF&I camps. In January 1916, with the passage of the Colorado state law enforcing prohibition, the YMCA continued to offer an alternative social center to CF&I employees. The YMCA operated in six camps. In three of these camps—Morley, Primero, and Rouse—the YMCA remodeled saloons to become association clubhouses. These buildings contained soda fountains, ice cream, pool tables, reading and writing materials.[13] The YMCA served as a place for social gatherings, religious meetings, and picture shows. "All nationalities avail themselves freely of the privileges," the *Industrial Bulletin* claimed.[14] Young men found leadership opportunities, and the women showed interest in sewing circles and women's social and recreational gatherings. Some women appealed to the wife of the secretary to be involved in gymnastic exercises.[15] The YMCA emphasized gender roles for women, but these women wanted to explore their own physical fitness.

Colorado Fuel and Iron incorporated ideas and standards of masculinity and femininity at their annual field days. These events centered on competitions within one's own gender and set an expectation for how the community and the company valued men and women. In 1915, CF&I inaugurated field days—company picnics with athletic events—as an attempt to improve social relations with their employees. It should be noted that employees had

FIGURE 5.3 "The Coal Miners" Trinidad Field Days, 1915 (courtesy of the Bessemer Historical Society / CF&I Archives)

organized field days since 1911 on a much smaller scale, but it was not until 1915 that the field days were heavily reported on in the *Industrial Bulletin*.

These all-day annual events included parades and athletic competitions and catered to all members of the family, regardless of age or gender. At these CF&I-sponsored field days, most of the events focused on competition between children; there were running races of all varieties: fifty- and hundred-yard dashes and sack races. The company sponsored "two basket ball games: one between boys, and one between girls under sixteen."[16] There was a hundred-yard dash for boys under sixteen, with the equivalent for girls under sixteen, the fifty-yard dash. This difference in distances established for the community the idea that CF&I held separate standards of physical fitness or endurance for girls and boys. Similarly, in the sack race competition girls under ten competed in a fifteen-yard race, while boys under ten competed in a twenty-five-yard race. For men and boys over sixteen there was a hundred-yard dash, but for girls and women in this age bracket no comparable event existed.[17] This established a paradigm for these children: CF&I

FIGURE 5.4 "The Spaniards" children at the Trinidad Field Days, 1915 (courtesy of the Bessemer Historical Society / CF&I Archives)

FIGURE 5.5 "Other Industries" Trinidad Field Days, 1915 (courtesy of the Bessemer Historical Society / CF&I Archives)

judged men and women by separate standards, girls did not compete with boys; nor did they compete at the same level as men. By segregating competitive events by sex, the competitions illustrated that there were two separate expectations for males and females.

Women did not compete in physically strenuous events. Girls over sixteen the company viewed as women, and their competitions no longer centered

FIGURE 5.6 "Finale" Trinidad Field Days, 1915 (courtesy of the Bessemer Historical Society / CF&I Archives)

on physical strength but rather on domestic accomplishments. Even for girls under twelve there was an opportunity to compete in a needle-and-thread race, otherwise known as a sewing competition. This domestic skill was not a part of the men's competition, and for the young women domestic duties and responsibilities became normalized in a company-sponsored public setting with athletic competition setting the groundwork for gender roles.

Perhaps it was that CF&I did not value the labor of women. For company management their labor force, except for some secretarial workers in Pueblo, were male laborers. They may have envisioned the wives and daughters of CF&I employees as not fit for athletic competitions in the same way that they envisioned their own wives in the private sphere. This illustrates a disconnect between company management and the women in CF&I camps, since these women lived strenuous lives not visible to the management and management's perception that women in the coal camps remained part of a separate sphere.[18]

The *Industrial Bulletin* of 1916 reported that for the wives of employees the field day included three events: a nail-driving contest, the largest-family contest,

FIGURE 5.7 Nail-Driving Competition, Trinidad Colorado Field Day, 1926 (courtesy of the Bessemer Historical Society / CF&I Archives)

and a heavyweight contest. The largest-family competition certified that the mother, not the father, bore the children; the mother won a pair of shoes for each child, but no prize for her "accomplishment."[19] In the heavyweight contest women were publicly weighed, with the heaviest woman winning her weight in flour. These events for women emphasized that a woman's reproduction was valued in this rural environment, and the flour prize revealed that the company acknowledged the woman's domestic role in the public sphere.

Nationally, the role of women during the Progressive Era centered on public life and organizing. From working in the textile trade to striking in the streets, American women linked their identity to public activities. Also, working women expressed their role in society through the act of consumption. With the buying of clothing, and the rise of participating in entertainment such as reading novels and watching motion pictures, women's roles as public figures reached into the capitalistic market. Middle-, upper-, and working-class women sought for public acceptance in the suffrage movement and brought about the idea that women envisioned themselves as political figures and consumers.[20]

FIGURE 5.8 Crested Butte's Heaviest Women Contest, winner from Floresta, 1917 (courtesy of the Bessemer Historical Society / CF&I Archives)

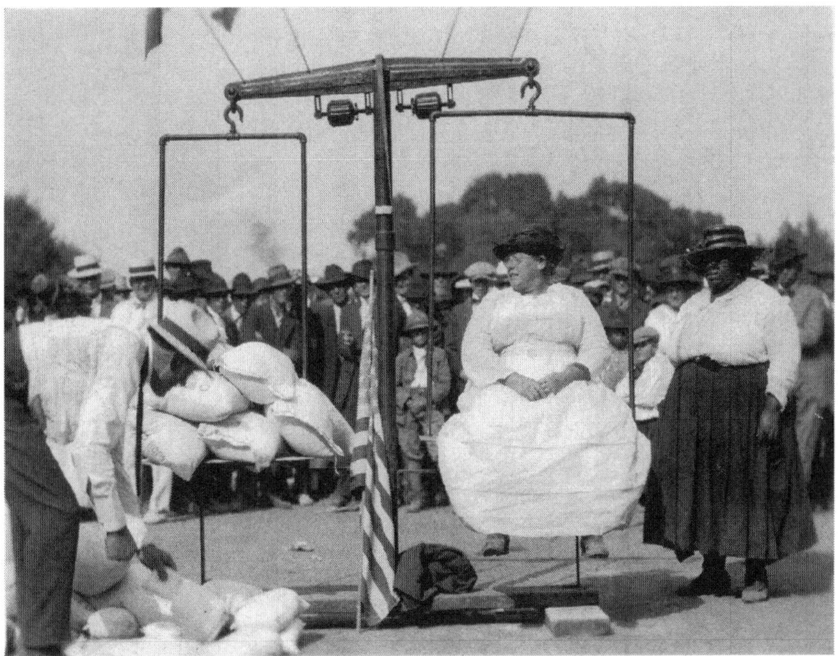

FIGURE 5.9 Women's Heavyweight Contest at the annual field day in Trinidad, 1919 (courtesy of the Bessemer Historical Society / CF&I Archives)

At the same time that women involved themselves in the suffrage movement on a national level, CF&I influenced women in southern Colorado since it controlled the towns and labor of the area. For these women, field days and YMCA activities instituted a standard by which CF&I judged and categorized men and women according to their daily roles. Women's participation in these field days and YMCA events illustrated that they accepted this new model of social betterment because they attended, continued to compete, and accepted their prizes at these field days.

Colorado Fuel and Iron acknowledged men based on their knowledge of the physical body, both in how to help others who had been injured and how best to complete manual labor. The first aid contest gave them an ability to show their knowledge in everyday activities, or enabled them to emphasize and validate the knowledge they gained in the workforce. This established the cultural and social expectation that an important component of masculinity was understanding one's field of work and the importance of being able to protect another man.

Instead of awarding an individual prize that would benefit a man's entire family, as it rewarded the women, the company awarded winners of the first aid contest with "a loving cup and banner." "The loving cup," an article in the *Industrial Bulletin* explains, will be contested for annually and will become the property of the camp winning it three times."[21] A man's knowledge of the workplace legitimized him in the eyes of his coworkers, and the longer his knowledge was superior to others, the more tangible it became to them, by literally taking a place within the camp. The women's prizes influenced households, while the men's prizes affected and reflected their coal camps.

While annual field days originated with the Industrial Representation Plan, as did much of women's competition, annual first aid contests were held as early as September 28, 1911. Images from a contest held in Trinidad, Colorado, reveal a competition among men, with few women in the audience. Each competing team included five male responders and one "injured" male.[22] A collection of CF&I photographs, an assortment of images from these field days, included material in which all of the men wore "work" clothes. These clothes included overalls and a work jacket with a white shirt and tie underneath. These work clothes, the overalls and the jacket, represented the clothing they wore in the coal mines, but the white shirts and ties showed that these men put on a performance of the skills that they learned in the workforce, since this was not clothing they would have worn while working in the mines. This performance of first aid or knowledge about the body was a performance emphasizing that these men contributed on a regular basis to their work environment and that their labor should be rewarded and praised by their respective communities. As the men stood posed for these photographs, the responders all held lanterns, dressed for work. This illustrated men outside of their work environment continuing to perform as employees and as men. When they were practicing for this role, the men in the photos removed their coats, revealing their cleaner clothing underneath. When these men worked in the camps, their cleanliness in appearance and their public performance were not valued the same as in a public setting or when the company celebrated their contributions to the company.

FIGURE 5.10 First Aid Contest at field day events in Trinidad and Walsenburg District, First Place Winners: Rockville Mine, 1917 (courtesy of the Bessemer Historical Society / CF&I Archives)

As field days expanded, men's performances extended beyond the first aid competition to include events for individual men. In 1916, field day individual events for men included the standing and running broad jump. Prizes for the winner included a box of cigars, an item that reflected men's leisure activities. In contrast, in the nail-driving contest in the women's competitions, the prize for the winners was a $35 kitchen cabinet, second place a $15 set of dishes, and third place a $12 washing machine or merchandise of equal value. The women's prizes reflected their household duties.[23] In other words, CF&I awarded men prizes that did not contribute to their roles as providers but as individual men; while CF&I rewarded women for their contributions to the family and awarded prizes that continued to associate them with domesticity or child rearing. The prizes women received assisted the family, not the individual woman. These prizes were associated with work or reproduction, while the prizes the men received reflected a contribution to the mine.

Within this context CF&I hoped to not just create a space for leisure but infused employee spaces with the company's own ideas of manhood and what made men better employers. The athletic events emphasized self-esteem and respect for others; at the same time, it developed a camaraderie between the laboring classes and management in an attempt to erase the labor/management conflicts of the past.[24]

Colorado Fuel and Iron publicized field days as family gatherings. The miners and other company employees took the day off, giving the wives and children an opportunity for a holiday. The company's publications emphasized

FIGURE 5.11 Young girls dressed to represent a columbine flower at a CF&I field day, 1915 (courtesy of the Bessemer Historical Society / CF&I Archives)

that the families sat and ate together. This implied that families of CF&I employees rarely had the opportunity to spend time in a recreational setting with their family members.

The company's emphasis on the family, and specifically on the girls, extended beyond field days into recreational activities. The Campfire Girl organization, an organization formed by CF&I management for the daughters of the coal camps and the steel mill, coordinated community service opportunities through the YMCA, allowing the girls a physical location to tutor them in femininity. The Campfire Girls found service opportunities at YMCA council dinners. The daughters of camp employees served dinner to company employees and their wives. The servers in this type of location found that the YMCA needed their feminine touch in assisting and organizing events. This experience emphasized that daughters of CF&I employees were part of the YMCA and CF&I community. The company's initial purpose in allowing these female children a space in company social gatherings may not have been to disseminate information about gender roles or for the girls to find a connection with the company. However, the experience gave the daughters of CF&I employees the opportunity to work within the structure of the YMCA and to learn what CF&I management considered to be appropriate gender roles, such as how to serve food to men and to care for one's house.[25] While the YMCA sponsored these activities, they occurred on CF&I property and included daughters of CF&I employees.

In June 1917, seventy-two Campfire girls from CF&I camps in Las Animas and Huerfano counties went on a ten-day camping trip to Stonewall. At this outing, YMCA community secretaries of other areas participated in organizing and implementing the trip. The campground was owned by CF&I, and the girls stayed in the clubhouse of the Stonewall Country Club. During the visit to the country club, CF&I personnel visited. This outing's sponsorship revealed that while these girls participated in a recreational activity, it was also a company-sponsored outing. Camp personnel exposed the girls to freedom and nature by allowing them to sleep where they wanted: in the house, on the porch, or on the ground outside. Activities during the camp included arts and crafts, stenciling, gathering wood, folk dancing, attending Sunday school, and hiking to the Stonewall rocks.[26] This event combined outdoor activities, which had traditionally been assigned to men, such as gathering wood and hiking. It also incorporated arts and crafts and Sunday School attendance. This company-structured program—while allowing the girls the opportunity to enjoy the outdoors, hiking, and camping—also set up standards and expectations of how to behave and act as women.

For the adult women, YMCA activities did not challenge their athletic abilities. Activities instead focused on women's domestic roles. In CF&I mining towns, the YMCA organized and held meetings at their own building. At these meetings, an *Industrial Bulletin* article notes, they "practice[d] housework and care of children, and with games and other entertainments."[27] YMCA buildings provided more than a training ground for young women on how to perform domestic crafts. They also included a gendered segregation of space. The Minnequa Steel Works YMCA had a gymnasium only for male employees. There were male and female locker and dressing rooms and restrooms. This spatial organization placed an emphasis on men's health over women's, because there were more facilities available to men and men's spaces. These male spaces were focused on their bodies, whereas women's spaces centered on domesticity.

FIGURE 5.12 Baseball games between Walsen and Starville at the Trinidad and Walsenburg District (courtesy of the Bessemer Historical Society / CF&I Archives)

For the men, the YMCA emphasized their physical strength at field days through running races and basketball competitions. The YMCA emphasized the need to be skilled and knowledgeable employees through the first aid competitions that rewarded the skills of the employees by their camps' contribution. Yet it was baseball that brought the ideas of physical strength and camp status to the forefront of CF&I's ideas of betterment.

Baseball represented a great American pastime and the strength of each camp, but it also gave men a break from the monotony of coal mining. Colorado Fuel and Iron included images of baseball games, and the *Industrial Bulletin* printed the results of games throughout CF&I-owned properties. The camps and the company viewed it as a great honor to be part of a winning team. In some instances there was recruitment from other camps in order to acquire stronger players. According to the *Industrial Bulletin*, though baseball was present in the camps prior to the entrance of the YMCA, "the advent of the YMCA has strengthened the already existing keen interest in sports, and the season promises a brisker competition than ever before."[28] Colorado Fuel and Iron's encouragement of baseball emphasized that men's physical strength and athleticism were together a valuable component of their employees outside of their work environment. An ideal man could contribute in the mines, in the steel mill, and on the baseball field.

The noted feature of the 1916 field day was the championship baseball game between the best teams of Las Animas and Huerfano Counties. This aspect of competition celebrated the competitive abilities of men in their regional areas and of their camps. The team that won at the field day for Huerfano and Las Animas counties played against the Canon District. Fifteen men were allowed to register, but they had to be "bonafide employees at

Figure 5.13 Teams of the Minnequa Steel Works Baseball League, 1916 (courtesy of the Bessemer Historical Society / CF&I Archives)

the camp on the date of registering."[29] The rules for the field day stated that the field day committee could investigate the registered employees, and "disqualify any employee who is hired on account of his ability to play ball or who has been induced to leave the service at one camp to go to another on account of his ability as a player."[30] It is obvious from this statement that the field day committee knew about the pressure to be successful in baseball and the risk that men might violate these rules. Baseball was the sporting activity for the field day that had the most rules, restrictions, and guidelines. In contrast, boy's basketball game rules contained the following information:

> There will be two basket ball games; one between boys, and one between girls under sixteen. Elimination games will be played in each county to determine which camp is to furnish the team for this contest, basketball games will be in charge of the basketball committee.[31]

There were no deadlines for basketball registration and no punishments or even concern that individuals would be hired for their basketball skills or recruited from other camps. In addition, the baseball game was the first event, and the prizes for this event were twelve uniforms or $100 in cash; for basketball the winning prize was a basketball and a pennant. The monetary value that the YMCA put up for the winning team reflected how they viewed baseball as central to the field days—baseball represented the first event, the contributions of men, and the success of a region. Colorado Fuel and Iron and the YMCA reflected their beliefs that baseball was an essential component of camp life.

Baseball games were played on a more regular basis than just during the annual field days; games were held for the Fourth of July, and a six-team baseball league was established at the steelworks. The company furnished a ballpark convenient to the steelworks complete with a grandstand that held large crowds.

By 1918, the baseball season plans were part of the joint committee meetings for recreation and education. Plans for the baseball season were outlined with no mention of other sporting activities. At these meetings the length of the season was discussed as well as the timing of games.[32] Baseball teams began to represent the strength of the camp, and playing on a baseball team reflected a higher standard of manhood than that represented by working in the mines or that achieved by competing in first aid contests and field days. For CF&I manhood was connected to athletic prowess.[33]

In 1915 John D. Rockefeller Jr. entered southern Colorado in an attempt to squelch the negative attention that eastern media outlets had focused on the Rockefeller family. He established the Industrial Representation Plan and subsequently the periodical the *Industrial Bulletin*, which encouraged communication between employees and management and the social betterment of the southern Colorado coal fields and the Pueblo steelworks. Company management disseminated ideals of masculinity and femininity through print material and physical recreation. As company employees and their families participated in CF&I activities, their ideas and standards of masculine and feminine identity came into line with company expectations. Masculinity focused on men being good miners and contributing to their mining camps. The company measured men's success through the awarding of individual prizes at competitions or through attempting to instill pride among men for being on a successful team. For women, their reproduction became central to their gender roles. The company rewarded them as mothers and caregivers, by giving them prizes that would help their families, not the individual women.

## Notes

1. Jonathan H. Rees, *Representation and Rebellion: The Rockefeller Plan at the Colorado Fuel and Iron Company, 1914–1942* (Boulder: University Press of Colorado, 2010).

2. The Towson Report documented the status of all CF&I mining camps and emphasized what the YMCA felt should be changed in the camps in regards to ideas about social betterment.

3. Colorado Fuel and Iron, *Industrial Bulletin*, Bessemer Historical Society and CF&I Archives, Pueblo, Colorado "Address of John D. Rockefeller," October 1915, 11–17.

4. Thomas Winter, *Making Men, Making Class: The YMCA and Workingmen, 1877–1920* (Chicago: University of Chicago Press, 2002).

5. CF&I, "Memorandum of agreement," 26. "Under direction of C.J. Hicks, Executive Assistant to the President," 3.

6. Ibid., 11–17.

7. CF&I, 1915–18.

8. Matthew Basso, *Across the Great Divide: Cultures of Manhood in the American West* (New York: Routledge. 2000); Gail Bederman, *Manliness and Civilization: A Cultural History of Gender and Race in the United States, 1880–1917* (Chicago: University of Chicago Press. 1995); Gary Gerstle, *American Crucible: Race and Nation in the Twentieth Century* (Princeton: Princeton University Press, 2002).

9. CF&I, October 1915, 4; ibid., "YMCA Extends Its Activities," April 26, 1916, 12–18.

10. CF&I, "Expert Aid for CF&I Clubs," December 22, 1915, 3.

11. Ibid., 3.

12. Alfred Montoya, "Oral Interview," California State University at Fullerton (CSUF), Coal Mining Oral History Collection, 15.

13. CF&I, "The YMCA in CF&I Camps," January 31, 1916, 8.

14. Ibid., 8.

15. Ibid., May 27, 1916.

16. Ibid., "Field Day 1916" and "Annual Field Day," September 15, 1916,3–7. "Annual Picnic and Independence Day Celebration of Minnequa Steel Works Employees and Their Families," July 31, 1919, 12, 13.

17. Ibid., "Field Day 1916, 5 Volume 1, #7–"Annual Field Day September 15, 1916, 7.

18. Stephen Norwood, *Strikebreaking and Intimidation: Mercenaries and Masculinity in Twentieth-Century America* (Chapel Hill: University of North Carolina Press, 202).

19. Ibid., "Annual Field Day September 15, 1916, 7.

20. Nan Enstad, *Ladies of Labor, Girls of Adventure: Working Women, Popular Culture, and Labor Politics at the Turn of the Twentieth Century* (New York: Columbia

University Press. 1999); Margaret Finnegan, *Selling Suffrage: Consumer Culture and Votes for Women* (New York: Columbia University Press, 1999); Susan Glenn, *Daughters of the Shtetl: Life and Labor in the Immigrant Generation* (Ithaca: Cornell University Press, 1990).

21. Colorado Fuel and Iron, *Industrial Bulletin*, September 15, 1916, 2.

22. Lemont Bowers, "First Annual First Aid and Helmet Contest," September 28, 1911, and Photo Collection, CF& I Lester Mine, "People," Bessemer Historical Society and CF&I Archives.

23. Colorado Fuel and Iron, *Industrial Bulletin*, "Annual Field Day," May 27, 1916, 4.

24. Thomas Winter, *Making Men, Making Class: The YMCA and Workingmen, 1877–1920* (Chicago: University of Chicago Press, 2002), 56–62, 65–74.

25. CF&I, "the CF&I Family: News from Bulletin Correspondents," January 31, 1917, 18. ""To Teach Housekeeping," April 21, 1917, no. 3-a, p. 4. June 22, 1917, 3–4d. Colorado Fuel and Iron, *Industrial Bulletin*, "Campfire Girls from CF&I Mining Towns at Their Annual Outing at Stonewall," July 31, 1917, 2.

26. Ibid., "Campfire Girls from CF&I Mining Towns at Their Annual Outing at Stonewall," July 31, 1917, 2.

27. Colorado Fuel and Iron, *Industrial Bulletin*, September 15, 1916, 7.

28. Ibid., May 27, 1916, 7.

29. Ibid., 3–4.

30. Ibid., July 31, 1916, 8, 9.

31. Ibid., March 28, 1918, 4.

32. Ibid., "Mr. Rockefeller's Denver Talk," July 31, 1918, 5–9.

33. Winter, *Making Men, Making Class*, 56–62.

SIX

# A Tale of Two Employee Representation Plans in the Steel Industry

## Pueblo, Colorado, and Sydney, Nova Scotia

*Greg Patmore*

Employee Representation Plans (ERPs) were a major feature of labor relations in Canada and the United States between the World Wars.[1] A major impetus for developing these ERPs was the "Colorado Industrial Plan" or the "Rockefeller Plan." The Rockefeller family had a substantial number of shares in the Colorado Fuel and Iron Company (CF&I), which owned coal mines and the Pueblo steel plant in Colorado. John D. Rockefeller Jr. (JDR Jr.) developed the plan following a strike at the company's coal mines and the adverse publicity surrounding the Ludlow Massacre. The company established the plan at its mines in October 1915 and at the Pueblo steelworks in 1916. It became a movement that spread throughout the United States and Canada to a range of industries and reached its peak by 1934, when, according to David Brody, ERPs in the United States covered probably 3 million workers and had more coverage than the unions. The plan continued to operate at the Pueblo steelworks in the United States until 1942.[2]

The ERPs' promoters viewed them as alternatives to both individual contracts and independent trade unions. The Rockefeller Plan involved workers

DOI: 10.5876/9781607323105.c006

electing representatives to a district conference, where they would meet with senior representatives of the company at least three times a year. The district conferences elected joint committees on employment issues, which consisted of three representatives of the employees and three representatives of the company. Workers could appeal to various levels of company management, and there was even a provision for appeal to an external court if mediation failed. The company paid for all costs associated with the plan, including reimbursement for the loss of work time by employee representatives. While there was no place for unions in the plan, the original Rockefeller Plan prohibited discrimination against employees on the grounds of union membership.[3]

The supporters of ERPs claimed that they were more effective than trade unions in raising employee grievances and contributing to firm productivity. The plans countered the growing gap between senior management and workers in large-scale enterprises. They provided a communication link, through which workers could bring minor grievances to management's attention and management could make workers realize that improved working standards depended upon reducing overheads and increasing efficiency. Trade unions, unlike the employer and employees, were "outside organizations," which were antagonistic to the firm and did not have as their primary interest the good of the company.[4]

Critics of ERPs argued that they did not provide an independent voice for workers, as employers established and managed the ERPs. The company generally has the right of veto over shop-floor initiatives in ERPs. Workers and their representatives were unwilling to raise grievances, fearing they could lose their jobs. The ERPs also generally dealt with minor matters and did not negotiate the general wage scale for the company or the plant. Without trade unions, workers were deprived of expert outside advice in putting their case and conducting their negotiations. Workers could not call upon outside help if employers decided to reduce wages and working conditions. As the ERP only covered a particular plant or company workers' knowledge of outside wages and conditions were limited.[5]

There has been some recent interest in refocusing on the ERPs as a solution to a "representation gap" and the need for employee involvement. As trade union membership has declined in many Western countries, scholars emphasize that workers without union representation no longer have a voice in the management of their workplaces. This "representation gap" reduces the potential of workers to contribute to improving productivity and the quality of working life. In the United States and Canada, academics explored their historical traditions particularly in regard to the Rockefeller Plan or ERPs prior to the outbreak of the Second World War. David Fairris and Bruce Kaufman have provided a favorable historical reexamination of ERPs during the interwar period. They argue that the ERP was part of a Progressive move in US industry to promote a greater interest in more sophisticated personnel management practices to improve worker commitment, morale, and productivity. The founders of the personnel management movement called for a recognition of the "human factor" and a more systematic approach to labor management. Jonathan Rees, in a recent study of the ERP at CF&I, has emphasized the benefits of ERPs for workers if management are committed to this idea as an alternative form of employee voice.[6]

This chapter compares two ERPs in the steel industry in United States and in Canada—Pueblo, Colorado, and Sydney, Nova Scotia. One of the problems with generalizing about the ERP experience at CF&I is that ERPs varied in terms of their jurisdiction and structure. Through a close comparison of the CF&I ERP with the ERP at Sydney, it is possible to generalize further about the benefits and limitations of this approach to employee participation. This chapter will explore the origins, practices, and demise of the two ERPs. Although this chapter reinforces Rees's argument that workers can make some gains under ERPs, it perpetuates the concern that ERPs are antiunion devices and may undermine freedom of association in the workplace.

## CF&I AND BESCO

A merger between the Colorado Fuel Company and the Colorado Coal and Iron Company led to the formation of CF&I in 1892. The company's interests included coal mines and the Pueblo steelworks. The Pueblo steelworks was virtually the only steel plant in the West until World War Two, and workers had "no chance of finding another job in steelmaking anywhere near Pueblo."[7] This relative isolation and the absence of an independent union could have weakened industrial militancy and encouraged an acceptance of the ERP. The average payroll for the steelworks peaked in 1920 with 7,783 employees. Pueblo had comparatively fewer immigrant workers than other

US steel plants, and American-born workers formed a slight majority of workers at the plant between 1915 and 1920. Colorado Fuel and Iron particularly employed immigrant workers as unskilled labor. From 1915 to 1920, there was a surge of Mexican workers in the plant, growing from 8 percent of the workforce in 1915 to 39.4 percent in 1920. The category of Mexican was misleading in the plant data, as 10 percent were born in the United States. Given that at least 60 percent of these workers did not speak English, their voice was limited in an ERP that emphasized communication in English. Mexicans remained an important component of the Pueblo workforce, constituting a third of the total workforce in January 1927. The company was severely hit by the Great Depression and went into receivership from August 1, 1933, until July 1, 1936. Employment dropped to an average payroll of 2,924 in 1932. It was renamed the Colorado Fuel and Iron Corporation and emerged from the receivership with a reduced debt. When the United States began to rearm for national defense in 1940, CF&I rapidly expanded production, with a peak average payroll employment of 6,480 in 1943.[8]

The involvement of the Rockefeller family in CF&I began in November 1902, when John D. Rockefeller paid $6 million for 40 percent of its shares and 43 percent of its bonds at the urging of George Jay Gould. Rockefeller's only son, JDR Jr., served as a director of CF&I until 1905 and again from 1909 to 1920. He gradually took over his father's duties and John D. Rockefeller Sr. withdrew from participation in all business activities in 1911. The Rockefeller family gained control of CF&I in 1907, when a panic in the financial market forced Gould to sell his securities. Although Rockefeller interests continued to dominate the company, JDR Jr. had "largely lost touch" with CF&I by 1933, as he had few personal ties with the company's officers. While JDR Jr. was in New York, the CF&I management was located in Denver. The company was also on an "economic rollercoaster" with slow growth and disappointing profits. Rockefeller Jr. had considered selling his interest as early as 1933, and the Rockefeller family eventually sold their controlling interest in the company in December 1944.[9]

The Rockefellers reinforced the long-standing hostility of CF&I management toward trade unions, which did not have legal support from either the state in Colorado or federally before the New Deal of the 1930s. Rockefeller Sr. saw unions as "frauds" and believed they stood for doing as little work as possible for the maximum pay. The management of CF&I generally did not recognize unions or engage in collective bargaining at the Pueblo steelworks. Unions found it difficult to organize the Pueblo plant because CF&I discharged or blacklisted union activists. Some workers were members of the International Molders Union, which claimed a majority of members in the steelworks foundry and was able to gain increases in wages in 1910 following discussions with the general manager. The company undertook labor espionage and blocked union attempts to organize the Pueblo plant during the 1919 Steel Strike.[10] While Rees emphasizes that the introduction of the ERP in the steelworks was motivated by JDR, Jr.'s interest in "promoting labor peace" rather than an immediate threat of union organization, the ERP was an extension of CF&I's policy of antiunionism in the Pueblo steelworks.[11]

Colorado Fuel and Iron had extensive welfare programs, which had a number of goals, including reducing labor turnover and thwarting labor organization, well before the adoption of the Rockefeller Plan in 1915. There was a hospital for the Colorado Coal and Iron Company's employees in Pueblo from 1881. The company formed a Sociological Department in July 1901, which provided educational facilities, recreational halls, and reading rooms for workers and their families. It abolished the Sociological Department in 1915, with the introduction of the Rockefeller Plan and handed over its activities to the industrial department of the Young Men's Christian Association (YMCA). The YMCA opened a clubhouse at the steel plant in March 1920 and included a bowling alley, cafeteria, swimming pool, library, gymnasium, and soda fountain. There was a separate building for African American workers called the "Colored Y," which also became the center for Pueblo's African American population. Following the introduction of the Rockefeller Plan, CF&I management published or sponsored several publications that highlighted the extensive welfare plans and the ERP.[12]

Sydney was founded in 1785 as the capital of the new colony of Cape Breton, which was a refuge for British loyalists following the American Revolutionary War. Its economy grew dependent on fishing, agriculture, shipping and a coal port, which froze during the bitterly cold winters. There was no tradition of iron and steel making in the town prior to the arrival of the Dominion Iron and Steel Co. (DISCO) in 1899. Dominion was a modern corporation with a board of directors that included some of Toronto and Montreal's leading capitalists. It and another provincial steel company, Nova Scotia Steel (NSS), merged in 1920 to form British Empire Steel Corporation (BESCO), which also covered extensive coal holdings and the Halifax shipyards. The consolidation did not prevent further economic problems. The corporation could not adjust to the shift in demand for steel away from railways to mass-produced consumer goods, faced import competition, and dealt with excessive transportation costs. With the closure of NSS's Sydney Mines steel plan, Sydney became the focus of BESCO's operations from 1921. Throughout its short history, BESCO remained in a financial crisis and accumulated a deficit of $5.7 million by the end of 1925. It went into receivership in 1926 and was reorganized by Canadian capitalists two years later as the Dominion Steel and Coal Corporation (DOSCO), with BESCO ceasing to exist in May 1930. There was further reorganization during the 1930s Depression, when the blast furnaces were idle for a period of eighteen months and steel in the open-hearth furnace was made from cold stock. As in Pueblo, the Sydney plant was isolated from the main centers of steel production in North America, which limited nearby employment opportunities in the steel industry and made workers more willing to accept an ERP rather than move. While employment data is more difficult to find for Sydney, the plant had a smaller workforce than Pueblo. While on June 28, 1923, there were 2,774 men on the day and 1,097 men on the night shift, the average daily workforce fell to merely 790 in 1932 during the midst of the Great Depression, when the steel plant was operating at 17 percent capacity. From this point production increased, and by 1936 the steel plant was operating at 93 percent capacity. The workforce was overwhelming Canadian born by 1923, with "rather more than" 10 percent being from "non-English speaking races" and approximately 8 percent "coloured men" from Barbados.[13]

Prior to the introduction of the ERP at Sydney, like CF&I, management was generally hostile to trade unions. An organizing campaign by the Provincial Workmen's Association (PWA), which commenced in 1902, culminated in June–July 1904 in a major strike, which was a victory for management. The demise of the PWA in the wake of the strike did not mean the end of labor activity at the Sydney plant. There were members of craft unions working in the plant, and unions continued to organize the plant—including the Amalgamated Association of Iron, Steel and Tin Workers (AAISTW), which in June 1911 established a lodge in Sydney, with at least sixty members. The lodge failed to gain recognition from a hostile management. There was a further campaign by the AAISTW to enroll during the First World War, with the organizing of a Sydney lodge on December 13, 1917. Despite management's refusal to recognize the union and supervisors discouraging union membership, the union formed another lodge for Sydney employees in October 1922, and the union claimed that they had organized 75 percent of steel workers by February 1923. The AAISTW was able to raise grievances through representation as a committee of employees. There were allegations that DISCO operated a system of labor espionage. During the organizing campaign by the AAISTW in 1911, "spotters," or spies, were responsible for the dismissal of five union activists. They also followed union organizers as they interviewed workers in their homes and attended union meetings to intimidate employees. British Empire Steel Corporation continued to use spies in the steelworks and encouraged loyalist employees to beat union activists with iron bars.[14]

Like CF&I, DISCO and its successors established welfare schemes to promote identification with the company. The company provided housing to attract employees and sponsored social clubs and benefit societies for employees. British Empire Steel launched a pension fund in January 1924 for employees with service of twenty-five years or more and was actively involved in promoting "safety first," which incorporated a safety committee, ambulance service, and an emergency hospital.[15] By contrast with CF&I, BESCO only showed a limited interest in publishing magazines for employees. In the mid-1920s it briefly published a four-page newsletter called the *BESCO Bulletin*, which called upon workers to cooperate with management in ensuring that the company was pointed to "as an example of good fellowship and loyalty and united endeavour."[16] The *BESCO Bulletin* praised the benefits of ERPs, including the Rockefeller Plan at CF&I, and criticized organized labor, for example, for making wage demands that deprived members of work and the opportunity of gaining a "livelihood."[17]

## The Origins of the ERPs at Pueblo and Sydney

Colorado Fuel and Iron introduced its ERP in the wake of the Ludlow Massacre on April 20, 1914, during a violent coal miner's strike in Colorado against the company and other coal firms. Public outrage flared against both CF&I and the Rockefeller family, which had the largest shareholdings in the company. It was possible that the Wilson federal administration would intervene and establish grievance procedures to settle disputes. The government proposal allowed local grievance committees chosen by the miners to settle grievances. If the grievance could not be resolved by the committee, then it would be referred to an arbitration board selected by the President. Rockefeller Jr. recruited W. L. Mackenzie King, a former Canadian minister of labor, to help him frame the Rockefeller Plan. With the union defeated in the strike, the miners gave their support to the plan in a secret ballot, where 84 percent of the 2,846 votes endorsed the scheme.[18]

Colorado Fuel and Iron extended its ERP from it coal mines to its Pueblo steelworks, where employees adopted it by a vote of 2,321 to 863 in May 1916. Rockefeller Jr. intervened and encouraged CF&I management to implement the ERP at the steelworks. He persuaded CF&I management to adopt his ideas including an internal appointment of an industrial representative of the company president to oversee the ERP and mediate grievances. There were no demands by the steelworkers for adoption of the ERP, and labor unions were not seeking recognition at Pueblo.[19] Warren Densmore, a leading activist in the ERP at Pueblo, was later to note that the employees accepted the ERP "because they felt conditions were so bad that any alternative was worth a trial."[20]

Under the ERP, the Pueblo plant was divided into eleven divisions and a number of subdivisions, which were based on occupations or geographical locations there. Each division was allowed one representative for every 150 employees, with a minimum of two employees for each. Employees had three months service at CF&I before they could vote. The election was by secret ballot with the company providing the ballot boxes and papers. There was no specific place for the holding of the elections, and the tellers—one appointed by management and the other by the representatives—carried the ballot boxes to workers on the job. The representatives held office for one year and could call meetings of employees in their division to discuss grievances provided it did not interfere with the work. Employees could raise grievances either individually or through their representative to their supervisor or the superintendent in the first instance and then to the CF&I President's Industrial Representative. All the representatives held joint conferences with management representatives and served on specialist joint committees, which had six employees and six managers.[21] Despite management's objections, representatives also began to meet together independently of management to consider issues as a "body."[22]

The introduction of the ERP at Sydney was set against the desire of BESCO to maintain an open shop. The growing strength of the AAISTW in the plant represented a major threat. The company rejected a proposal by union members to set up a scheme for formation of worker committees in September 1922 on grounds that it would not recognize the union. Henry Bischoff, the general superintendent of the Sydney plant tried to introduce an ERP in December 1922, but workers and the AAISTW defeated the proposal in a ballot by a vote of 1,562 to 1,021. Opponents linked their hostility to the ERP to the demand for union recognition. The scheme involved a general works council, elected by the workers. This general works council elected a group of representatives to meet with a similar number of management representatives on a joint council. Bischoff described the scheme as a form of "co-operative bargaining," which dealt with problems of mutual interest. The major influences in shaping the "Bischoff Plan" were Whitleyism, which was a system of workplace committees used in the United Kingdom, ironically with union involvement, and a similar plan at the Bethlehem Steel Corporation in the United States.[23]

Tensions between the AAISTW and BESCO continued. Union members walked out on February 13, 1923, following the dismissal of a unionist for disobeying orders. The AAISTW accused management of dismissing the employee because of union activities. Management faced pickets, the prospect of serious damage to the plant in subzero temperatures, and the possibility of miners joining the dispute. While management agreed to meet a committee of employees, they refused to meet any official union delegation. They agreed on February 17 to reconsider the case of the dismissed unionist. Union leaders considered the strike a victory and believed that the company would give them full recognition upon returning to work. However, BESCO investigated the case of the dismissed unionist and upheld it on the grounds of insubordination. The police arrested more than thirty steelworkers on various charges, including intimidation and trespassing, and BESCO increased the size of its employment blacklist. The board of directors of BESCO formally rejected the request for union recognition in June 1922. Roy Wolvin, president of BESCO, saw "Cape Breton Bolshevism" as the cause of the strike and issued a warning to the local business community that unless "Cape Breton Bolshevism" was driven out, he would withdraw his capital.[24]

The conflict between the AAISTW and the company ultimately resulted in its demise and management's implementation of the ERP. The union continued to pursue its demands for union recognition, particularly for a check-off system for union dues. Other demands included a general wage increase of 30 percent and an eight-hour day. Management, while still refusing to recognize the union, granted a 10 percent increase in wages on April 16, 1923. The tensions culminated in a strike on June 28, 1923, which saw military and provincial police intervention and the deployment of machine guns. "Bloody Sunday" on July 1—when strikers and bystanders outside the Sydney steelworks, including women and children, faced charges by mounted police and steel halted soldiers advancing with fixed bayonets—undermined further collective action by the strikers. The steelworkers gained the support of 8,500 Cape Breton miners, who left work on July 3 in protest against the use of force by the state. However, John L. Lewis, president of the United Mine Workers of America (UMW), moved against the Cape Breton militants, following their refusal to end the sympathy strike and revoked the charter of the UMW local on July 17. Lewis was in direct contact with Wolvin and was concerned that the action of the miners in Cape Breton would jeopardize UMW negotiations with anthracite coal operators in the United States. Lewis alleged political intrigue between the local's leaders and their "revolutionary leaders in Moscow." While the strike continued until August 2, the AAISTW was defeated.[25]

Management introduced an ERP in August 1923 without a vote by employees. This event followed a deputation of a committee of employees to Bischoff on August 14, calling for the plan to be put into effect and claiming that employees "whole heartily favoured" the plan.[26] The local newspaper, the *Sydney Record*, which supported the ERP, noted that the "level-headed section" of the steelworkers, "who have never been stamped by songs in Russian and flags of red," were in control of the plant. With the defeat of the AAISTW, some workers took the view that the Bischoff Plan was "better than nothing." Management hoped unsuccessfully that the scheme would make a proposed federal commission to inquire into labor relations at the plant "inopportune." The commission, however, did make favorable recommendations concerning the ERP and did not force the issue of union recognition.[27]

The plan was identical to that proposed the previous December, with a general works committee, which consisted of thirty-eight employee representatives elected by workers and by elected representatives to a joint committee with management representatives. The worker representatives on the joint committee also constituted a central works committee. The Rockefeller Plan did not provide for these worker forums and envisaged that employee representatives would not meet separately. This explicit provision for independent worker meetings was to lead to greater autonomy for employee representatives under the Bischoff Plan, though in both plans managerial prerogative remained paramount. As in the Rockefeller Plan, employee representatives could raise grievances on behalf of constituents if they were not satisfied with the response of their supervisor. If the employee representative failed to get satisfaction, then the representative could take the matter to the joint committee. The Bischoff Plan dealt with suggestions for safety and improvements in a similar manner. There was to be a secret ballot for the employee representatives; however, employees would elect two fellow workers in each department to assist employees as requested in filling out the ballots. While all employees over eighteen could vote, there were restrictions on voting by supervisors and managers. Candidates had to be twenty-one and have a total of one year's service at the plant. The first ballot occurred on August 29 and 30, 1923, with sixty-eight employees nominating for thirty-six positions and 2,729 employees, or about 93 percent of the workers in the plant voting. In the wake of the strike, the blacklisting of union activists by BESCO and the establishment of the ERP, the Sydney lodges of the AAISTW eventually became moribund. Although management publicly justified the plan on the grounds of keeping the "personal touch and human touch with the men" that was being lost by the growing size of the business and the "absentee management" by the BECSO directors; this context highlights the importance of the ERP as an antiunion strategy.[28]

## What Did the ERPs Do?

The committees at Pueblo dealt with a range of issues. There was a joint conference of thirty-six employee representatives and thirty-six management representatives in February 1918. The president of CF&I, J. F. Welborn, chaired the meeting, the management representative acting as secretary. The issues discussed included the employment of returned soldiers, the company magazine, and concerns about the conduct of the recent election for representatives from the wire mill. Some workers were taking ballot papers from immigrant workers to vote for their preferred candidates. In March and April 1918, there were four specialist joint committees: industrial co-operation and conciliation; safety and accidents; sanitation, health and housing; and recreation and education. The committees met separately once a month. A management representative chaired these committees. The industrial cooperation and conciliation committee dealt with issues such as lockers, drinking water systems, and mail. In the context of the First World War, one representative was concerned about the disloyal sentiments of particular employees. While the manager requested that employees inform him of any disloyal acts, he advised against hasty actions that could lead to injustice to fellow employees. Whereas the safety and accidents committee dealt with issues such as lighting, safe handling practices, and dangers such as falling coal, the sanitation, health and housing committee dealt with the water supply, housing, medical services, and laundry facilities. The recreation and education committee dealt with education programs, the steelworks band, and sporting activities. The ERP did generally improve working conditions in the plant through the construction of large modern washhouses with toilet facilities and the installation of drinking fountains.[29]

The ERP became a mechanism for changes in wages and conditions at Pueblo. Following frequent requests by employee representatives over several years and conferences between company officials and employee representatives, a reduction of the working shift took place from twelve to eight hours on November 1, 1918. There were also implemented 10 percent increases in the hourly tonnage and piece rates. The reduction in hours led to increases in productivity rates beyond those when the twelve-hour shift was operating. One disadvantage for CF&I steelworkers compared to CF&I miners was that while both groups of workers' wages were linked under the ERP to CF&I's competitors, the miners' rates were determined by collective agreement negotiated between the UMW and major coal companies and the steelworkers' wages were determined by reference to the nonunionized United States Steel Corporation.[30]

In the wake of the 1919 steel strike and the defeat of unions at Pueblo and elsewhere, according to David Brody, generally steel companies in the United States, "having booted out the agitators, were eager to restore good feelings."[31] Senior management of CF&I took a more sympathetic view of their employees and the ERP. Senior management believed that with the defeat of unionization, the representatives had no alternative but to support the ERP. In February 1920, senior management allowed a joint committee of representatives and management to visit steel plants in the eastern states to investigate wage increases as a prelude to granting wage increases. This met a long-standing criticism by the representatives that they could not contribute to the adjustments of wage rates at the plant, as they did not know what was going on elsewhere. Senior management also showed a greater willingness to reverse the decisions of supervisors following complaints by the employee representatives.[32]

While there was greater sympathy of senior management for the ERP, and some supervisors decided to cooperate with the employee representatives in order to avoid having their decisions overturned by senior management, there were still supervisors who opposed the ERP. This resulted in a wide variation in the way the ERP functioned across the plant. In the Rod Mill, there was a good relationship between the superintendent and the employee representative. The two men were able to settle grievances, and by 1928 no grievances had gone from the Rod Mill to the Joint Committee on Co-operation, Conciliation and Wages. By contrast, an employee representative in the Casting Foundry complained in January 1924 that there was a lack of cooperation between management and labor. He had to follow up 90 percent of grievances, and there were long delays in replies from local management. In the By-Product Coke Plant, Superintendent H. B. Carpenter suppressed the operation of the ERP because, as he put it, "we have practically 100% harmony." Carpenter was strongly opposed to the ERP and stopped his employee representatives from attending one joint conference. Senior CF&I management had to intervene and overrule Carpenter. Carpenter believed that the ERP committees were "inefficient" and workers showed "poor judgement" in electing their representatives.[33]

The CF&I ERP delivered favorable responses to worker grievances. During 1920, employees at the steelworks and lime quarries raised 118 issues with management. Of these issues 44.9 percent related to working conditions, 13.6 percent to living conditions such as company housing, 9.3 percent to medical treatment, and 7.6 percent to wages. Employees respectively received favorable outcomes in at least 83 percent, 75 percent, 73 percent, and 67 percent of cases. By comparison, at the Bethlehem, Steelton, Lebanon and Maryland plants of Bethlehem Steel, the ERP settled 71 percent of 2,365 grievances in favor of the employee between October 1918 and June 1923. There is evidence that management manipulated CF&I data on the outcome of grievance settlement.[34]

While workers made some gains through employee representation at Pueblo, management still asserted its authority on crucial issues such as general pay and promotion. In January 1920, the company asked the Pueblo workers to accept a 20 percent wage cut due to a recession. Employee representatives argued that this was too severe and requested a 15 percent cut, which management accepted. The representatives said that they could make up for the other 5 percent by increased efficiency and elimination of waste. Two employee representatives did argue that the workers in their sections of the Pueblo plant believed that there should be no cuts in their wage rates, but accepted the majority view. There were further cuts of 15 percent in August 1921 following more discussions with employee representatives and a further 10 percent cut in January 1922. Employee representatives initially rejected the 10 percent cut in wages in January 1922. Only after management began to issue dismissal notices and threatened to place the remaining staff on short time did the employee representatives agree. Management in the middle of this dispute also obtained permission from employee and management representatives in December 1921 to change the eligibility rules for employee representatives; duration of employment increased from three months to twelve months. The employee representative now also had to be a US citizen and over twenty-one, rules that reduced the threat of outside agitators becoming employee representatives.[35]

Senior CF&I management also insisted that promotion be by merit rather than seniority. In March 1924, the six employee and six management representatives on the Joint Committee on Co-operation, Conciliation and Wages unanimously ranked one first helper over two others based on strict seniority. His supervisor, however, considered this worker inefficient compared to the others. Welborn, the president of CF&I, believed that this ruling had gone far beyond what management had considered appropriate for adjudication by the joint committees and ruled that the "direction of working forces" rests "unquestionably" with "managing officers."[36]

By 1927, the ERP at the Steelworks was, rather than producing mutual understanding, institutionalizing conflict between employees and management. In contrast to the mining camps, there was "legalistic wrangling" over the meaning of the ERP, and employee representatives threatened to appeal against plant management to Welborn and Rockefeller. Local management believed they did not get the backing from senior management in dealing with the representatives and that the representatives could "wear down" local management in long and exhausting meetings. However, local management continued to emphasize that the ERP was subordinate to managerial prerogative and the requirements of steel plant operations. The employee representatives were also now holding meetings on a monthly basis independently of management. They elected their own chair, vice-chair, and secretary and invited management to discuss important issues. As noted previously, the ERP never assumed that the employee representatives would act collectively. The *Industrial Bulletin* published the minutes of these meetings as well as the joint committees. While management did edit out questionable material in the published minutes of all meetings, the airing of the grievances of employee representatives before being heard by the joint committees exacerbated the criticism of management, who did not have right of reply.[37]

Tensions between the representatives and CF&I flared further during the economic downturn of the Great Depression. The company newspaper, *The Blast*, published letters praising the ERP for assisting the company's economic survival by allowing workers to raise grievances and management to settle those complaints that had merit. The company, however, was forced into equity receivership on August 2, 1933. The receiver's economy measures included shutting the YCMA clubhouse building, discontinuing employee group insurance and cutting company pensions. Andrew Diamond, chair of the employee representatives at the Pueblo steelworks and employed in the rod mill, was angered that despite management's promise that the representatives would be informed of the receivership, they learnt about it from the press. Diamond had publicly supported the Rockefeller Plan by arguing that employee representation created a better spirit among employees and cooperation by fostering closer contact between workers and management. At a meeting of steel representatives with the receiver on August 10, Diamond argued that JDR Jr. would not "stand for" the closure of the YMCA building and would intervene to stop it. He appealed directly to JDR Jr. and his father concerning the YMCA clubhouse, group insurance, and pensions. The Rockefeller family, however, believed such "sacrifices" were necessary to save the company from bankruptcy.[38] JDR Jr. rejected a request by Diamond to personally fund the YMCA building and the pension fund. He already had forgone dividends from CF&I to allow these schemes to operate and argued that philanthropy was unwise as it could prevent employees from thinking "all the more of the extraordinary advantages they have."[39]

Although extensive records survive for the operation of the ERP at Pueblo, only limited records survive for Sydney, sufficient, however, for noting some similarities and differences. The Sydney meetings were held on company premises, and the representatives received payment for meetings but not for other representative duties such as raising grievances. By 1925 the workload was such that the general works committee found it necessary to set up subcommittees to deal with wages, safety and personnel matters, such as promotion, discipline, and dismissal. Meetings could be lengthy, with one general works committee meeting in January 1934 lasting for two hours and twenty minutes. Critics recognized that the Bischoff Plan did provide protection for representatives taking up worker grievances and removed some injustices. Two of the activists associated with the 1923 strike remained on the general works committee for most of its existence. The general works committee provided a forum to discuss issues of general concern and assisted management in rationing work during periods of economic downturn. Management also discussed the financial position of the company with the representatives and allowed the representatives to distribute company charity to needy families during Christmas. There could be lively campaigning and a large turnout in the elections for employee representatives. Workers in the electrical department in May 1935 successfully petitioned management for the recall of their representative on the grounds of "misrepresentation." The elected representatives tended to have worked at the plant for long periods, with average service of the thirty-six representatives in 1925 being eleven years and maximum service twenty. During the mid-1930s, there were complaints about workers names being placed on nomination forms without their consent by management and supervisors voting despite the prohibition.[40]

While the ERPs obtained unofficial autonomy at Pueblo, the explicit provision for a worker-only forum at Sydney gave employee representatives a great deal of autonomy to pursue issues outside the company and gain support from politicians and other outside groups. Former union activists, elected on the general works committee, pushed for the same demands as they pursued through the unions. The general works committee in 1925 called for improved tariff protection for the Canadian steel industry and in May 1930 even rejected linking a government bonus on steel to the eight-hour day. The secretary, P. W. McDougall, noted that the employees had confidence that management would reduce working hours as soon as conditions warranted it. In 1929 the workers' representatives embarrassed BESCO by persuading the Social Service Council of Canada, a Protestant churches reformist body, to investigate the twelve-hour day at the Sydney plant. Sydney workers employed on continuous production, such as the blast furnaces and open-hearth furnaces, gained the eight-hour day in 1930. Workers in other parts of the plant had their hours reduced from twelve to ten. There were compensating wage increases for workers on hourly rates.[41]

A good run of minutes for the ERP at the Sydney plant have survived for 1934. As Table 6.1 indicates, the primary category of issues raised at the general works committee related to recruitment and selection, particularly of former employees who had lost their jobs due to the economic depression. Production was reviving at the plant, and the representatives wanted to ensure that management gave preference to former workers over newcomers. The second-largest group of items related to industrial relations issues, particularly wages, hours and conditions. In May 1934 the general works committee forwarded a petition, with 1,700 signatures, to the Nova Scotia Government supporting eight-hour day legislation. In May 1934, management refused to increase wages, previously cut due to the depression, because they were making losses on exports. In response, the representatives requested that an external board of conciliation check management's claims concerning the losses. While management rejected the request, they were prepared to allow two or three representatives to check the relevant financial records. The representatives rejected this on the grounds that they were not experts and it was a job for "Price Waterhouse." Welfare issues included pensions and company housing. Safety issues included the response time in transporting accident victims to the hospital and the dangers associated with railway operations around the plant. The general works committee was able to persuade management in November 1934 to institute monthly safety inspections of departments by the departmental superintendent, the safety engineer, and an employee representative. The representatives also showed concern for other issues beyond the steelworks. In May 1934, they sent a letter to the local municipal authority condemning the low wages being paid to highway workers. The general works committee referred matters to the joint committee, which did not generally make decisions, but referred matters to management for further consideration. Frustrations arose over the failure of management to follow through with issues and on occasions ignore recommendations by the joint committee. In December 1934, one representative even suggested that they go on strike over issues such as the restoration of wage reductions and old-age pensions. Later management claimed that they granted 69 percent of the claims submitted by general works committee, which was lower than the rate for the plans at CF&I and Bethlehem Steel.[42]

Despite this relative autonomy of the Sydney ERP compared to Pueblo, there was still discontent concerning the usefulness of the ERP for employees. Critics noted that the ERP's success for employees depended on how "management felt" and how they responded to external pressure.[43] One former steelworker remembered that the plan was not beneficial because, as he put it, "you had no strength."[44] Some former members of the AAISTW flirted with the idea of the One Big Union (OBU) during the mid-1920s. In 1930, Rannie McDonald, a former representative and critic of the managerial right of veto under the plan, organized a lodge of the International Association of Machinists. Management, however, laid him off along with approximately fifty other employees in the machine shop on the day they received their charter from the union. One exception was the financial secretary of the lodge, also an employee representative. Management in 1932 dismissed Dan Mackay, a former OBU organizer and the chair of general works committee, after he began advocating for a union.[45]

## The Demise of the ERPs at Pueblo and Sydney

The ERP at CF&I came under challenge during the 1930s. Section 7 (a) of President Roosevelt's *National Industrial Recovery Act* of June 1933 recognized that workers had the right to bargain and organize collectively through their own representatives without employer interference. Unionism took off, and employers rushed to set up ERPs to stop unions organizing in their workplaces. The number of workers covered by these ERPs grew from 1.8 million in 1934 to 2.5 million in 1935. Critics condemned these ERPs as "sham organizations" that impeded economic recovery; they were outlawed in the National Labor Relations Act of 1935, or Wagner Act. The National Labor

Table 6.1 Issues raised at General Works Committee, Sydney, Nova Scotia, 1934

| *Issues* | *Number* | *Per Cent (Rounded)* |
|---|---|---|
| Recruitment, selection and employment | 41 | 38 |
| Industrial relations | 28 | 26 |
| Welfare | 17 | 16 |
| Safety | 11 | 10 |
| Improvements and repairs | 4 | 4 |
| Rules and procedures | 3 | 3 |
| Others | 4 | 4 |
| Total | 108 | |

*Source*: Drawn from minutes held at BI, MG19/17/D, minutes for general works committee, January 15, 1934, are located at USWA Collection, PANS, Microfilm Reel 14877.

Relations Board (NLRB), the agency of the act, moved against ERPs after the Supreme Court upheld the legislation in 1937. In 1939, the board won a major case against Newport News Shipbuilding and Dry Dock, when the US Supreme Court ruled that an ERP in existence since 1927 was illegal. The ERP was illegal despite that the employer no longer funded employee representatives' expenses and that workers had voted for it in a secret ballot in preference to independent trade unions. The decision spelt the effective end of the movement inspired by the Rockefeller Plan.[46]

The favorable climate for unions meant the end of the ERP at the CF&I mining camps. In October 1933, CF&I miners voted for collective bargaining through the UMW and against the ERP by 877 votes to 275. While CF&I officials recognized the wishes of the miners, they regretted the defeat of the ERP. They concluded that passive resistance was preferable to overt resistance, which "would lead to serious labor disturbances and probably bloodshed."[47] Rockefeller Jr. took the view that the ERP at CF&I was "eminently satisfactory." However, if the National Recovery Act directed them to deal with unions in issues of wages and hours, they had to comply. He hoped that the ERP could continue to deal with "other matters of common interest."[48]

Despite JDR Jr.'s views concerning the mining activities of CF&I, the ERP remained in operation longer at the Pueblo Steelworks. Management of CF&I believed that the ERP could continue there because the steelworks were not organized to any extent and that the National Recovery Act recognized ERPs. The CF&I newspaper the *Blast* published articles that supported the ERP, and management credited the ERP with providing steelworkers with one week's vacation with full pay in July 1936 and wage increases in December 1936. The company newspaper reinforced the advantages of the ERP by carrying news of other steel plants where workers supported ERPs in preference to "outside unions" in collective bargaining. It also claimed that unions were forcing steelworkers to join them. When the *Blast* covered elections for the ERP, it highlighted the high voter turnout and the fairness of the elections. Management continued to employ spies to monitor any labor organizing in Pueblo and further ensure the survival of the ERP.[49]

Although management saw the ERP as preferable to unions, tensions still occurred between the representatives and local management. There was a tied vote between employee and management representatives on the Joint Committee on Co-operation, Conciliation and Wages over the reinstatement of an employee named Anderson. Management fired him because he allowed a furnace bottom to burn out. The employee representatives wanted arbitration, whereas the management representatives upheld the decision. Employee representatives called for a revision of the ERP to remove the requirement for CF&I's consent before any question was referred to arbitration. With the threat of unionization looming, the company agreed to amend the ERP in 1936 to allow the referral of any deadlocked matter at the request of either management and the employee representatives for final arbitration to a board consisting of an employee representative, management representative, and a third person selected by mutual agreement.[50]

Management faced the threat of growing unionization. The Steel Workers Organizing Committee (SWOC), which was affiliated to the Congress of Industrial Organizations (CIO), began organizing the plant in 1937 and chartered a lodge in Pueblo on August 3, 1938. During the SWOC's campaign for recognition, it alleged that supporters of the ERP assaulted union organizers, and there was strong sympathy for CF&I by the local media and public authorities. In February 1938, the company asked its employees to ratify the ERP and designate the representatives as their collective-bargaining agent. The subsequent vote was 2,426 votes in favor and only 198 against the ERP. Many of the employees who voted for the ERP, however, believed that the continuation of their insurance, pension, and medical plans depended on a positive vote. The company changed the name of the ERP to the Employees' Representation Organization (ERO) to indicate a break with the past, but most of the officers administering the ERP were the same, with Diamond being president. Despite the vote and the changes, the full NLRB ruled on appeal in March 1940 that the ERP was company dominated and directed CF&I to withdraw recognition. At the first ballot in March 1941, the employee representatives made a strong appeal in the local newspaper for workers to vote against any outside representation. A. T. Stewart, the ERP lawyer, in one local radio broadcast, compared the union's organizing campaign with Hitler's invasion of Norway and warned of "bloodshed" and a loss of earnings if the union replaced the ERP. The supporters of the ERP were victorious, as 2,670 workers voted for no representation and 1,783 voted for the CIO out of 4,838 votes cast. The CF&I meanwhile petitioned the Tenth Circuit Court of Appeal for a review of the NLRB direction, but the Court upheld the NLRB direction in June 1941. The ERO reorganized itself again and became ERO Inc., which the company identified as the collective-bargaining agent for its employees on December 1, 1941. The Tenth District Court of Appeals ordered the company in June 1942 to withdraw recognition from ERO Inc. ruling that there was an insufficient break of continuity with the disestablished ERO and that ERO Inc. was not a truly independent labor organization. During the final representation election in July 1942, ERO Inc. tried to persuade workers to vote against the union by hinting that the CIO was led by Communists and un-American. They were unsuccessful, however, in saving the final vestiges of the Rockefeller Plan and the result was 58 percent in favor of the union. The primary reason for the defeat of the ERP was a major influx of new employees as steel mill production expanded to meet wartime demand.[51]

As the Canadian economy recovered from the Great Depression, there was also an upsurge in labor militancy and trade unionism. While there was no national equivalent to the Wagner Act, workers rushed to join new industrial unions, which were organized initially by the Communist-led Workers' Unity League and later by the CIO. Management again established ERPs to try to stop unionization. Sydney steel workers used their ERP as a platform for organizing unions. Several activists believed that they could use the council to build a "real union." Some of them successfully stood for the plant council, which gave them some freedom to move around the plant. When management rejected a request for a wage increase, four employee representatives formed a workers' committee. The committee became the basis for the independent Steelworkers' Union of Nova Scotia, which became a SWOC affiliate in December 1936. The union soon organized the majority of workers at the Sydney plant. It successfully lobbied with other workers for the Nova Scotia provincial legislature to pass a Trade Union Act in April 1937. This legislation forced employers to recognize and bargain with the trade union representing the majority of workers and fined companies for discriminating against trade unionists. This was the first Wagner-influenced legislation in Canada and contained provisions for a vote on a union check-off if employers already had a system for checking off deductions for any other purpose. Management at the Sydney plant tried to undercut the SWOC drive for union members by offering wage increases and retrenching workers. They also tried to mobilize workers to fight the menace of "foreign controlled" international unions. Within a week of the passage of this legislation, however, the employee representatives on the plant council, who were all union members, resigned en mass. The plant council held its last meeting on April 22, 1937, and the steelworkers' union subsequently won a ballot for a check-off system for union subscriptions.[52] Ron Crawley notes, "As with many SWOC locals in the United States, SWOC steel workers at Sydney had essentially occupied and subverted the plant council."[53]

## Conclusion

While there may have been a Progressive desire to give workers a voice through the ERPs at Pueblo and Sydney, the ERPs also undermined the appeal of union representation. Rockefeller Jr. introduced the ERP for CF&I miners following a strike and the adverse publicity of the Ludlow Massacre to block any public or government pressure to recognize unions and engage in collective bargaining. Although there was protection against victimization for being a union member, the ERP did not recognize the right of unions to represent its members. While there was no effort to organize the Pueblo plant at the time of the introduction of the ERP, there was a long history at the plant of union avoidance, reinforced by the Rockefellers' dislike of unions before the Ludlow Massacre. Management at Sydney first called for an ERP during a union-organizing campaign and introduced the ERP in the wake of the union defeat in the 1922 strike. Both CF&I and Sydney management were hoping to preempt possible government intervention into labor relations at their plants. After the introduction of the ERP, it remained an important management tool for union avoidance at Pueblo and Sydney. The ERP at Pueblo played an important role in fighting the surge of unionism that accompanied the New Deal during the 1930s. Management tried to restructure the ERP into a legal-bargaining unit under the Wagner Act and tried to weaken union organizing by crediting the ERP with wage increases and other improvements.

The ERPs at Pueblo and Sydney did allow workers to challenge arbitrary decisions by supervisors and provide improvements in working conditions. It did give workers the potential for "voice" and opened up new lines of communication between workers and senior management. The ERPs at Pueblo and Sydney played a role in reducing working hours. While it was a vehicle for wage increases, the rule that wages had to be linked to wage levels in the Eastern steel mills in the United States limited the wage benefits of the Pueblo ERP. Management at Pueblo also used the ERP to legitimize wage reductions during periods of economic downturn and defended the rights of employers in areas such as promotion.

There was some degree of autonomy for employee representatives both at Pueblo and at Sydney. In the face of management opposition, the Pueblo representatives organized themselves, held regular meetings, and elected their own leaders. Some managers complained about the time involved in negotiating with the employee representatives and their adversarial nature. With the defeat of the unions in the 1919 strike, the representatives were willing to accept the ERP and some, such as Andrew Diamond, became advocates of it as a way of improving employee and management relations at Pueblo. These attitudes may have contributed to the continuation of the ERP at Pueblo after its demise at the CF&I mines. At Sydney, unlike Pueblo, the ERP explicitly recognized the rights of representatives to meet without management on the general works committee. The general works committee referred issues to the joint committee but also took matters up with external agents such as politicians and even clergy. Whatever benefits these ERPs obtained for the employees have to be balanced against the role of ERPs in weakening the desire by employees to join unions and engage in collective bargaining.

## Notes

1. This research was supported by an Australian Research Council Discovery Grant (2010-00047). I would like to thank Jonathan Rees, Yasmin Rittau, and the Bessemer Historical Society for their assistance.

2. David Brody, *Labor Embattled: History, Power, Rights* (University of Illinois Press, Urbana/Chicago, 2005), 52; Greg Patmore, "Employee Representation Plans in the United States, Canada and Australia: An Employer Response to Workplace Democracy," *Labor* 3, no. 2 (2006): 41–65.

3. Patmore, "Employee Representation Plans in the United States," 43.

4. Ibid., 44.

5. Ibid.

6. David Fairris, "From Exit to Voice in Shopfloor Governance: The Case of Company Unions," *Business History Review* 69, no. 4 (1995): 494–529; B. E. Kaufman, "The Case for the Company Union," *Labor History* 41, no. 1 (2000): 321–51; Jonathan Rees, *Representation and Rebellion: The Rockefeller Plan at the Colorado Fuel and Iron Co., 1914–1942* (Boulder: The University Press of Colorado, 2010).

7. Rees, *Representation and Rebellion*, 137.

8. Greg Patmore, "Employee Representation Plans at the Minnequa Steelworks, Pueblo, Colorado, 1915–1942," *Business History* 49, no. 6 (2007): 847; "Pueblo Payroll from 1915 to 1940," typescript, n.d., MSS 1051, box 6, file 130, Colorado Historical Society (hereafter, CHS); H. Lee Scamehorn, *Mill & Mine: The CF&I in the Twentieth Century* (University of Nebraska Press, Lincoln, 1992), 140–41.

9. Patmore, "Employee Representation Plans at the Minnequa Steelworks," 847, 858.

10. Ibid., 847, 852–54; J. Rees, "'X,' 'XX' and 'X-3': Labor Spy Reports from the Colorado Fuel and Iron Company Archives," *Colorado Heritage* (Winter 2004): 28–41.

11. Rees, *Representation and Rebellion*, 106.

12. Patmore, "Employee Representation Plans at the Minnequa Steelworks," 848; Greg Patmore and J. Rees, "Employee Publications and Employee Representation Plans: The Case of Colorado Fuel and Iron," *Management and Organisational History* 3, nos. 3–4 (2008): 257–72.

13. Dominion Steel and Coal Corporation, Joint Committee Minutes, December 21, 1933, Beaton Institute, University College of Cape Breton (hereafter, BI), MG19/17/D; DOSCO, General Works Committee Minutes, January 15, 1934, December 29, 1936, United Steel Workers of America, Sydney Lodge collection, Provincial Archives of Nova Scotia, Halifax (hereafter, USWA collection, PANS), microfilm reel 1487; David Frank, "The Cape Breton Coal Industry and the Rise and Fall of the British Empire Steel Corporation," in *Cape Breton Historical Essays*, 2nd ed., ed. D. Macgillivray and B. Tennyson (Sydney, NS: College of Cape Breton Press, 1981), 121–22, 127; C. Heron, *Working in Steel: The Early Years in Canada, 1883–1935* (Toronto: McClelland and Stewart, 1988), 24–29, 75; *Labour Gazette*, February 1924, supplement, 13, 20; Greg Patmore, "Iron and Steel Unionism in Canada and

Australia, 1900–1914: The Impact of the State, Ethnicity, Management and Locality," *Labour / Le Travail* 58, (2006): 81–82.

14. David Frank, *J. B. McLachlan: A Biography* (Toronto: James Lorimer & Co., Toronto, 1999), 294; Heron, *Working in Steel*, 97; *Labour Gazette*, February 1924, supplement, 6–8; Paul MacEwan, *Miners and Steelworkers: Labor in Cape Breton* (Toronto: A. M. Hakkert, 1976), 94; Patmore, "Iron and Steel Unionism in Canada and Australia," 85–88, 99; *Amalgamated Journal*, December 27, 1917, 4, May 6, 1920, 32, February 17, 1920, 20, November 9, 1922, 28; *Sydney Record*, February 14, 1923, 1.

15. *Besco Bulletin*, February 21, 1925, 3, June 13, 1925, 3, February 27, 1926, 4; *Amalgamated Journal*, March 4, 1920, 11; *Sydney Record*, April 23, 1930, 5.

16. *Besco Bulletin*, February 1925, 1.

17. Ibid., May 9, 1925, 4, May 16, 1925, 4, May 23, 1925, 1–3, December 5, 1925, 4.

18. Patmore, "Employee Representation Plans in the United States," 45.

19. Ibid., 850.

20. Letter from Elton Mayo to Arthur Woods, November 20, 1928, box 3B, folder 19, Elton Mayo Papers, Baker Library, Harvard Business School.

21. B. M. Selekman, *Employees' Representation in Steel Works: A Study of the Industrial Representation Plan of the Minnequa Steel Works of the Colorado Fuel and Iron Company* (New York: Russell Sage Foundation, 1924), 53–60.

22. Letter from Elton Mayo to Arthur Woods, November 20, 1928, box 3B, folder 19, Elton Mayo Papers, Baker Library, Harvard Business School; Selekman, *Employees' Representation in Steel Works*, 162–63.

23. *Besco Bulletin*, April 11, 1925, 1; M. Earle, "The Building of Steel Union Local 1064: Sydney, 1935–1937," in *Industry and Society in Nova Scotia: An Illustrated History*, ed. J. E. Candow (Halifax: Fernwood Publishing, 2001), 45; *Labour Gazette*, February 1924, supplement, 16–17; *Sydney Record*, December 18, 1922, 1, September 1, 1923, 4, 12, September 1, 1924, 6.

24. Frank, *J. B. McLachlan*, 294–97; *Labour Gazette*, February 1924, supplement, 9–12; G. MacEachern, *George MacEachern: An Autobiography* (Sydney: University College of Cape Breton Press, 1987), 28–29; *Sydney Record*, February 14, 1923, 1–2.

25. Frank, *J. B. McLachlan*, 300–315; *Labor Gazette*, February 1924, supplement, 12–16; D. Macgillivray, "Military Aid to the Civil Power: The Cape Breton Experience in the 1920's," *Cape Breton Historical Essays*, 2nd ed., ed. D. Macgillivray and B. Tennyson (Sydney: College of Cape Breton Press, 1981), 102–4; *Amalgamated Journal*, June 14, 1923, 15.

26. *Sydney Record*, August 15, 1923, 1.

27. Ibid., p. 11.

28. *Labour Gazette*, February 1924, supplement, 12–16; MacEachern, *George MacEachern*, 36; Patmore, "Employee Representation Plans in the United States,"

58; *Amalgamated Journal*, November 17, 1924, 2–3; *Sydney Record*, August 15, 1923, 1, August 22, 1923, 1, August 25, 1923, 4, 12.

29. Patmore, "Employee Representation Plans at the Minnequa Steelworks," 851.

30. Ibid., 851–52.

31. D. Brody, *Steelworkers in America: The Nonunion Era* (New York: Harper & Row, 1969), 264.

32. Patmore, "Employee Representation Plans at the Minnequa Steelworks," 854.

33. Ibid., 854–55.

34. Ibid., 855.

35. Ibid.

36. Ibid.

37. Ibid., 857.

38. Ibid., 857–8.

39. JDR Jr. to C. J. Hicks, September 7, 1933, box 14, folder 114, Record Group III2C, Rockefeller Family Archives (RFA), Rockefeller Archives Centre (RAC). Jonathan Rees, *Representation and Rebellion: The Rockefeller Plan at the Colorado Fuel and Iron Company, 1914–1942* (Boulder: University Press of Colorado, 2010)

40. *Besco Bulletin*, April 11, 1925, 1–3; MacEachern, *George MacEachern*, 36; DOSCO, General Works Committee Minutes, January 15, 1934, Joint Meeting Minutes, December 21, 1933, December 20, 1934, Joint Committee, January 3, 1934, May 9, 1935, BI, MG19/17/D.

41. *Besco Bulletin*, October 24, 1925, 1; Heron, *Working in Steel*, 109; T. Power, "Steel Unionism in Eastern Canada" (BA thesis, Saint Francis Xavier University, 1942), 17–18; *The Sydney Record*, 23 May 1930, p. 1.

42. DOSCO, General Works Committee Minutes, January 15, 1934, December 29, 1936, USWA Collection, PANS, microfilm reel 14877, May 1, 1934, May 12, 1934, November 20, 1934, December 4, 1934, BI, MG19/17/D.

43. MacEachern, *George MacEachern*, 36.

44. Interview with Emmerson Campbell in *Cape Breton's Magazine*, no. 22, 1979.

45. MacEachern, *George MacEachern*, 36–7, 62; MacEwan, *Miners and Steelworkers*, 207–8.

46. Patmore, "Employee Representation Plans in the United States,"43–44.

47. Arthur Roeder to Colonel Arthur Woods, October 31, 1933, box 15, folder 122, record group III2C, RFA, RAC.

48. JDR Jr. to Arthur Woods, July 24, 1933, box 14, folder 114, record group III2C, RFA, RAC.

49. Arthur Woods to JDR Jr., July 18, 1933, box 14, folder 114, record group III2C, RFA, RAC; Patmore and Rees, "Employee Publications and Employee

Representation Plans," 268–69; Spy report on IWW dance/meeting, March 14, 1936, box 1, RG 2.1.1, Bessemer Historical Society and CF&I Archives.

50. "In the Matter of The Colorado Fuel and Iron Corporation and International Union of Mine, Mill and Smelter Workers, Local 442."; "In the matter of the Colorado Fuel and Iron Corporation and Steel Workers, Organizing Committee," 22 NLRB, no. 14, 1940, 200–203.

51. J. Dodds, *They All Come to Pueblo: A Social History* (Virginia Beach: Donning, 1994), 195–96; National Labor Relations Board, Decision and Direction of Election, Case No. R–2190, February 12, 1941, 3. The US National Archives, Rocky Mountain Region, Denver, R 276, Records of the United States Courts of Appeal, Tenth Circuit Denver, Colorado, Transcripts of Records on Appeal 1929–54, case 2097; Patmore, "Employee Representation Plans at the Minnequa Steelworks," 855; "Proceedings of the Third Annual Convention, Colorado State Industrial Union Council, Pueblo, Colorado, September 20 and 21, 1940," typescript, 3–4. Frank and Fred Hefferly Collection, box 3, folder 4, Norlin Library, University of Colorado, Boulder; Rees, *Representation and Rebellion*, 193–205; A. T. Stewart, radio broadcast recording, KGHL Pueblo, 1941. Hefferly Collection, box 8; G. W. Zinke, *Minnequa Plant of Colorado Fuel and Iron Corporation and Two Locals of United Steelworkers of America* (Washington, DC: National Planning Association, 1951), 31–33.

52. Patmore, "Employee Representation Plans in the United States," 59–60.

53. R. Crawley, "What Kind of Unionism: Struggles among Sydney Steel Workers in the SWOC Years, 1936–1942," *Labor / Le Travail*, no. 39 (1996): 104.

SEVEN

# Putting the "I" in CF&I

## The Struggle over Representation, Labor, and Company Town Life on the Edge of *Aztlán*

*Ronald L. Mize*

In the not-too-distant past, my maternal family was irrevocably altered after a workplace incident that permanently disabled my late maternal grandfather, Theodore Herrera. The Herrera family had followed the migrant trail, after being displaced from their land near Gallup, New Mexico, to work sugar beets in Central Wyoming. Far, far from home, the Herreras were one of several Mexican American families that left northern New Mexico during the Depression as land speculators and Anglo squatters used a legal system, fully designed with Anglo interests in mind, to wrest control over land and resources. Census records confirm that the Herrera family lived in New Mexico since at least 1820, when Patricio Herrera was born in Socorro County. The Herreras were one of several hundred thousand Mexicans who did not cross the border to enter the United States. The border crossed them with the signing of the Treaty of Guadalupe Hidalgo in 1848, when Mexico was forced to cede nearly one-half of its northern territory to the United States. My family does not share details about the land loss but still talks of the *enganchadores* (labor contractors) who represented the Great Western

DOI: 10.5876/9781607323105.c007

Sugar Company. The enganchadores waited for local economic downturns to start recruiting the resident New Mexican population with the promise of good, steady wages and housing. Sarah Deutsch has thoroughly detailed these practices in *No Separate Refuge*.[1]

After returning from World War II and a short stint laying railroad track, rather than working in the sugar refinery in Wheatland or with a *cortito* (short-handled hoe) in the surrounding fields, my grandfather relied upon the long family history as miners to secure employment at Colorado Fuel and Iron's iron-ore mine in Sunrise, Wyoming. Unlike the seasonal and temporary nature of agricultural work, mining operations offered year-round employment. Work was constant with the exception of production downturns and intermittent strikes or work stoppages to protest unsafe workplace conditions. Even though wages were just above destitute levels, they were dependable. But for the Herrera family, all that changed at precisely 8:00 a.m. on September 12, 1946.

Town residents knew the accident occurred because an alarm sounded whenever a worker was injured in the mine. Mine injuries happened all too often in Sunrise. The first two weeks of September 1946 bore witness to fifteen accidents.[2] When my eldest uncle graduated from the company's Sunrise High School, eleven of his thirteen fellow senior classmates either lost their fathers in a mine accident (three), had fathers seriously injured (two), or had an injury that prevented them from working for a significant period of time (six). The two unscathed fathers were employed as a railroad engineer and a farmer. Hard work in the mine was synonymous with workplace injuries. Operating a jackhammer, Theodore Herrera unknowingly hit unexploded dynamite, and the resulting explosion embedded iron-ore pellets under his exposed skin, in his lungs, and in one eye, which eventually went blind. The company reported the accident in the worker injury ledger as "Injuries both eyes, contusions both hands and chest; Drilled into misfired shot; 75% loss vision both eyes."[3] His accident was preceded by his brother-in-law's loss of a hand in a mine accident in New Mexico and followed by his son's (my Uncle Trinidad or "Doc" Herrera's) breaking his back after falling fifty feet down a mineshaft.

The Herrera family of seven lived in a four-room company house and attended the company school. Even though they avoided the company store, they unwittingly purchased their staples from a local merchant who, on at least one documented significant occasion, doubled as a company informant. Their dislocation from their long-standing ancestral homelands in New Mexico was partially mitigated by the neighbors, friends, and family who accompanied them on the migrant trail. In 1940, many of those families would have been found in the beet fields of Platte and Goshen counties or working in the sugar refineries of Wheatland and Torrington.[4] Mexican miners, other than a few transient single men or one or two families, did not arrive in earnest in CF&I's Sunrise until after the Second World War.

Yet, as early as 1915, the United States Commission on Industrial Relations recognized the inherent flaws in mining company towns. As the author of the report, George P. West, noted: "The employees were forced not only to depend on the favor of the Company for the opportunity to earn a living, but to live in such houses as the Company furnished, to buy such food, clothing and supplies as the Company sold them, to accept for their children such instruction as the companies wished to provide, and to conform even in their religious worship to the Company's wishes."[5] To allay their concerns, what were workers given? They received a company union that narrowly set the terms for how workers could express grievances. Even though a conduit to management was created with employee representation, in reality the majority of workers eschewed participation in the Employee Representation Plan (ERP). As Jonathan Rees notes, it was almost exclusively the skilled, white, native worker who benefited.[6] It comes as no surprise that the intensity that led to organized labor's initial inroads was not assuaged by the development of company unions. By the 1940s, CF&I's coal miners were represented by the United Mine Workers of America (UMWA), Minnequa Steel Works millers in Pueblo by United Steel Workers of America (USWA), and the Sunrise iron miners by International Union of Mine, Mill, and Smelter Workers (Mine-Mill). For Mexican American miners in particular, the unions brought the hope and appearance of representation that the ERPs were never designed to provide.

One factor that coincided with the increasing union recognition was the postwar demographic shift leading to a more complex rank-and-file, in Sunrise adding a Mexican American presence to the multiethnic European immigrant base. Unbeknownst to Mexican American families, their arrival in Sunrise landed them in the center of a union battle that involved the red-baiting of the CIO's Mine-Mill, the business unionism of the AFL's USWA, and the smoldering debris of the employee representation plan that left the remnants of Rockefeller's company union all over the town (from the garages, medical dispensary, YMCA, housing, school, company store, to a constant rotation of company doctors). Entering into postwar labor management relations, Mexican American mine workers were recognized as an ascendant bloc to account for in negotiations. Part of Mine-Mill's achievements, as a multiracial union, included Mexican American organizers translating flyers into Spanish and negotiating on behalf of all workers regardless of race, and never far from the labor struggles was the specter of the Ludlow Massacre.

In this chapter, I address the central role of Colorado Fuel and Iron to illustrate the dynamics of labor, unions, adjustment, and Americanization in relation to the formation of Chicano/Hispano communities in central Wyoming. By combining oral and family histories with archival analysis, I highlight the central role of labor organizing in protecting the health, safety, and cultural conflict concerns embedded in the daily lived experiences of Mexican Americans and their fellow workers in CF&I's largest supplier of iron—Sunrise, Wyoming.[7]

## On the Fringes: The Case of Sunrise, Wyoming

In the hinterlands of southeastern Wyoming, the sparsely populated area was nonetheless quite abundant in the iron ore, embedded in hematite, known to exist prior to European contact. Those recruited to extract the valuable resource out of the ground are emblematic of the comparative labor and ethnic relations in the West. Greek and Italian immigrants worked along Hispanos from northern New Mexico and Midwest and East Coast transplants.[8]

If one were to travel to central Wyoming today, it would take more than a few turns down the roads less traveled and special permission to access the ghost town associated with what was once one of the world's largest open-pit iron-ore mines. The ore had to be separated from the massive deposit of red hematite that once gave the appearance, prior to reclamation, of a forty-four-acre wound carved into the earth releasing a torrent of dry blood that leaves its red dust mark on everything it comes in contact with (e.g., cars, clothes, shoes, trees, company records, family photos, and the abandoned buildings of the town). Even as a company town, Sunrise followed the mixed

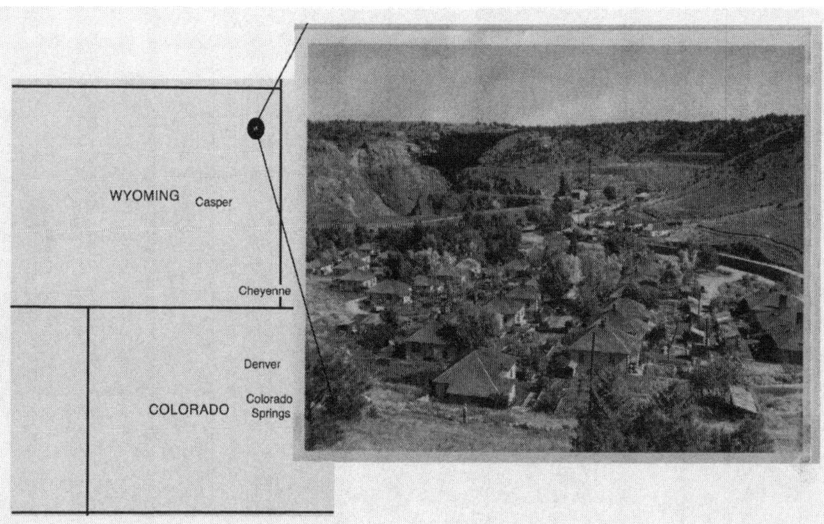


FIGURE 7.1 Map and photograph of Sunrise, Wyoming (ca. 1945) (courtesy of the Bessemer Historical Society / CF&I Archives)

development pattern witnessed in southern Arizona and southern Colorado. Vicki Ruiz defines these zones of regional development as "mining towns next to villages with ranches and homesteads marking the landscape."[9]

The sugar beet industry was the main pull bringing Mexican Americans from northern New Mexico to central Wyoming. With sugar beet cultivation and ranching as the main land tenure forms, including a Great Western Sugar refinery in nearby Wheatland and Holly Sugar's refinery in Torrington, many families from northern New Mexico followed the promises of high wages and steady work by *enganchadores* (labor contractors), through the beet fields of Colorado, to their eventual destination. The employment records at the Sunrise Mine note that many listed Homer Oxley, a beet farmer in Lingle, as their place of previous employment prior to locating mine work.[10] Like many other mining towns, the community was segregated by race / ethnicity / class with the mine managers living in the largest brick-constructed houses closest to amenities (known as brick row), white ethnic families living closer in wood frame or brick homes but separated into their own ethnic enclaves, and the Mexican American mining families living furthest from the company-owned store, YMCA, school, medical dispensary, electrical lines, and sewage system.

FIGURE 7.2 Colorado Supply Company Store at the Sunrise Mine, Wyoming, 1907 (courtesy of the Bessemer Historical Society / CF&I Archives)

For many Mexican American families, this meant going without running water and electricity in the most poorly constructed homes.

The dangerous nature of the work was constantly on miners' and their families' minds. Town residents knew an accident had occurred because the alarm was sounded whenever a worker was injured in the mine. Death, dismemberment, occupational diseases, and various types of injuries were endemic to underground mining. These dangerous working conditions were coupled with substandard housing. Living quarters for Mexican American mine workers' families consisted of either three or four rooms, but (particularly for the larger families) the miners' pay was not enough to meet expenses. Summertime was reserved for sugar beet harvesting completed by wives and children. Finally, differential treatment was integral to the everyday practices in a town defined by corporate ownership. For instance, the mine-owned school enforced a rule that speaking Spanish was strictly forbidden,

FIGURE 7.3 Sunrise Mine, Wyoming (courtesy of the Bessemer Historical Society / CF&I Archives)

and Mexican American students faced corporal punishment if they strayed into their home language. These cultural conflicts were equally relevant to miners as stock employment concerns (wages, health and safety, hours and promotion, and the like). Recognized as points for negotiation by both CF&I management and workers, the company union and two collective-bargaining agents (Mine-Mill 442 and USWA 4709) addressed cultural conflict concerns over the sixty-five-year history of union representation. The context for these labor battles are rooted in the coal mines of southern Colorado, where all-out battles were waged over workplace health and safety regulations, minimum wages, company towns, payment of wages in company scrip, eight-hour days, forty-hour work weeks, weekends, child labor restrictions, overtime pay, and rights to collective bargaining. The events of the Ludlow Massacre have justly attracted attention unparalleled in Western labor history but the postwar labor battles (often between AFL and CIO unions) are just as important for understanding the West, especially on the northern frontiers of the Mexican American Southwest.[11]

## Rockefeller's Company Union for Iron Miners, 1915–40

Out of the ashes of Ludlow and the southern Colorado coal wars, CF&I embarked upon the first public relations campaign to vindicate the Rockefeller name so thoroughly demonized by Upton Sinclair and organized labor. To be fair, Rockefeller did himself no favors in federal testimony when he attempted to distance himself from the working and living conditions of miners subjected to the violent actions of the company and its hired goon squads. While he offered unwavering support for the company's union-busting practices, in response to being asked: "If it [keeping the union out] costs all your property and kills all your employees," Rockefeller testified: "It [the open shop] is a great principle."[12] What became known as the Rockefeller Plan was the first attempt to create a company union that in many ways prefigured the modern-day human relations department, where grievances would be brought to the corporation but in an environment clearly aimed at protecting first and foremost corporate interests.

Coal miners were the first to sign up for the ERP, followed by the Minnequa millworkers in Pueblo, and finally the iron miners in Sunrise. On October 29, 1915, J .B. McKennan, general manager of CF&I, explained the plan to all Sunrise employees; then a vote was required. It is not clear, but most likely there was no secret ballot option given to employees. The results of the vote went as anticipated with 124 yes and 12 no votes. At the time, hourly pay rates varied from 19 to 55 cents per hour depending on the job task.[13] Workers were charged $13 per month for company housing in a five-room house or $15 for a six-room house.

The ERP remained remarkably consistent over the nearly twenty-five years of its existence. The twenty-six provisions of the April 14, 1938, agreement remained similar to the original terms of agreement. The agreement between the company and employee representatives at the Sunrise Mine comprised four provisions for the representation of employees and terms of agreement; three on wages and working conditions; two on the right of the company to hire and fire at will; an arbitration, or "adjustment of differences," process; two on conferences or meetings to discuss the ERP; five on subcommittees; and three on legal rights for employees to hold meetings and not be discriminated against for belonging to an organization or union as long as all federal, state, and company laws were obeyed; holidays from work on Christmas, July Fourth, and Labor Day; two on housing, wash houses, and utilities; coal for domestic use; and employees not obliged to trade at company stores. The subcommittees addressed topics including cooperation; wage conciliation; safety and accidents; sanitation, health, and housing; and recreation and education. Employees were elected annually according to job classifications, so three representatives came from the underground (one from the open pit, one from the block-caving section), one from the transport crew, one surface representative, and one representative of the railway shops for a total of five employee representatives.[14]

Particularly at the coal-mining towns, the issue of the increasing rise of domestic coal costs became a major bone of contention. In the ERP, Provision 21 stated: "Prices for domestic coal to be charged employees shall be substantially its cost to the Company, so far as is legally permissible."[15] By 1918, the only serious concern raised in the annual joint conference of the coal and mill employee representatives with management over those initial two years was the increasing cost of coal to heat homes.[16] Wellborn and management all rationalized it away in that it was 50 cents less than retail, but what was lost on them was the fruits of the labor of coal miners were taken and then resold to workers at ever increasing rates, in effect cancelling out pay raises. Estrangement from the fruits of one's labor was certainly front-and-center at the southern Colorado coal camps, but in the far northern operations of CF&I, the employees at iron-ore mine in Sunrise, Wyoming, similarly benefited from the improvements promised in the ERP.

The first mention of the Sunrise Mine is in the January 26, 1916, Pueblo Joint Conference minutes: "I should say that the Plan was offered to the employees of the Sunrise iron mine in Wyoming the latter part of October and adopted by a large majority vote. The representatives elected at the same time were reelected on January 8th, and the district conference at that point as held last week."[17] Even though major improvements were made to the company town in 1917, no mention surfaced in the minutes of Sunrise's new medical dispensary, school, or the dedication of the YMCA.[18] The dispensary was subsequently touted as funded by Rockefeller, and the creation of the company school and Y was a hallmark of the Rockefeller Plan. But it was clear from

FIGURE 7.4 YMCA at the Sunrise Mine, Wyoming (courtesy of the Bessemer Historical Society / CF&I Archives)

the minutes that the public relations aims were not aimed at fellow workers to show parity between coal and iron towns, as improvements were simply not mentioned to the coal towns and Pueblo employees. It is unclear even as late as 1919 whether Sunrise representatives participated in the annual joint conference, as they do not appear as participants in the minutes. If they were present at the meetings, they were silent nonparticipants. It is unlikely that they attended at all, as all the coal mine and Minnequa representatives were asked to respond at some point during the meeting. The Sunrise mine was by and large invisible to coal miners, and its only presence in the Pueblo steel mill was the iron that came from up north on railcars. It was not until 1925 that for the first time the official newsletter of the ERP, "Industrial Bulletin," provided a public relations piece on the quarries in Monarch and Cañon City and the Sunrise Mine.[19] Designed to introduce readers to the sources of calcite, dolomite, and iron necessary to the steel-making process, the article also mentions the value added by the ERP by featuring images of the school and YMCA. Interviews with employees were conducted for the same issue, yet from the report of survey results on the level of satisfaction with ERP, it becomes clear the quarry and iron miners were not interviewed to assess their satisfaction with the company union.[20] Rockefeller's eye was always aimed at the legacy of Ludlow and his perceived satisfaction of coal miners, so much of the ERP public presentation was aimed at demonstrating contented coal towns.

CF&I management did visit Sunrise quarterly, but the only rectified grievance to surface in the records of the ERP minutes is mentioned in a letter from the president's industrial representative B. J. Matteson to E. S. Cowdrick, assistant to president, on March 18, 1919:

> In regard to the matter of carpenters being idle at Sunrise. On the first afternoon while at Sunrise the representatives and I inspected a number of old houses which were in very bad condition. We interviewed the boss carpenter, and he informed me that the three carpenters referred to started to work on that day. In regard to the community cow barn at Sunrise, which was also taken up. In company with the representatives, while at Sunrise, we selected a location for a community cow barn, a few hundred feet above the laboratory, which met with the approval of the superintendent and Mr. Weed, should it be found advisable to build such a building.[21]

From recollections of families that lived in Sunrise, there is no evidence that a barn was ever built. Yet, the inferior condition of housing became a larger rallying point as it related to discriminatory access to higher-quality housing; this became a basis for of union organizing and mounting strikes.

The company union did not preclude the miners' proclivity to strike when bargaining broke down. Often it originated with white ethnic immigrant communities where labor unrest manifested. "A note from the weeks before the 1919 strike described a similar ethnic-centered protest at the CF&I's Sunrise Mine in Wyoming. 'Two or three Greeks spoke about the houses of the foreigners not being repaired', wrote the anonymous management author. 'They seem to think there was some discrimination in that the foreigners' houses were not taken care of. One Italian spoke in behalf of other Italians.' "[22] The discontent over housing was connected to two interrelated factors. First, quality of housing varied widely in the company towns, and some of the worst housing was dilapidated, without a furnace or running water, small and cramped.[23] Second, the town of fewer than 500 families was remarkably segregated into ethnic sections so that Sunrise had, as residents decried, Greek Row and Little Italy.[24] A 1938 map drawn by three Sunrise

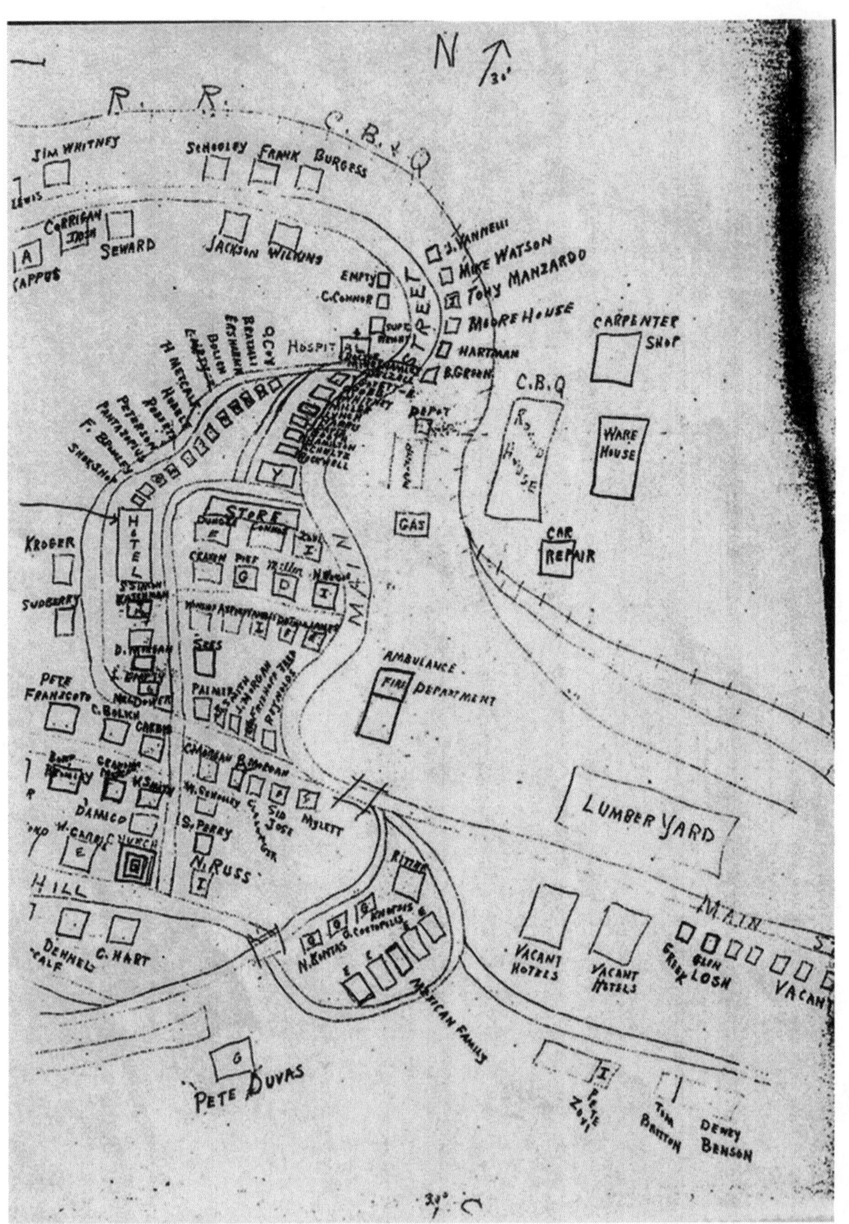


FIGURE 7.5 Making a model camp, Sunrise, Wyoming Plan, 1917 (courtesy of the Bessemer Historical Society / CF&I Archives)

high school students identifies the conglomeration of Greek-surnamed families residing together and Italian-surnamed families similarly situated. The Mexican section of town was only marked by the generic label "Mexican family" as it stands out that every other family name is identified on the map. Letters "G" and "I" were designed to identify Greek and Italian households, and though Italians were more widely dispersed, it is clear that Greeks and Mexicans were relegated to the Southeast section of town.

What the ERP did not specifically address was the ethnic and racial discrimination in housing that plagued the company towns. What the discrimination clause of the ERP (18) barred was "discrimination by the management or by any of the employees on account of membership or non-membership in any society, fraternity, or union."[25]

In Sunrise, the presence of the Dante Alighieri Society among Italian immigrants became the major institutional nexus for union organizing.[26] Throughout the mining towns, Italian and Greek fraternal organizations became the site for union organizing activity, and CF&I management was well aware of that fact. Though the ERP conceded the rights to free association, miners found themselves constantly infiltrated with company spies and informants. No better example of this can be found than the first attempts of the Italian community to organize Sunrise miners in 1935.

A Union Pacific mediator named Sam Moraldo set up a meeting at the Dante Alighieri Society Hall in nearby Hartville (frequented by Italian miners) to discuss organizing efforts among railroad workers and coal miners in Rock Springs, Wyoming. The rail lines that went through Wyoming became another labor source for the mine that brought particularly Japanese, New Mexicans, and southern and eastern European immigrants into the area for work once track construction was completed.[27] Moraldo contacted fellow Italian Tony Francescato, a timber framer, to set up the meeting. The plan was to sign up at least twenty men for the union so that a full-fledged organizing campaign could be initiated. Only Francescato and fellow timberman Joe Corollo signed up at that time. Unbeknownst to the organizers, the company had two men at the meeting to monitor what was said and report back to management. Even though the meeting was by and large unsuccessful, the company took an extra step to ensure that the organizing efforts would be squelched. The company never determined whether the organizers represented the Western Federation of Miners or the United Mine Workers, as the representatives were a bit sketchy in describing their affiliations and masking their insurance scheme that they intended to add onto union dues.

The company enlisted the help of the Hartville grocer Dante Testolin, whom management identified as "the most influential Italian in Hartville," to track down the parties responsible for the union meeting and put an end to the discussions of organizing.[28] Testolin's store offered the only alternative to the company store, and he was often very generous with the extension of credit to destitute families, many relying on him for comparatively cheaper goods and repayment terms that did not lock miners into the type of debt peonage that company stores were infamous for. Miners' families had no idea that Testolin was probably a company informant and one of the first men directly responsible for ending organizing efforts among Italian miners.

Testolin and Victor Birleffi (Moraldo's brother-in-law and Sunrise mine supervisor) traveled with mine superintendent Harry A. Wright to Cheyenne to visit with Moraldo directly, though Wright dropped the men off to attend his scheduled visit with a Wyoming state senator. The men exposed the insurance plot of Moraldo and his associate known only by the last name of Cole at that time. When George Cole returned to organize Mine-Mill Local 442, he had the financial backing of the union and majority support of the miners to successfully organize the men within five years of his original ill-fated visit. However, Moraldo agreed to cease and desist all organizing efforts and cut all ties between the union and Italians residing in Hartville and Sunrise. As news of these events traveled to miners, Birleffi became the target of an anonymous death threat letter signed by "The American" who described Italians as "all snakes." "A snake of the lowest grade that nature made on earth. You especially," referring to Birleffi." "People telling lies to you of your own race." As a mine foreman, Birleffi had a supervisory role that particularly distressed the letter writer but that did not override a sentiment of ethnic hatred. The letter writer was never located. In the final analysis, what began as a long-standing complaint about the quality of housing, which was temporarily addressed piecemeal by the ERP, eventually became the touchstone for successful union organizing efforts.[29]

Quarterly meetings were expected but often only annual meetings were recorded, with the director of mining, mine superintendents, foremen, and employee representatives present. These meetings brought together management and employee representatives to discuss issues that arose, for instance, in 1924 that included utilities (an issue around water rent increase for bathing and some discussion of lights, rent, water, high cost of living), but nothing seemed to improve as result of the airing of grievances.[30] Yet, by 1937, the ERP had been reduced to three representatives, and during most of the year the mine was down to one representative. The ERP was so ineffective and unimportant that a vote on September 1, 1937, to elect a new representative was carried out with seven men present out of two hundred eligible voters.[31] Unbeknownst to the company, each person elected to the ERP was organizing for Local 442. The ERP had not delivered on its promise to represent workers, and the disinterest in the company union was readily apparent.

One of the last grievances filed under the ERP concerned the quality of medical care available to the men and their families. In 1937, correspondence about the workers' request for a nurse, an ambulance to transport the injured to the nearest hospital—in effect to fully staff the Rockefeller medical dispensary—exposed an underlying complaint about the quality of medical care.[32] Management's response was captured in notes to Sunrise mine superintendent H. A. Wright from manager of mining department George H. Rupp: "Complaint on the ambulance. Do you actually need a new one? Or is this just agitation?"[33] Even when employee representatives DeFond, Albee, and Palmer successfully raised legitimate concerns about medical care, raises for hazard pay or general wage increase, or days off, the mine superintendent summarily dismissed them on all counts. The lone victory was management's willingness to allow two days off in a row instead of a midweek break with Sundays off.[34] However, the agreement was made with the proviso that this arrangement would be barred if it created situations requiring overtime pay. "This leads to time over the forty hours per week and may be payable at time and one half. In all fairness to the Company I cannot allow it, if at all possible [need] to prevent [it]." In the end, no nurse was appointed to Sunrise, a treadmill of poorly performing care cycled doctors through the dispensary, no ambulance was provided, and in terms of labor demands—no paid days off, hazard pay, or general wage increase.

The following year, representatives aired essentially the same grievances; the response they received was in response to a pay increase requested for jobs similar between the Pueblo Plant and iron mine: "Mr. Rupp stated that as the wage rates paid at Sunrise conform substantially with wage rates for like work under similar conditions [ 'at the mines' was added in pencil] in effect with Companies whose products are sold in active competition with products of this Company, it would be impossible to make a comparison with the Steel Works also."[35]

The underlying reason it would be "impossible" to compare is the mill-workers made substantially more per hour than iron-ore miners. In response to a vacation time request of 1 week vacation for 2 years of service and 2 weeks for 5 years of service, "Mr. Maxwell replied that the Company would be unable to grant this request since they were doing as much as any competing Company along that line now." Competitiveness was always the key justification to refuse requests above and beyond the industry standard.[36] A request that house rents be reduced during work slowdowns or stoppages was met with "In reply Mr. Maxwell advised Rep. Palmer to take this up when it occurred, as they were anticipating something in the future, but if taken up at the proper time and through the proper channels, they would give the matter all consideration." Proactive planning and negotiation were not the purpose of the ERP, so requests to fix problems in advance were summarily dismissed. Finally, a long-standing request regarding a reduction of old house and garage rentals in arrears was more unequivocally requested as a cancellation of past rents due. Even when work stoppages occurred and wages were not earned, the debts for rent and utilities mounted. Representatives further requested all old light, water, and coal accounts be "stricken as families cannot break even as is." In response "Mr. Maxwell requested Rep. DeFond to take this up in the customary manner so it could be acted on by the proper persons." With these responses, it becomes readily apparent that the debt peonage engendered by the ERP would only be countered by an independent union if miners sought collective-bargaining rights that would allow for real bargaining power and their social improvement.

## International Union of Mine, Mill and Smelter Workers (Mine-Mill Local 442): 1938–1954

Even with earlier failed attempts by primarily Italian miners, organizing efforts were emboldened by the passage of the 1935 Wagner Act, the law that gave employees the right to collective bargaining as secured by the National Labor Relations Board (NLRB), and previously unsuccessful outside organizers found their subsequent efforts were paying off. In the late 1930s, significant under-the-surface organizing occurred, and miners always kept one step ahead of the company's spying and subversion tactics. Sunrise miners found their efforts to build a union realized, with federal recognition stemming from the creation of the National Labor Relations Board and the ruling of the act that forbid company unions. "On March 29, 1940, the federal NLRB issued its decision against the Rockefeller Plan. The basis of the decision was the fact that the ERP continued to be a 'creature' of management even after the post-NLRA changes, which therefore invalidated it under Section 8(a)(2) of the NLRA . . .This decision applied to both the steel plant in Pueblo and the iron-ore mine in Sunrise, Wyoming."[37] Even though the company fought unionization efforts every step of the way with every tactic at their disposal, the union persevered.

Representing Sunrise miners, the International Union of Mine, Mill, and Smelter Workers Local 442 filed an amended unfair labor practices charge that was filed on April 20, 1939. Their first filing, on March 7, 1938, claimed unfair labor practices. The NLRB was asked to investigate:

> The said Corporation has interfered with, restrained, and coerced its employees at the Sunrise mine in the exercise of their rights guaranteed in Section 7 of the National Labor Relations Act. This interference, restraint, and coercion began on about February 1, 1938 and has continued up to and including the present time and has consisted of numerous statements and acts intended to discourage membership in the Sunrise Miners Union Local No. 442. Further, the Colorado Fuel and Iron Corporation, starting on about October 30, 1938 and continuing up to and including the present time, has interfered with the formation and administration of the Independent Union of Sunrise Mine and Surface Workers and has contributed financial and other support to it so as to encourage membership in this labor organization. Further, the Colorado Fuel and Iron Corporation has discriminated against individuals at its Sunrise Mine in regard to hire, term and condition of employment, and tenure of employment so as to discourage membership which began on about October 30, 1938 and are being continued at the present time.[38]

Specific examples included denial of work—totaling four thousand man hours—to about thirty-five miners who were all union sympathizers, refusal of employment to six men, underpayment of three men for work completed, and demotion of two men. The amazingly detailed chronology of events is listed in the ruling that required CF&I to disband their company union in Pueblo and Sunrise and required the corporation to officially recognize the Steel Workers' Organizing Committee in Pueblo and Mine-Mill Local 442 in Sunrise. The NLRB decision was based on both the illegality of the ERP as well as the company's efforts to thwart unionization efforts by in one instance, creating an "independent union" (covertly sponsored by company management and devoted to continuing the employee joint representation plan). Even though the Mine-Mill local had majority worker support in 1938, its recognition was stalled by CF&I until decisions by both the NLRB and the National War Labor Board finally forced the company to recognize and bargain with the union on March 13, 1942. Mine foremen intimidated the elected leaders of 442 and threatened dismissal if organizing activities continued. They also threatened lockouts or shutdowns if the company were required to recognize the union.

When labor struggles arose, industries sensitive to the war effort fell under the jurisdiction of the National War Labor Board (activated during both world wars). As CF&I was a major supplier of steel, the company's refusal to recognize unions wound the CF&I into the bureaucratic machinery of the federal arbitration system. The state had become a central site of class struggle. The War Labor Board's official mandate was the: "protection of unions against disruptive forces, or withholding such protection in case of strikes, job evaluation, vacation practices, and settlements of disputes which, in part, fall within the jurisdiction of the NLRB."[39]

The 1942 War Labor Board decision was rendered on October 31. Points adjudicated by the board included (1) union security and check-off, (2) general wage, (3) vacations with pay, and (4) probationary period for new employees.[40] The union was granted something closer to a closed shop on the closed-open continuum, if a check-off system and maintenance of membership agreement are accurate indicators of a closed shop. What appeared to be a victory was the 15 percent wage increase ruled in the workers' favor, yet in reality the raise was nonexistent as it was shown that a 15 percent raise, consistent with the overall Little Steel settlement, was already achieved in Sunrise and that miners had thus been given a 1 cent per hour adjustment. The board concurred with CF&I's reference to comparable wage rates among ranching and beet farming in the local area, thus placing mining wages at a higher scale. The ruling on vacation benefits brought Sunrise roughly to the same standard employed in Pueblo. Finally, a four-month probationary period was decided whereby workers could voluntarily join but the union could not file grievances on behalf of probationary employees. Even though the War Labor Board affirmed the NLRB ruling for Mine-Mill, they noted the company's unwillingness to come to terms with the union even after miners passed an affirmative strike vote on February 19, 1942. That strike was averted due to an appeal and request for US Conciliation Services. But throughout the War Labor Board's report, the specter of the Rockefeller plan loomed large with the miners, and the report went to great lengths to identify the ERP's lack of worker representation. So vehemently opposed to the closed shop, CF&I would go on to contest the maintenance-of-membership process (a provision granted consistent with the Little Steel decision), and company general counsel Fred Farrar led the battle. The maintenance of membership consisted of union dues drawn directly from workers' paychecks and deposited into a union account, and union membership was recognized according to a voluntary check-off, per the company's preference for level-of-union security. The language of the maintenance of membership in the contract was contested, and later the overall practice with the employer favored Taft Hartley Act of 1947, the law that limited the scope of the Wagner Act by defining "unfair labor practices" as actions committed by unions, not employers.

Two central actors at the negotiating table are emblematic of the management-organized labor struggles that came to define the period. On the side of management, CF&I general counsel Frederick Farrar represented the depth of antiunion sentiment by the corporate elite. On the side of labor, "Sam" Embree was a longtime Mine-Mill organizer who experienced nearly every labor battle from Ludlow to red-baiting. Their connection was inextricably linked in the battles over CF&I recognition of the Sunrise Miners' Union. In a letter dated June 28, 1943, which referred to the ongoing wage dispute mediated by the War Labor Board, Mine-Mill president Reid Robinson wrote to Thomas Howshar, secretary of Local 442: "I understand that Mr. Maxwell, the [CF&I] President, is due back in Denver either today or tomorrow and International Representative Sam Embree is in constant contact with Farrar to arrange a negotiating meeting."[41]

Fred Farrar served as the Colorado state attorney general during the Ludlow Massacre and refused to press charges against CF&I or hold the Colorado National Guard culpable for the lives lost. However, he was vehement in pressing murder charges against labor leaders such as John Lawson and other agitators. His subsequent employment, after serving as attorney general and ruling in favor of CF&I by finding no wrongdoing for the company's role in the Ludlow Massacre, was as a corporate lawyer for CF&I. From 1918 to 1952, he became general counsel for the company and the main opponent to unionization. Throughout his battles against recognizing unions (UMWA Local 15 in the coal fields, SWOC in Pueblo's Minnequa mill, Mine-Mill Local 442 in Sunrise), he deployed every legal mean at his disposal to maintain the ERP while delaying implementation of federal NLRB findings.

He also resorted to extralegal means of working with miners in Sunrise to create an "independent union" to compete with Mine-Mill Local 442. The challenge of the Independent Union president S. H. Whitney was likely funded but most certainly aided based on correspondence with Farrar and what appears to be a company-created blue pamphlet, "Bylaws for Independent Union of Sunrise Mine and Surface Workers." Many ERP representatives had a major leadership role in the Independent Union. In a one-page debate challenge by Local 442 organizer John Krionderis, he identified the "Independent" Union as a company tool for undercutting 442 organizing efforts. "Of course, the 'Independent' Union also uses the time worn propaganda that the C.I.O. is controlled by Communists and supported by aliens. That argument is always used when all other arguments fail."[42] The War Labor Board, in its order to disband the Independent Union, noted the main organizers were former representatives in the ERP and that, it was clear from company records, men were receiving advice and encouragement from management, particularly Farrar. When the company assessed the union membership question in 1940,[43] management determined that of the 152 men, the majority were supportive of Mine-Mill Local 442, even if the support was not necessarily unequivocal (see Table 7.1). The term *radical* might have referred either to anticapitalist sentiments or strong supporters of the respective unions, as the letter with this table does not analyze the numbers.

The ascendant anti-CIO sentiment was clearly exploited by the supporters of the independent union, and it appears the company assumed their "independent" union had slightly more strong support than Local 442 but that organizing efforts should concentrate on those neither "not too enthusiastic" nor "afraid to abandon union." After the NLRB ruling, it was clear they

TABLE 7.1 CF&I estimate of union support, 1940

| *Mine Mill Local 442* | *Independent Union* |
|---|---|
| 30 Radicals | 36 Radicals |
| 25 Strong union men | 20 Strong union men, anti-CIO |
| 20 Not too enthusiastic | 6 Not interested in union |
| 15 Afraid to abandon union | |
| 90 Total | 62 Total |

*Source*: Adapted from The Bessemer Historical Society and CF&I Archives, box MIN-0437, "Iron Ore Mines, Sunrise Mine, Operations files, including files on industrial relations (union files) and medical correspondence, 1928–1975," folder 1940.

overestimated the draw of the "independent" union and severely underestimated worker allegiances to Mine-Mill's Local 442.

On the other side of the labor relations battle, Mine-Mill was committing some of its most seasoned organizers to unionize Sunrise miners. Adolphus Stewart (Sam) Embree embodied the very struggles that necessitated the formation of the Western Federation of Miners (WFM) that eventually became Mine-Mill. From miner to labor organizer, Embree finished college in his native Canada and joined the WFM in British Columbia. He eventually moved among several mining locales—Coeur d'Alene, Idaho, southern Colorado, and Bisbee, Arizona—to witness firsthand the depths to which mine owners would resort to cast out union organizers and worker sympathizers. He was involved in the Ludlow Massacre, he worked as a copper miner and served on the local Industrial Workers of the World (IWW) board before being deported from Bisbee, and was eventually jailed for trying to return after being left in the middle of the desert with 1,200 fellow striking miners. In 1927, Colorado coal miners struck in solidarity to protest the executions of Nicola Sacco and Bartolomeo Vanzetti. During that year, Embree was originally the lead IWW organizer but was again jailed, this time for violating the antipicket policy of Colorado. Embree had written at the time, "The end in view [the revolution] is well worth striving for, but in the struggle itself lies the happiness of the fighter." Although United Mine Workers predicted the IWW's strike would fail, Embree wrote, Sheriff Harry Capps of Huerfano County had identified "fully two-thirds of the miners in the [Walsenburg] district [who are] members of the I.W.W. When the walkout occurred, out of a total 1,167 miners, 1,132 stayed off the job, and only 35 went to work."[44]

Embree continued to organize for Mine-Mill, and his daughter married executive secretary Maurice Travis, while she eventually worked as President Reid Robinson's personal secretary.[45] The entire leadership group was eventually red-baited with Embree one of the first convicted under charges of syndicalism. Yet, it was Embree's visit to Sunrise, as a lead organizer, that solidified Mine-Mill's commitment to Local 442.

The management of CF&I was aware of the "outside agitators," as they characterized Embree and his fellow organizers, but they were not particularly knowledgeable of who the men were. To rectify this lack of information, they were not above using local law enforcement to conduct their surveillance: "It might be well at Sunrise to have Sam Embree's record. It need not be advertised, of course. As a matter of fact, we shouldn't advertise it. I asked the F.B.I. to get it, but labor leaders are in a very special privileged class, as you may know, and the F.B.I. will give us nothing on him. His record, however, can be obtained through local law enforcement officers. You might talk to Bud Jones and see if Bud will or can get it."[46] It is interesting that management would assume radical union organizers held a privileged status given the long prison record of Embree and his constant life of turmoil based on the consequences paid for his organizing efforts.[47] The gains of Mine-Mill for the Sunrise miners were short lived, for as soon as they officially began contract negotiations and were officially recognized by CF&I, competing unions aimed their efforts at raiding those remaining postwar locals held by unions directly under attack by red-baiting politicians.

In 1948, mining department head G. H. Rupp assessed that year's annual negotiating terms with Mine-Mill: "The new contracts proposed by the union are extreme. They demand a 30 cent-per-hour general wage increase, a Health and Wellness plan, pensions, improved vacation and holiday clauses, a modified check-off and union security, anti-discrimination, protection of the union against suits arising from secondary boycotts." "For the last two or three years," he continued, "we have managed to get the union to accept practically the same contract as we negotiated with them in Washington, D.C. some years ago."[48] The eventual agreement concerned only wages, which management raised by twelve cents per hour. It was not until 1951 that the remaining amount of the requested raise was conceded by the company. One of the last wins of Mine-Mill was the securing of a Health and Wellness fringe benefits plan that was already granted to millworkers in Pueblo, and the company fully intended to extend the benefit to Sunrise miners but delayed granting access until parties entered into contract negotiations.

The annual contract negotiations required attention to a new community that began arriving at the end of World War II. Entering into the town were families with last names such as Apodaca, Herrera, Martinez, Otero, and Ramirez. Looking for year-round employment and recognizing that there would be no returning home to Aztlán, or their ancestral lands in New Mexico, the pressure to make central Wyoming a permanent home would coincide with securing stable jobs at the Sunrise mine. It also put another set of faces, cultural conflicts, and interests at the contract bargaining table.

One particular clause on the list of union demands was "The Company will not discriminate against any employee on account of his membership in the Union or on account of Union activity nor on account of his race, color, national origin, religion or political beliefs." In the CF&I mining department's files, the word *NO* was handwritten in the margins next to this clause. The company was well aware that Mexican American families were living in the mining camps as a result of a post–World War II influx. The director of the YMCA characterized the changes thusly:

> We are very busy here at the "Y" especially during the cold weather, and we have a different kind of people to deal with. I refer to the Mexicans. I get along fine with them, as I had lots of experience with them before, but it is hard for the people here to get used to them, at first they would not mix at all, but now they play cards, and bowl, and sit around and talk to each other, and gradually are becoming one of the big family, it takes a lot of patience, and a lot of head [*sic*] work to get these two factions to work in harmony with each other.[49]

At the time, as evidenced by the YMCA letterhead of the time, the mining camp Ys were still segregated; for example, Pueblo Steel Works miners belonged to Steel Works YMCA 1 Pueblo or Steel Works YMCA 2 Pueblo (Colored). A policy of segregation was not in place in Sunrise, but Mexican American families likely steered away from using the facilities until it became clear that they were not barred. Though the director seemingly states his acceptance of Mexicans' difference, he does identify the initial isolation they experienced upon arrival.

Though the company stood firm in allowing Mexican Americans to work in Sunrise but not expressly protecting their civil rights, Mine-Mill had shifted its organizing and bargaining approach to reflect the demographic changes in the workforce of the Sunrise iron mine. An organizer based in Leadville, Colorado (300 miles from Sunrise), named Leo Ortiz was assigned to represent Local 442. In 1950 Ortiz reported that the union "settled for 16 cents per hour wage increase" as of December 31, 1950.[50] Organizers cycled through, including Joe Mason and Harlow Wildman, but Ortiz remained the lead representative of Local 442 due to the Mexican American presence in the mining camp. In fact, Ortiz was commended by Wildman for his skill in organizing Mexicans.[51] Many flyers and letters created by Ortiz for the rank-and-file were bilingual. Access to union materials and protocols translated into inclusion, power, and solidarity, with language the key to access. Ortiz noted on January 14, 1951, when first fears of a Steelworkers' raid were identified: "Local [442] voted to have me mimeograph an outline of the grievance procedure and seniority clause in English and Spanish."[52] Ortiz often noted in his monthly reports that building and maintaining a strong Mexican American base of support was essential for a local's success. Solidarity among Anglo and Mexican miners was an overt theme in Ortiz's bilingual leaflets, pamphlets, and flyers.

On April 15, 1951, Ortiz presented his plan for saving Local 442 from a Steelworkers raid: "The membership of the Local is around 240 out of a possible 275. I worked out a series of Leaflets with the Officers and Stewards to launch a campaign to sign up the plant 100% and to increase the membership of the Ladies Auxiliary Local in Sunrise."[53] Adhering to the strength-in-numbers rationale, full union membership made sense, but increasing the membership of Ladies Auxiliary 71 in Sunrise was called for in the context of an auxiliary comprised almost exclusively of Anglos, with exception of Mrs. Baros, Julia Ramirez, and Phyllis Chavez (who signed a withdrawal card dated November 30, 1950).[54] Though the main draw of the auxiliary was their holding of weekly bingo games, other expenditures included sick benefits ($50 paid out) and funeral flowers for workers lost to fatal accidents. Auxiliary 71 ceased to operate when Mine-Mill Local 442 lost the election to USWA. For Ortiz, the plan dated in April would be the last monthly report filed until November 7, 1951, when the election was clearly a loss and USWA established itself as the favored union among Sunrise miners.

It is curious though that Ortiz never mentioned in his reports the very visible part of the battle between USWA and Mine-Mill, which included the

FIGURE 7.6 View of the town of Sunrise, Wyoming, with mining structures in the background, 1950 (courtesy of the Bessemer Historical Society / CF&I Archives)

children of miners wearing buttons to display if their families were Steel Worker or Mine-Mill supporters. The subtle choosing of sides, the perennial "Which side are you on?" question, put the recently arrived Mexican American families in the middle. Were they good Americans who supported anticommunist unions? Were they rabble-rousers who put ethnic allegiances over American identity? My uncle recalls wearing a Steel Worker pin to school during the fight. Yet, I recall visiting my grandparents' Guernsey home in the early 1980s and spending time reading the old Mine-Mill/CF&I contract pamphlets from 1946 and 1948 cover to cover, over and over in the hopes of one day understanding the legalese. I vividly recall the union magazines that also sat on stacks in the house with crossword puzzles on the back cover of the Mine-Mill "News from the Mines." At ten, I learned from these crossword puzzles the terms *solidarity*, *capitalism*, *profit*, and *scab* for the first time. The conflicted Mexican Americans, whose allegiances were often challenged as being un-American or their very identities as "a different kind of people," underwent exclusion from social gatherings, corporal punishments for speaking Spanish in school, and a constant pressure to assimilate and Americanize. Their main hope appeared to be the efforts at solidarity building through multiracial representation by Mine-Mill organizer Leo Ortiz.

Yet, it was unclear if Ortiz prioritized his representation of Sunrise miners as he was often working in Leadville and nearby mines to hold off raiding unions. After successful contract negotiations in 1950, Ortiz identified five priorities: (1) Raise dues from 1.50 to 2.50 per month, (2) create a two-man committee to police Pension and Social Insurance, (3) reorganize the grievance committee, (4) hold classes on grievance process, (5) and codify rules about seniority.[55] The following year, his quarterly report would read: "Lost election in Sunrise to Steelworkers. Mine-Mill 113, Steel 115, Challenged 1."[56] He never succeeded in securing full union membership among Sunrise miners. Most of the locals under his purview were lost in 1951, but he was not the only Mine-Mill representative who did not foresee the United Steel Workers Association raid. In a 1950 letter to President John Clark by W. Mason, he wrote, "As I told you the other day some head mogul in the steel outfit in Pueblo has been casting proprietary remarks concerning the Sunrise Mine but the guys in Local 442 are good and the relationship we developed with the Mining Department of the CF&I over the years places the Company on the side of the group with Mine-Mill and I do not think we will have any trouble there."[57]

## United Steel Workers of America, Local 4709, 1952–1980

Though Ortiz distributed a plethora of flyers in support of Mine-Mill, the opposing USWA campaign was directed by Minnequa-based USWA organizer Michael Soldren. He distributed a series of anti–Mine-Mill flyers highlighting its communist influence and in particular indicting secretary/treasurer Maurice Travis. Flyers documented Travis's forced resignation from the Communist Party (IWW) to sign the non-Communist affidavit, and he was subsequently labeled "Red" Travis in USWA pamphlets.[58]

The CF&I management was actually conflicted about the raid. Their negotiating experiences with USWA were not perceived as positive. They most feared a "substantial wage increase." The basis of that fear was a recently negotiated raise of ten cents per hour in Utah between USWA and US

Smelting, Refining, and Mining Company.[59] Rupp contacted peers at the Utah Mining Association (his contacts were college classmate Ed Snyder, who owned Combined Metals Reduction Company, and Jim Ivers, president of Park City Consolidated Copper Company) and was told the negotiations have "been tied up and almost idle because he [the Utah Mining Association representative] cannot agree with the United Steelworkers on any such arrangement as stated above. It looks as though we are in for some trouble on job classifications and their resulting wage rates." At the same time, officials were unsure about their prognosis of negotiations with the USWA, they also pined for the amiable relations with Mine-Mill. In letter to Vice President J. C. Martin, G. H. Rupp wrote, "While we have been very happy in our relationship with the Mine, Mill, and Smelter Workers, they were expelled from the C.I.O. because they were a Communistic-dominated union. We would be in real trouble any time the Mine, Mill, and Smelter Workers produced a pension plan different from that now in effect with the C.I.O. I hope that we shall be as happy under the Steel Workers union as we have been with the Mine, Mill, and Smelter Workers union."[60]

In the end, the USWA contract was almost a verbatim copy of the Mine-Mill—negotiated contracts.[61] The initial difference between contracts is a USWA push for job descriptions in order to bring Sunrise Local 4709 into conformity with the overall USWA policy of removing wage inequities in classifications. The wage inequity language in the contract was modeled on Tennessee Coal, Iron, and Railroad Co.-USWA agreement. The negotiated issue stated that "the parties agree to establish a program for the ultimate elimination of wage rate inequities similar to such inequity programs effective in the principal collective-bargaining units in the iron ore mining industry represented by the USWA-CIO."[62]

Interestingly, even in the last days of Mine-Mill representation, the local leadership consisted of at most one Mexican American officer. The racially inclusive CIO Mine-Mill Local 442 was often only represented by Ollie Ramirez along with a consistent Greek representation. The USWA Local 4709 expanded the number of officers, and they were also organizing at a time when a larger Mexican- Mexican American workforce was in place, but throughout the 1950s to 1970s, at least two Mexican Americans were officers representing the union in any given year. One clue in terms of the shifting ethnic composition of the workforce is available in a 1973 list of mining safety trainees, or employees who qualified for training based on their job title. At the time, a significant minority (30%) of Sunrise employees were Spanish surnamed as of September 19. The employment list for ensuring mining evacuation and self-rescuer training included 46 Mexican Americans among the 153 employees eligible. [63] Compared to 1930 Census records, nearby Hartville primarily housed Italian and Greek immigrants yet no Mexican American residents. In 1930, Sunrise was home to two single male Japanese laborers and three Mexican immigrant families (by the last names of Albares, Refugio, and Ramirez) who lived next to each other in a town of then-approximately 623 residents.[64] All of the Mexican men were listed as "laborers" in the iron mine.

By the late 1970s, the population of Sunrise was in serious decline due to financial woes at CF&I and the decline in iron-ore extraction at the mine. In 1980, CF&I declared bankruptcy and closed the mine in the same year. The corporation quit claim deeded the property to the state of Wyoming (in effect, abandoning the property), yet the lands were rejected by the state's governor as the site's air and soil was determined to be contaminated. The former mine site was eventually sold to a private entity who received reclamation funds to secure the safety of the mine and remedy its most contaminated areas. When CF&I was purchased by Oregon Steel in 1993, the Sunrise mine was not included in the purchase. Today, the steel mill is owned by the Russian firm Evraz Group SA and consists of limited operations in Minnequa with the Sunrise property still for sale and literally a ghost town. The boom/bust of cycle of Sunrise is now complete as the lands have been restored on the surface to premining days with only a few abandoned structures on the site (the Y and a few homes) still intact. But the memories linger and the records available in archives such as the Bessemer Historical Society point to a history long forgotten but not lost. The next generation of scholars would be well served to continue expanding their analysis of labor history beyond the events at Ludlow and into some of the less explored areas of inquiry analyzed herein.

## Conclusion

The legacy of the early twentieth-century Colorado labor wars is immeasurable in the annals of US Western history. In the aftermath of Ludlow, workers' rights to collective bargaining were subverted by the introduction of company unions, or employee representation plans, that sought to keep the peace on company terms. This peace did not allay the dangers associated with mining operations and the outright class warfare that came to a head in 1913. Records collected by Colorado Fuel and Iron (CF&I) list forty-eight mines from 1902 to 1922 that lay claim to 485 deaths associated with 18 "mine disasters" (mostly explosions) as distinct from "accidents" that took far more individual miners' lives.[65] They document nearly forty days when mob violence, shooting incidents, and intentional explosions left at least nineteen dead. Class war was being waged beginning with the first strike call on September 23, 1913, to the initiating strike at the Ludlow tent colony on April 20, 1914, which eventually resulted in the Ludlow Massacre. All totaled, "more than seventy-five people died, most of them shot to death in the first eight months of the coal strike that lasted eighteen months and that the miners lost . . . [No other strike] reached the level of pitched warfare that erupted here in Colorado's southern coalfields, where East Coast money and power collided with immigrant poverty and need."[66] The majority of those killed were strikers but miners vehemently fought back, and casualties among guards, detectives, and Colorado National Guard troops mounted, particularly after April 20, when strikers burned Empire, Royal, and McNally mines in retaliation. Violence on both sides continued until federal troops were called out on December 10, 1914, to effectively end the strike. The context was irrevocably set for analyzing labor struggles embedded in company unions versus organized labor and the daily lived experiences in a company town.

Yet, the experiences of miners in Sunrise point to the false promises of the company union and the attempts in response to build labor unions across racial and ethnic lines. The success of Mine-Mill in Sunrise was in many ways a direct result of the failings of the company union. Missing in the resurgent interest on the topic is an attention to the role of iron ore mining and the steelmaking side of the CF&I operations (excusably due to the high-profile labor wars in the coal mines and the events at Ludlow). Often overlooked are the CF&I's mining operations located in Wyoming, where one mine produced only one percent of the nation's steel, yet the vast majority of iron used in Pueblo's steelmaking operations. The company town and mine in Sunrise, Wyoming, had an employee representation plan, and due to relatively lower levels of labor unrest the community received a lot of early attention in the development of Rockefeller's plan. Yet, unrest was never far from the surface; at the first opportunity iron miners organized in 1938 to be represented by the International Union of Mine, Mill, and Smelter Workers Local 442 (the only Mine-Mill local that entered into contracts with CF&I). The changing social character of the town in the postwar years and the eventual Taft-Hartley vote by Sunrise miners in 1951 resulted in the workers' affiliating with the United Steelworkers of America, Local 4709. Americanization in company schools, high degrees of social division in such a small town, and too often second-class citizenship became a reality for Mexican American miners and their families. From the unstated but often felt Colorado Supply Company and YMCA for whites only, to job classifications negotiated by USWA that opened up hope for advancement and union leadership positions, all too often Mexican Americans found themselves caught in the middle. Their loyalties were divided by two unions and a company offering some economic opportunity in spite of its inability to fully provide for families or upward social mobility. The transition from company union to Mine-Mill to Steel Workers intersects with the historical patternings of race relations, labor organizing, residential segregation, Americanization, immigration, and exploitation. Being able to write about these events, two generations removed, represents a full-circle vindication of the power of listening to the stories of elders and recognizing the historical relevance of those daily lived experiences often lost to more conventional retellings of history.

## Notes

1. Sarah Deutsch, *No Separate Refuge: Culture, Class and Gender on an Anglo-Hispanic Frontier in the American Southwest, 1880–1940* (New York: Oxford University Press, 1987).

2. Colorado Fuel and Iron Corporate Archives, Bessemer Historical Society and CF&I Archives, Pueblo, CO, box MIN-0004, "Safety Letter and Reports, 1927–1959."

3. Bessemer Historical Society and CF&I Archives, box MIN-0004.

4. US Census, 1940 rolls, Platte County, Wyoming, roll T627_4574, page 6B, Enumeration District 16-2, 1940 United States Federal Census, http://www.ancestry.com, accessed 2012.

5. George P. West, United States Commission on Industrial Relations, *Report on the Colorado Strike* (Barnard and Miller, 1915), 55.

6. Jonathan Rees, *Representation and Rebellion: The Rockefeller Plan at the Colorado Fuel and Iron Company, 1914–1942* (Boulder: University Press of Colorado, 2010), 104. At the time, not all European immigrants were allowed to stake claims on whiteness to the same degree, so it was African Americans, Mexican Americans, Greeks, and Italians that were relegated to the worst jobs with the least amount of employee representation (and not surprisingly, then, the most militant in advocating for CIO-union representation). Company unions were expressly outlawed with the passage of the National Labor Relations, or Wagner, Act in 1935.

7. The opening of Bessemer Historical Society's CF&I archives initiated my interest in approaching my family's history in the archival records, as my grandfather worked in the Sunrise mine and my mother grew up in the company town. Since initial trips to Pueblo, I have also benefited from the labor collections of the Denver Public Library, Cornell University's Kheel Center, the Pennsylvania State University Labor Archives, University of Colorado at Boulder Archives, and the massive archival digitization projects across the country that have enabled access to collections too numerous to identify here.

8. Demographic data were calculated by triangulating company employee records and US Census rolls from 1920 to 1940.

9. Vicki Ruiz, *From Out of the Shadows: Mexican Women in Twentieth-Century America* (Oxford: Oxford University Press, 1998), 24.

10. Bessemer Historical Society and CF&I Archives, box MIN-0073, "Personnel Cards, Sunrise Mine." Personnel cards filled out by new employees contained a box to identify prior employer. In Sunrise, a few workers transferred from other mines but more often were employed in railroads or agriculture.

11. The terminology employed in this chapter is quite intentional. My selection of the terms *Ludlow Massacre*, *company union*, and similarly *loaded* word choices is based on how these terms were most often discussed in the mining camps by miners themselves. Referring to the Ludlow Massacre, I recognize the long-standing role of the Colorado National Guard in perpetrating massacres (including the events of Sand Creek but also including subsequent campaigns to eradicate Cheyenne, Arapahoe, Ute, and other native nations). Referring to Ludlow as a massacre does not lessen resistance on the part of strikers but does connote the difference between minimally armed strikers and government-appointed strikebreakers firing machine guns into canvas tents behind the armor of a "Death Special." I retain the term *company union* as well because an ERP is a company union in name only as a term preferred almost exclusively by the company management.

12. Jonathon Rees, *Representation and Rebellion*, 14.

13. Bessemer Historical Society and CF&I Archives, box MIN-0375. Handwritten on a wage sheet of retrieved notes from the Sunrise mining superintendent's office,

"Sunrise Wage Scale 1910–1921" show that wages varied from .16 to .655 per hour, and includes the assessment: "THE GOOD OLD DAYS!!"

14. The iron-mining operations began as an open-pit mine that was eventually dug over six hundred feet below the surface. As the faces became too dangerous to scale—though one crew's job was to repel down the sheer sides on ropes—the engineers designed an intentional cave-in system called block caving that exploded deposits into a chutes below, where iron was separated, extracted, and loaded onto carts. The process was incredibly dangerous but recognized as a technological innovation in the mine-engineering literature. See George H. Rupp, "Block-Caving at the Sunrise Iron Mine, Wyoming," *Mining Technology* American Institute of Mining and Metallurgical Engineers, 1939] for a description of the technical process.

15. Bessemer Historical Society and CF&I Archives, "Agreement by and between the Colorado Fuel and Iron Corporation, Colorado and Wyoming Railway Company Northern Division and Employees' Representatives," Sunrise Mine, folder 3, (1938), 11.

16. Bessemer Historical Society and CF&I Archives, box INR-1292, SG 2.1.1, folder 1.

17. Bessemer Historical Society and CF&I Archives, folder 1, "Employee Representation Plan Joint Conference Minutes, 1916."

18. Bessemer Historical Society and CF&I Archives, folder 2, "ERP-JC Minutes, 1917."

19. The article was penned by the former Sunrise mine superintendent L. B. Weed, *CF&I Industrial Bulletin* (April 25, 1925).

20. ERP Minutes, March 1919.

21. CF&I Archive, INR 1293, folder 6, "ERP: Letters from ERP evaluating plan."

22. Rees, *Representation and Rebellion*, 104.

23. The house my grandparents lived in was the same model of CF&I company home in which they raised their family in Sunrise. Homes were moved from the older Chicago Mine encampment to their current locations in nearby Guernsey. It has the same dimensions the house my mom and her four siblings grew up in and is 624 square feet with two bedrooms(12' × 12'), a kitchen and living room (12' × 14'), two closets. There was a bathroom added after its relocation.

24. In recalling these social divisions, my uncle expressed how these disparagements worked to stereotype and segregate communities. In an oral interview, he stated, "Thank God that we didn't have Black people in Sunrise, as you can guess what their section would have been called."

25. Bessemer Historical Society and CF&I Archives, "ERP," 11.

26. Mutual aid societies did not exist for the small numbers of Mexican families and the handful of single Japanese men who cycled through the mine. There is no

record of African Americans in Sunrise from employee and census records, and the sizable Mexican influx was clearly post–World War II. The Veterans of Foreign Wars (VFW) Hall, set up by the company according to the YMCA director, was not established on company property but in the nearby town of Guernsey. The VFW became the main gathering place for all veterans, regardless of race, after World War II.

27. The number of Japanese workers was extremely small. Census records from 1920 and 1930 triangulated with Sunrise personnel cards identify that two single Japanese men worked in the mine and lived in the town's hotel (boarding house) in 1920 and another two in 1930. "Track Work" was their listed previous occupation.

28. Bessemer Historical Society and CF&I Archives, personal letter from George H. Rupp, manager, CF&I Mining Department, to William A. Maxwell Jr. CF&I vice president, January 25, 1935.

29. From the first report on "Complaint about interior of some of the dwellings. Weed arranged for temporary repairs." This concession was repeated in subsequent reports to Rockefeller as a measure of progress in Sunrise labor relations, Bessemer Historical Society and CF&I Archives, box INR-1292, "Employee Representation Plan: Minutes, 1916," (6), folder 4.

30. Bessemer Historical Society and CF&I Archives, Box INR-1298, "General Correspondence: SW-117 Elections, Sunrise," folder 80.

31. National Labor Relations Board, Cases Nos. C-983, R-1100, and C-984.—Decided March 29, 1940, http://mynlrb.nlrb.gov/link/document.aspx/09031d458006 1b6f, 222–23.

32. This complaint resurfaced about ten years later in a letter dated February 10, 1948, from Samuel Potter, chief doctor of Corwin Hospital to Mining Department Manager G. H. Rupp: "Since sending my recent letter to Dr. Wood, I have had communication with him in which he states that he believes his services are 85% satisfactory to the people of Sunrise. He says most of the difficulty comes from the fact that there are two or three men, rather Communistic in nature who are supporting Wallace for president, who have leveled off on him and seem to keep leveling off on him." Potter stated earlier there was no need to replace him even though there were complaints by "labor." "They have accused you of not being interested in medicine, as being indifferent to their ills and that you are too lazy to make calls and take care of them. They have also said that you have made some bad errors in judgment, which, of course, they very likely know nothing about since judgment in medicine cannot accurately arise from their minds." Bessemer Historical Society and CF&I Archives, letter from Potter to Wood, January 30, 1948.

33. Bessemer Historical Society and CF&I Archives, letter from George H. Rupp, Manager of Mining Department, to Henry A. Wright, Sunrise Mine Superintendent, April 22, 1937.

34. Bessemer Historical Society and CF&I Archives, "Minutes on ERP Representative and Management at Sunrise Mine," March 27, 1937.

35. All company responses can be found in the Bessemer Historical Society and CF&I Archives, "Minutes of meeting held between Employees Representatives and Management of the CF&I Corporation at Sunrise, March 25, 1938."

36. CF&I mining files provide ample documentation that companies were very knowledgeable about each other's wages and benefits and that it was primarily Big Steel labor relations (US Steel and the United Steel Workers Association) that set standards for the Little Steel corporations.

37. Rees, *Representation and Rebellion*, 201.

38. National Labor Relations Board, Case Numbers C-983, R-1100, and C-984, Decided March 29, 1940.

39. War Labor Reports, *Reports of Decisions of the National War Labor Board with Headnotes and Index-Digest*, vol. 4 (Bureau of National Affairs, 1943), iv.

40. Ibid., 271.

41. Western Federation of Miners and International Union of Mine, Mill, and Smelter Workers Collection, Archives University of Colorado at Norlin Library, box 163, "Sunrise, WY Miners Union, 1943–1946," folder 12.

42. John Krionderis, "Independent Union vs. International Union, Debate Challenge," reproduced in R. W. MacCannon, *Sunrise: A Chronology of a Wyoming Mine* (Pueblo, CO: Bessemer Historical Society, 2003), 97.

43. The 1940 Census, taken in April, identifies the 129 households and 32 unaccompanied residents (listed on 13 census roll sheets) as being all white, non-Hispanic surnamed. This confirms my family's recollections that the sizable Hispano population did not arrive in Sunrise until after World War II.

44. Donald J. McClurg, "The Colorado Coal Strike of 1927—Tactical Leadership of the IWW," *Labor History* 1 (1963): 69–72; Joseph R. Conlin, *At the Point of Production: The Local History of the IWW* (Westport, CT: Greenwood Press, 1981), 199.

45. Michael Solski and John Smaller, *Mine Mill: The History of the International Union of Mine, Mill, and Smelter Workers in Canada since 1895* (Reno: Steel Rail Publishing, 1984).

46. Bessemer Historical Society and CF&I Archives, letter to H. A. Wright, superintendent of Sunrise Mine from G. H. Rupp, Manager of Mining Department December 28, 1943.

47. The close relationship between the International Workers of the World (Wobblies or IWW) and Mine-Mill is well documented, and the inner circle of Robinson, Travis, Embree, and other Mine-Mill officers in the late 1940s was one of dual membership with both organizations.

48. Bessemer Historical Society and CF&I Archives, personal letter, G. H. Rupp, manager of Mining Department, to M. Sisson, Sunrise Mine Superintendent, May 17, 1948.

49. Bessemer Historical Society and CF&I Archives, personal letter, C. L. "Banty" Wendel, Sunrise YMCA director to G. H. Rupp, Mining Department Manager, February 6, 1947.

50. University of Colorado Boulder Archives, Mine Mill Papers, "Ortiz, Leo—96 (1950), 97 (1951)—Local Rep. reports."

51. Ibid., "Wildman, Harlow—98 (1951)—Local Rep. reports."

52. Ibid., "Ortiz, Leo—96 (1950)—Local Rep. reports."

53. Ibid., "Ortiz, Leo—97 (1951)—Local Rep. reports."

54. Ibid., "Ladies Auxiliary 71, Sunrise WY160 (1947–1951)."

55. Ibid., letter from Ortiz to W. Mason, January 19, 1950.

56. Ibid., September 15, 1951.

57. Ibid., letter dated January 5, 1950, from William Mason, region director to John C. Clark, President Mine-Mill.

58. Flyer found in Travis's files, University of Colorado Boulder Archives, box 144, "Sec Treas Local Correspondence, 7/50–12/52," folder 442, 1952.

59. Bessemer Historical Society and CF&I Archives, box INR-471 11a/b, "USWA Local 4709 2-5-52."

60. Ibid., letter to J. C. Martin, vice president from G. H. Rupp.

61. Ibid., box INR-471, "Industrial Relations Sunrise IUMMSW 1948–1950," folder 1A, 1952.

62. Folder 1B identifies that consent election takes place on December 12, 1951.

63. MacCannon, "Mine Evac. and Self Rescuer Training, September 19, 1973," 233.

64. Wyoming Platte Sunrise 1930 census. Ancestry.com.

65. Bessemer Historical Society and CF&I Archives, Pueblo, CO. Forty-four of the forty-eight mines on the list of disasters and strikes, not all CF&I owned, included Aguilar, Berwind, Bowen, Brookside, Cameron, Cardiff, Coal Basin, Coal Creek, Cokedale, Cornell, Crested Butte, Cuatro, Delagua, El Moro, Engle, Floresta, Frederick, Fremont, Gulch, Hastings, Hezron, Ideal, Lester, Lime Quarry, Maitland, Marion, McNally, Morley, Nonac, Pershing, Pictou, Piedmont, Primero, Rockvale, Rouse, Segundo, Sopris, Starkville, Sunrise, Tabasco, Tercio, Tioga, Toller, and Walsen.

66. Scott Martelle, *Blood Passion: The Ludlow Massacre and Class War in the American West* (Brunswick, NJ: Rutgers University Press, 2008), 2.

EIGHT

# The Legacy of Ludlow

*Maria E. Montoya*

Is Ludlow unique in the lexicon of US labor history and strife? Certainly, the horrific vision of women and children lying dead amidst the rubble of the burnt-over and decimated tent colony shocked Americans, who were used to labor violence but not to the image of dead women and children. Ludlow also incited an intense public response that wholeheartedly sided with workers to the point that striker-provoked violence and death were almost virtually ignored by the press.[1] Rarely had the American public been so anticapitalist and proworker. During earlier strikes, such as the Great Railroad Strike of 1877, public opinion had quickly turned against the striking workers. Once that happened, the strikers lost their edge. Not since the Triangle Shirtwaist Factory Fire of 1912 had the American public press been so in favor of workers and reforms that would improve working conditions.[2]

Yet, as horrific as the events at Ludlow were, the violence was not unique, either qualitatively or quantitatively, to the American West or to US labor/management relations during the years surrounding the late nineteenth century and early twentieth. With the emergence of the Industrial Age after the

DOI: 10.5876/9781607323105.c008

close of the Civil War, the divisions between capitalists and their workers only became more apparent. Fueled by immigration and urbanization, the American workplace emerged as a complex web of laborers who brought with them their own sense of what it meant to be a worker, a citizen, and an economic provider for one's family. Some had left their farms to take jobs in the newly industrialized workplace, while others came with much experience from their homelands as miners or craftsmen. As these workers confronted one another, as well as their bosses and business owners, the results were predictable, and in many cases quite horrible.

Two strikes are particularly illustrative for understanding the national context of Ludlow: the Great Railroad Strike of 1877, and the Homestead Strike of 1892. The end of the nineteenth century and the beginning of the twentieth were wracked by economic instability. The panics of 1873, 1893, 1901, and 1907 periodically threw the US and global economies into turmoil resulting in reduced wages, fewer benefits, and layoffs. Consequently, laborers responded with one of the few tools available to them: the strike.[3] This period saw dozens of strikes with thousands of laborers leaving their jobs to protest labor conditions, long hours, child labor, and wage cuts.

The Great Railroad strike stemmed from the financial panic of 1873 brought on by the overinvestment in railroads after the close of the Civil War.[4] Up until the 1930s, the 1873 economic downturn had been labeled the Great Depression, with thousands thrown out of work, plants closed down, and families suffering deeply. The depression lasted until 1879, and the Great Railroad Strike of 1877 revealed the frustration of workers as their strike shut down most of the railway traffic nationally.

When local and state militias, in places such as Baltimore, refused to fire on striking workers, President Rutherford B. Hayes sent in federal troops from city to city to put down the strike, which ended forty-five days after it started. The loss of life as well as the millions of dollars in wages lost, time lost, and property loss showed the devastation that strikes could wreak on a national economy. But, the real lesson that both capitalists (including the Rockefeller Family) and workers took away from the strike was that when the federal government was willing to get involved and send in troops, the tide could be turned and swayed against workers. Certainly this was the pattern at Ludlow . . . a drawn-out strike that ended with government intervention shifting the balance of power. It was in the wake of this massive Railway Strike that unionization got a boost; workers flocked to emerging unions such as the Knights of Labor, the American Federation of Labor, and the United Mine Works to name a few.[5]

By 1892 the power of union organization was being felt across the industrial landscape. Andrew Carnegie, and his associate Henry Clay Frick, feared the power of the Amalgamated Association of Iron and Steel Workers (AAISW) at their Homestead Iron Works in Pittsburgh, Pennsylvania.[6] After a series of bitterly fought strikes during the 1880s, Andrew Carnegie admitted that the union virtually ran the steelworks, so complete was its control over the pace of work, wages, and hours. Carnegie heeded Frick's advice and used the 1892 contract negotiations to break the union and bring in unskilled and nonunionized workers to his increasingly mechanizing works.

After failed contract negotiations, Frick locked out the workers and called in Pinkerton and Baldwin agents to confront the strikers. The battle was bloody and eventually resulted in a complete route of the strikers and the destruction of the union.[7] Again, the presence of violence, and state-sponsored violence in particular, tipped the balance in favor of capitalists. Furthermore, the other lesson that capitalists, like Rockefeller, took from Homestead was that virtual monopoly and domination of an industry—steel in the case of Carnegie and oil and coal in the case of the Rockefellers—meant that workers had nowhere else to turn when strikes did not boost their cause. The Carnegie Steel works remained a nonunion shop for forty years. The Colorado Coal fields remained nonunion until the passage of the 1935 Wagner Act, more than twenty years after Ludlow.

By looking at these two strikes in particular, and the general history of labor relations in the United States at the turn-of-the century, we can see Ludlow as just one event on a continuum of violence between labor and capital. Ludlow fit the pattern as workers attempted to make qualitative changes to their workplace. And like the Homestead strikers, they faced a paternalistic company owner who believed he knew what was best for his workers: a stable work environment with no independent union. But what made Ludlow different from Homestead and other strikes was the very public and horrific deaths of women and children. Although not entirely true, the American public perceived strikes as a contest between men: labor on one side and capitalists on the other. The death of those fourteen women and children made clear that strikes and labor in America were family events that involved every aspect of peoples' lives. . . . No one could escape the hardship of the labor practices in Colorado's coal fields.

In the face of this shifting public perception, pushed by women like Mother Jones and Josephine Roche, John D. Rockefeller Jr. felt that he needed to shift the terms of the compromise and not merely make it about wages and hours, but get the root of the problem as he saw it: how to remake the American workplace and how to influence workers. It is easy to dismiss the Industrial Relations Plan as paternalistic, with its obvious shortcomings, which are eloquently covered in this collection of essays. Nevertheless, the Industrial Plan shifted the national conversation about the nature of the relationship between employers and their workers and, at the very least, suggested that capitalists had some obligation to the working class beyond wages and safety. When compared to the rhetoric that industrialists such as Henry Clay Frick and Andrew Carnegie were espousing at Homestead or George Pullman was espousing during the Pullman Strike, Rockefeller was at least interested in working toward a more progressive and fair workplace, but only on his terms.[8] At no point did Rockefeller or the Industrial Plan consider the idea of union recognition and negotiation as a means to creating a better workplace an option.

The Industrial Plan was a step on the path toward reform in the American workplace. The document laid out a half dozen areas in which management would negotiate with workers about how to accommodate workers' demands.[9] The plan went beyond the scope of the workplace and addressed issues of home life and social life, which had come to be a major part of CF&I's industrial workplace. The plan also established a hierarchy of decision making, but more important, it created a system by which employees could lodge complaints and see them dealt with by their representatives and management. It is easy to dismiss the Industrial Plan and the systems that were put in place as paternalistic, one-sided favoring of management, and a charade of a process. All of this is true. Nevertheless, it is wrong to overlook the power of creating such a system and the process that emerged. It laid the groundwork for what would eventually emerge in the 1930s during the New Deal, which remade labor relations both in Colorado and nationally.

The most significant shortcoming of the Industrial Plan, and the one due to which all the others faltered, was the lack of real and independent representation of the workers by an independent union. Although the plan created representation, it was essentially a company union that always had to balance the immense demands of the company with the scattered demands of the workers. Nevertheless, working and living conditions among CF&I's workers improved. If we were to compare the wages and conditions of coal miners in the Rocky Mountains to those in Appalachia, the comparison would favor Rockefeller and the Industrial Plan. Yet, despite these improvements, workers still yearned for an independent union. As Mary Abby Van Kleeck noted during her observations of the Industrial Plan's implementation, the men were looking for something more than just wages, but also the need to be recognized by the company as "men."[10]

In 1927, Colorado coal miners again went out on strike to protest working conditions and low wages, and most of all to demand the right to unionize freely. They wanted to be released from CF&I's paternalistic hold on them as a result of the Industrial Plan.[11] Two unions—the United Mine Workers (UMW) and the Industrial Workers of the World (IWW)—competed for their membership. Of the two, the IWW was the more radical and tainted with charges of communism and a reputation for violence.[12] The UMW historically had a presence in Colorado since the earlier strikes of 1894 and 1914, but because of Rockefeller's stronghold on the industry had been unable to make any real progress in organizing the coal miners. In November of 1927 violence broke out in both the southern and northern coal fields. It lasted for almost two weeks and resulted in dozens injured and almost another dozen workers killed. The former was aimed at CF&I and the latter at Rocky Mountain Fuel, which was just being taken over by Josephine Roche, a leading Colorado Progressive.[13]

The difference in management style and ideas about workers between Rockefeller and Roche was stunning. Rockefeller and the CF&I management team were intent on making sure that unionization did not come into the CF&I camps. Roche, on the other hand, quickly recognized the UMW and began negotiations with them to end the strike. Roche's reasons for recognizing the UMW were complex. First, she wanted to keep the IWW from getting a foothold in the state; while she was a Progressive she was not a radical who wanted to see an overthrow of the capitalist system. Second, she sought an advantage over CF&I. She hoped that by producing union coal, she could gain market share from the unpopular Rockefeller and CF&I. Finally, and perhaps more central to her ideals, was her belief that corporations should not be in the business of regulating people's lives and involving themselves in areas that she clearly thought were the province of the family. Roche believed that negotiating a fair wage and safe working conditions between a company and its workers' union representatives was the way to create the best American workplace. She had no desire to implement her own Industrial Plan or paternalistically (or maternalistically in her case) manage her workers.

By 1929 the labor strife came to an end just as the United States began to sink into what became the largest and most devastating global depression. The economic downturn sent the price of coal plummeting and the industry became unstable, which led to slowdowns, shuttering of mines, and eventually massive layoffs. Rockefeller was quicker to shut down production, while Roche desperately tried to keep her workers on the payroll. Her UMW members even postponed wages in order to keep the mines open longer. But by 1932, the US coal industry was decimated and would not recover until after World War II. The Colorado Coal fields were stagnate through most of the Depression, while Rockefeller and Roche moved on to other ventures. Rockefeller spent the Depression building Rockefeller Center, the Cloisters Museum, and Colonial Williamsburg. Roche took a position as assistant secretary of treasury, where she helped draft legislation that would become the Social Security Act and the Wagner Act.

Legislation that emerged out of the New Deal took a lesson from Rockefeller's Industrial Plan and put the government in the business of directly aiding American workers. The Wagner Act (also known as the National Labor Relations Act) as well as the 1937 Fair Labor Standards Act put in place a set of laws that gave workers, such as those fighting against Rockefeller, the kind of protections they needed. Under these provisions, they were allowed to freely organize and bargain collectively. It is easy to interpret the New Deal legislation as a set of laws meant to combat the likes of Rockefeller and the Industrial Plan, but really these laws were an outgrowth from the paternalistic policies that industrialists like Rockefeller had been pushing. The difference was that the New Deal federal government thought that worker protection should not be under the direction of the private sector, but instead placed in the hands of the federal government, which could be a fair arbiter of workplace conflicts.

The labor history of the United States has been fraught and disjointed. Historians have been puzzled by the ways in which American workers backed away from Socialist or Communist organizations to trying to create the kind of workplaces they demanded. Instead, major union organizations, like the AFL under the leadership of Samuel Gompers, worked to create change within the prevailing US capitalist system. A horrific event such as Ludlow upon reflection is not a breaking point in which American workers rejected the role of capitalism, but instead a touchstone on the way to slow Progressive reform of the American workplace. Out of Ludlow emerged the Rockefeller Industrial Plan, a plan with a myriad of faults but which nevertheless laid the groundwork for a working relationship between management and capital. And it was from the likes of Rockefeller's Industrial Plan and other Progressive thinkers, such as Josephine Roche, Robert Wagner, and Franklin D. Roosevelt (none of whom were radicals), that the sweeping legislation of the New Deal remade the American workplace in postwar America. While this was a legacy that would be challenged later by the Taft-Harley Act and again in the 1980s with the President Reagan's firing of the PAATCO (Professional Air Traffic Controllers' Organization) workers, many of those reforms became the foundation of American workers' rights.

## Notes

1. Sarah Deutsch, "Learning from Ludlow," in *Making an American Workforce: The Colorado Fuel and Iron Company's Construction of a Work Force During the Rockefeller Years*, ed. Fawn Amber Montoya (Boulder: University of Colorado Press, 2014, xx.

2. For general works on the Triangle Shirtwaist Fire, see Leon Stein, *The Triangle Fire* (Ithaca: Cornell University Press, 2001); David Von Drehle, *Triangle: The Fire That Changed America* (New York: Atlantic Monthly Press, 2003).

3. Regarding the impact of the boom-and-bust cycle on Americans, see Scott Reynolds Nelson, *A Nation of Deadbeats: An Uncommon History of America's Financial Disasters* (New York: Random House, 2013).

4. Richard White, *Railroaded: The Transcontinentals and the Making of Modern America* (New York: W.W. Norton, 2012) 414–52.

5. Melvyn Dubofsky and Foster Rhea Dulles, *Labor in America: A History* (Wheeling, IL: Harlan Davidson, 2004) 138–52.

6. David Montgomery, *The Fall of the House of Labor: The Workplace, the State, and the American Labor Activism, 1865–1925* (London: Cambridge University Press, 1987), xx.

7. Montgomery, *The Fall of the House of Labor*, xx.

8. In general, see Jonathan H. Rees, *Representation and Rebellion: The Rockefeller Plan at the Colorado Fuel and Iron Company, 1914–1942* (Boulder: University Press of Colorado, 2010).

9. "Industrial Plan," Appendix I in ibid., 221.

10. Ben M. Selekman and Mary Van Kleeck, *Employees Representation in Coal Mines: A Study of the Industrial Representation Plan of the Colorado Fuel and Iron Company* (New York: Russell Sage Foundation, 1924), 116.

11. Maria E. Montoya, "Creating an American Home: Contest and Accommodation in Rockefeller's Company Towns," in *Mapping Memories and Latina Lives*, ed. Vicki Ruiz and John Chavez (Urbana: University of Illinois Press, 2008).

12. Melvyn Dubofsky, *We Shall Be All: A History of the Industrial Workers of the World* (Urbana: University of Illinois Press, 2000).

13. Elinor McGinn, *A Wide Awake Woman: Josephine Roche in an Era of Reform* (Denver: Colorado Historical Society, 2002).

# Bibliography

## Newspapers and Periodicals

*Albuquerque Morning Journal*
*The Amalgamated Journal*
*Association Men, YMCA*
*Besco Bulletin*
*The Blast*
*Camp & Plant*
*Denver Post*
*Industrial Bulletin*
*Labour Gazette*
*New York Times*
*Pueblo Chieftain*
*Pueblo Star Journal*
*Raleigh News and Observer*

DOI: 10.5876/9781607323105.c009

*Rocky Mountain News*

*The Sydney Record*

*YMCA Railroad Men and Industrial Magazine*

## Archival Sources

*Baker Library, Harvard Business School, Boston, Massachusetts*
Elton Mayo Papers

*Beaton Institute, University College of Cape Breton, Sydney, Nova Scotia, Canada*
Dominion Steel and Coal Corporation (DOSCO), General Works Committee Minutes

*Bessemer Historical Society and CF&I Archives, Poeblo, Colorado*

*California State University at Fullerton (CSUF), Coal Mining Oral History Collection, Fullerton, California*

*Colorado State Archives, Denver, Colorado*
Colorado State Department of Military Affairs Collection
Papers of Governor Elias Ammons
Papers of Roady Kenehan
Records of the Treasurer of Colorado

*History Colorado, Denver, Colorado*
Papers of Captain Hildreth Frost

*Denver Public Library, Western History Collection, Denver, Colorado*
Papers of Captain Hildreth Frost
Papers of Edward Doyle

*Kautz Family Archives, Minneapolis, Minnesota*
YMCA publications

*Norlin Library, University of Colorado, Boulder, Colorado*
Frank and Fred Hefferly papers
Papers of Josephine Roche
Western Federation of Miners and International Union of Mine, Mill, and Smelter Workers Collection

*Provincial Archives of Nova Scotia, Halifax, Canada*
United Steel Workers of America, Sydney Lodge collection

*Rockefeller Archives Center, Sleepy Hollow, New York*

Papers of the Colorado Fuel and Iron Company

Rockefeller Family Papers

*Simon Flexner Papers, American Philosophical Society, Philadelphia, Pennsylvania*

## Government Documents

*The Colorado Coal Miners' Strike, 64th Cong., 1st sess., 1916.*

*Commission on Industrial Relations, Report on the Colorado Strike, 64th Cong.*

*National Labor Relations Board*

*Records of the United States Courts of Appeal*

*United States Census*

*War Labor Reports*

## Books and Articles

Andrews, Thomas G. *Killing for Coal: America's Deadliest Labor War.* Cambridge, MA: Harvard University Press, 2008.

Ammons, Elias M. "The Colorado Strike." *The North American Review* (July 1914): 38.

*A Report on Labor Disturbances in the State of Colorado from 1880 to 1904, Inclusive with Correspondence Relating Thereto.* Prepared under the direction of Carroll D. Wright, Commissioner of Labor, 58th Congress, 3rd sess., 1905, S. Doc. 122, 360.

Basso, Matthew. *Across the Great Divide: Cultures of Manhood in the American West.* New York: Routledge, 2000.

Bederman, Gail. *Manliness and Civilization: A Cultural History of Gender and Race in the United States, 1880–1917.* Chicago: University of Chicago Press, 1995. http://dx.doi.org/10.7208/chicago/9780226041490.001.0001.

Bender, Daniel E. *American Abyss: Savagery and Civilization in the Age of Industry.* Ithaca, NY: Cornell University Press, 2009.

Berlin, Ira, ed. *Power and Culture: Essays on the American Working Class.* New York: New Press, 1987.

Berman, David R. *Radicalism in the Mountain West, 1890–1920: Socialists, Populists, Miners and Wobblies.* Boulder: University Press of Colorado, 2007.

Beshoar, Barron B. *Out of the Depths: The Story of John R. Lawson, A Labor Leader.* Denver: Golden Bell Press, 1958.

Black, Edwin. *The War against the Weak: Eugenics and America's Campaign to Create a Master Race.* New York: Four Walls Eight Windows, 2003.

Boemeke, Manfred F. "The Wilson Administration, Organized Labor, and the Colorado Coal Strike, 1913–14." PhD diss., Princeton University, 1983.

Brody, David. *Labor Embattled: History, Power, Rights*. Urbana: University of Illinois Press, 2005.

Brody, David. *Steelworkers in America: The Nonunion Era*. New York: Harper & Row, 1969.

Canadaonline.about.com.

Chace, James. *1912: Wilson, Roosevelt, Taft & Debs—The Election that Changed the Country*. New York: Simon & Schuster, 2004.

Chernow, Ron. *Titan: The Life of John D. Rockefeller, Sr.* New York: Random House, 1998.

Chipman, James O. "Ammons Biography." http://www.colorado.gov/dpa/doit/archives/govs/eammons.html.

Conlin, Joseph R. *At the Point of Production: The Local History of the IWW*. Westport, CT: Greenwood Press, 1981.

Corwin, R. W. "Report of the Joint Committee on Health Problems in Education, National Education Association." (1913): 418–20.

Crawley, Ron. "What Kind of Unionism: Struggles among Sydney Steel Workers in the SWOC Years, 1936–1942." *Labor / Le Travail* 39 (1996): 104.

Crocker, Ruth Hutchison. *Social Work and Social Order: The Settlement Movement in Two Industrial Cities, 1889–1930*. Chicago: University of Illinois Press, 1992.

DeStefanis, Anthony R. "The Road to Ludlow: Breaking the 1913–14 Southern Colorado Coal Strike." *Journal of the Historical Society* 12, no. 3 (September 2012): 341–90. http://dx.doi.org/10.1111/j.1540-5923.2012.00373.x.

DeStefanis, Anthony R. "Violence and the Colorado National Guard: Masculinity, Race, Class, and Identity in the 1913–14 Southern Colorado Coal Strike." In *Mining Women: Gender in the Development of a Global Industry, 1670–2005*, ed. Jaclyn Gier Viskovatoff and Laurie Mercier, 195–212. New York: Palgrave/MacMillan, 2006.

Democratic Party of Colorado. *Democratic State Platform: Progress in Every Plank*. Denver: Democratic State Central Committee, 1912.

Deutsch, Sarah. *No Separate Refuge: Culture, Class and Gender on an Anglo-Hispanic Frontier in the American Southwest, 1880–1940*. New York: Oxford University Press, 1987.

Dodds, Joanne. *They All Come to Pueblo: A Social History*. Virginia Beach: Donning, 1994.

Donovan, Brian. *White Slave Crusades: Race, Gender, and Anti-Vice Activism, 1887–1917*. Chicago: University of Illinois Press, 2006.

Drehle, David Von. *Triangle: The Fire That Changed America*. New York: Atlantic Monthly Press, 2003.

"Dr. Richard Corwin." Pueblo Hall of Fame. http://www.pueblocc.edu/AboutUs/Foundation/AnnualFundraiser/1992_Inductees.htm. Accessed April 25, 2008.

Dubofsky, Melvyn. *We Shall Be All: A History of the Industrial Workers of the World*. Chicago: Quadrangle, 1969.

Dubofsky, Melvyn, and Foster Rhea Dulles. *Labor in America: A History*. Wheeling, IL: Harlan Davidson, 2004.

Dyer, Thomas G. *Theodore Roosevelt and the Idea of Race*. Baton Rouge: Louisiana State University Press, 1980.

Earle, M. "The Building of Steel Union Local 1064: Sydney, 1935–1937." In *Industry and Society in Nova Scotia: An Illustrated History*, ed. J. E. Candow. Halifax: Fernwood Publishing, 2001.

Engs, Ruth Clifford. *The Eugenics Movement: An Encyclopedia*. Westport, CT: Greenwood Press, 2005.

Enstad, Nan. *Ladies of Labor, Girls of Adventure: Working Women, Popular Culture, and Labor Politics at the Turn of the Twentieth Century*. New York: Columbia University Press, 1999.

Fairris, David. "From Exit to Voice in Shopfloor Governance: The Case of Company Unions." *Business History Review* 69, no. 4 (1995): 494–529. http://dx.doi.org/10.2307/3117143.

Finnegan, Margaret. *Selling Suffrage: Consumer Culture and Votes for Women*. New York: Columbia University Press, 1999.

Fosdick, Raymond B. *John D. Rockefeller, Jr.: A Portrait*. New York: Harper and Brothers, Co, 1956.

Frank, David. "The Cape Breton Coal Industry and the Rise and Fall of the British Empire Steel Corporation." In *Cape Breton Historical Essays* 2nd ed., ed. D. Macgillivray and B. Tennyson, 121–22, 127. Sydney, NS: College of Cape Breton Press, 1981.

Frank, David. *J. B. McLachlan. A Biography*. Toronto: James Lorimer & Co, 1999.

Gerstle, Gary. *American Crucible: Race and Nation in the Twentieth Century*. Princeton: Princeton University Press, 2002.

Gitelman, Howard M. *The Legacy of the Ludlow Massacre: A Chapter in American Industrial Relations*. Philadelphia: University of Pennsylvania Press, 1988.

Glenn, Susan. *Daughters of the Shtetl: Life and Labor in the Immigrant Generation*. Ithaca, NY: Cornell University Press, 1990.

Green, James, and Elizabeth Jameson. "Marking Labor History on the National Landscape: The Restored Ludlow Memorial and its Significance." *International Labor and Working Class History* 76 (Fall 2009): 6-25. http://dx.doi.org/10.1017/S0147547909990032.

Green, Marcus E. "Gramsci Cannot Speak: Presentations and Interpretations of Gramsci's Concept of the Subaltern." In *Rethinking Gramsci*, ed. Marcus E. Green, 73. New York: Routledge, 2011.

Gutman, Herbert. "The Braidwood Lockout of 1874." *Journal of the Illinois State Historical Society* 53 (1959): 5–28.

Gutman, Herbert. "Class, Status, and Community Power in Nineteenth-Century American Industrial Cities, Paterson, New Jersey: A Case Study." In *Work, Culture, and Society in Industrializing America: Essays in American Working-Class and Social History*, ed. Herbert Gutman, 234–60. New York: Random House, 1977.

Heron, C. *Working in Steel: The Early Years in Canada, 1883–1935*. Toronto: McClelland and Stewart, 1988.

Heron, C. *Working in Steel: The Early Years in Canada, 1883–1935*. Toronto: University of Toronto Press, 2008.

Hiebert, Ray Eldon. *Courtier to the Crowd: The Story of Ivy Lee and the Development of Public Relations*. Ames: Iowa State University, 1966.

Hoare, Quintin, and Geoffrey Nowell Smith, eds. *Selections from the Prison Notebooks of Antonio Gramsci*. New York: International Publishers, 1971.

Horowitz, Helen Lefkowitz. *Rereading Sex: Battles over Sexual Knowledge and Suppression in Nineteenth-Century America*. Amherst: University of Massachusetts Press, 2002.

Hunt, Geoffrey R. *Colorado's Volunteer Infantry in the Philippine Wars, 1898–1899*. Albuquerque: University of New Mexico Press, 2006.

Jacobson, Matthew Frye. *Whiteness of a Different Color: European Immigrants and the Alchemy of Race*. Cambridge: Harvard University Press, 1998.

Jameson, Elizabeth. *All That Glitters: Class, Conflict, and Community in Cripple Creek*. Urbana: University of Illinois Press, 1997.

Johnson, Marilynn S. *Violence in the West: The Johnson County Range War and Ludlow Massacre*. Bedford / St. Martin's, 2009.

Kaufman, B. E. "The Case for the Company Union." *Labor History* 41, no. 3 (2000): 321–50. http://dx.doi.org/10.1080/713684492.

King, Joseph. *A Mine to Make a Mine: Financing the Colorado Mining Industry, 1859–1902*. College Station: Texas A&M University Press, 1977.

Leonard, Thomas C. "Eugenics and Economics in the Progressive Era." *Journal of Economic Perspectives* 19, no. 4 (Autumn 2005): 207. http://dx.doi.org/10.1257/089533005775196642.

Long, Priscilla. "The Women of the Colorado Fuel and Iron Strike, 1913–14." In *Women, Work, and Protest: A Century of U.S. Women's Labor History*, ed. Ruth Milkman. Boston: Routledge & Kegan Paul, 1985.

Long, Priscilla. *Where the Sun Never Shines: A History of America's Bloody Coal Industry*. New York: Paragon House, 1989.

Lukas, Anthony. *Big Trouble: A Murder in a Small Town Sets off a Struggle for the Soul of America*. New York: Simon & Schuster, 1997.

MacCannon, R. W. *Sunrise: A Chronology of a Wyoming Mine*. Pueblo, CO: Bessemer Historical Society, 2003.

MacEachern, George. *George MacEachern: An Autobiography*, 28–29. Sydney, NS: University College of Cape Breton Press, 1987.

MacEwan, Paul. *Miners and Steelworkers: Labor in Cape Breton*. Toronto: A. M. Hakkert, 1976.

Macgillivray, Don. "Military Aid to the Civil Power: The Cape Breton Experience in the 1920's." In *Cape Breton Historical Essays*. 2nd ed., ed. D. Macgillivray and B. Tennyson, 102–4. Sydney, NS: College of Cape Breton Press, 1981.

Margolis, Eric. "Western Coal Mining as a Way of Life." *Journal of the West* 24, no. 3 (July 1985).

Martelle, Scott. *Blood Passion: The Ludlow Massacre and Class War in the American West*. New Brunswick, NJ: Rutgers University Press, 2008.

McClurg, Donald J. "The Colorado Coal Strike of 1927—Tactical Leadership of the IWW." *Labor History* 1 (1963): 69–72.

McGinn, Elinor. *A Wide-Wide Awake Woman: Josephine Roche in an Era of Reform*. Denver: Colorado Historical Society, 2002.

McGovern, George, and Leonard Guttridge. *The Great Coalfield War*. Boston: Houghton Mifflin Company, 1972.

Milkman, Ruth, ed. *Women, Work, and Protest: A Century of U.S. Women's Labor History*. Boston: Routledge & Kegan Paul, 1985.

Mink, Gwendolyn. *Old Labor and New Immigrants in American Political Development: Union, Party, and State, 1875–1920*. Ithaca, NY: Cornell University Press, 1986.

Montgomery, David. *The Fall of the House of Labor: The Workplace, the State, and American Labor Activism, 1865–1925*. New York: Cambridge University Press, 1987. http://dx.doi.org/10.1017/CBO9780511528774.

Montoya, Maria E. "Creating an American Home: Contest and Accommodation in Rockefeller's Company Towns." In *Mapping Memories and Latina Lives*, ed. Vicki Ruiz and John Chavez. Urbana: University of Illinois Press, 2008.

Nankivell, John H. *History of the Military Organizations of the State of Colorado, 1860–1935*. Denver: W. H. Kistler Stationery Company, 1935.

Nelson, Daniel. "The Company Union Movement: 1900–1937: A Reexamination." *Business History Review* 56, no. 3 (Autumn 1982): 340–42.

Nelson, Scott Reynolds. *A Nation of Deadbeats: An Uncommon History of America's Financial Disasters*. New York: Random House, 2013.

Norwood, Stephen. *Strikebreaking and Intimidation: Mercenaries and Masculinity in Twentieth-Century America*. Chapel Hill: University of North Carolina Press, 2001.

Papanikolas, Zeese. *Buried Unsung: Louis Tikas and the Ludlow Massacre*. Salt Lake City: University of Utah Press, 1982.

Papanikolas, Zeese. *Buried Unsung—Louis Tikas and the Ludlow Massacre*. Lincoln: University of Nebraska Press, 1991.

Patmore, Greg. "Employee Representation Plans at the Minnequa Steelworks, Pueblo, Colorado, 1915–1942." *Business History* 49, no. 6 (2007): 844. http://dx.doi.org/10.1080/00076790701710340.

Patmore, Greg. "Employee Representation Plans in the United States, Canada and Australia: An Employer Response to Workplace Democracy." *Labor* 3, no. 2 (2006): 41–65.

Patmore, Greg. "Iron and Steel Unionism in Canada and Australia, 1900–1914: The Impact of the State, Ethnicity, Management and Locality." *Labour / Le Travail* 58 (2006): 81–82.

Patmore, Greg, and J. Rees. "Employee Publications and Employee Representation Plans: The Case of Colorado Fuel and Iron." *Management and Organisational History* 3, no. 3–4 (2008): 257–72. http://dx.doi.org/10.1177/1744935908094088.

Pivar, David J. *Purity and Hygiene: Women, Prostitution, and the "American Plan," 1900–1930*. Westport, CT: Greenwood Press, 2002.

Rees, Jonathan. *Representation and Rebellion: The Rockefeller Plan at the Colorado Fuel and Iron Company, 1914–1942*. Boulder: University Press of Colorado, 2010.

Riker, William H. *Soldiers of the State: The Role of the National Guard in American Democracy*. Washington, DC: Public Affairs Press, 1957.

Rodgers, Daniel T. *Atlantic Crossings: Social Politics in a Progressive Age*. Cambridge: Belknap Press, 2000.

Ruiz, Vicki. *From out of the Shadows: Mexican Women in Twentieth-Century America*. Oxford: Oxford University Press, 1998.

Rupp, George H. "Block-Caving at the Sunrise Iron Mine, Wyoming." In *Mining Technology*. Englewood, CO: American Institute of Mining and Metallurgical Engineers, 1939.

Scamehorn, H. Lee. *Mill & Mine: The CF&I in the Twentieth Century*. Lincoln: University of Nebraska Press, 1992.

Selekman, B. M. *Employees' Representation in Steel Works: A Study of the Industrial Representation Plan of the Minnequa Steel Works of the Colorado Fuel and Iron Company*, 53–60. New York: Russell Sage Foundation, 1924.

Selekman, Ben M., and Mary Van Kleeck. *Employees Representation in Coal Mines: A Study of the Industrial Representation Plan of the Colorado Fuel and Iron Company*. New York: Russell Sage Foundation, 1924.

Senger, Dr. William. *Colorado and Its People*. Vol. 4. New York: Lewis Historical Publishing Co, 1948.

Solski, Michael, and John Smaller. *Mine Mill: The History of the International Union of Mine, Mill, and Smelter Workers in Canada since 1895*. Reno: Steel Rail Publishing, 1984.

Stein, Leon. *The Triangle Fire*. Ithaca, NY: Cornell University Press, 2001.

Stern, Alexandra Minna. *Eugenic Nation: Faults and Frontiers of Better Breeding in Modern America*. Berkeley: University of California Press, 2005.

Suggs, George G., Jr. "The Colorado Coal Miners' Strike, 1903–04: A Prelude to Ludlow?" *Journal of the West* 12 (January 1973): 36–52.

Suggs, George H. *Colorado's War on Militant Unionism: James H. Peabody and the Western Federation of Miner*. Detroit: Wayne State University Press, 1972.

Taylor, Paul S. *Mexican Labor in the United States*. 6 vols. Berkeley: University of California Press, 1928–1934.

War Labor Reports. *Reports of Decisions of the National War Labor Board with Headnotes and Index-Digest*, vol. 4. Washington, DC: Bureau of National Affairs, 1943.

Weed, Frank J. "The Sociological Department at the Colorado Fuel and Iron Company, 1901–1907: Scientific Paternalism and Industrial Control." *Journal of the History of the Behavioral Sciences* 41, no. 3 (Summer 2005): 269–84. http://dx.doi.org/10.1002/jhbs.20104.

West, Elliot. "Cleansing the Queen City: Prohibition and Urban Reform in Denver." *Arizona and the West* 14, no. 4 (Winter 1972): 338–43.

White, Richard. *Railroaded: The Transcontinentals and the Making of Modern America*. New York: W. W. Norton, 2012.

Wiebe, Robert H. *The Search for Order, 1877–1920*. New York: Hill and Wang, 1967.

Winter, Thomas. *Making Men, Making Class: The YMCA and Workingmen, 1877–1920*. Chicago: University of Chicago Press, 2002.

Wolff, David A. *Industrializing the Rockies: Growth, Competition, and Turmoil in the Coalfields of Colorado and Wyoming, 1868–1914*. Boulder: University Press of Colorado, 2003.

Zinke, G. W. *Minnequa Plant of Colorado Fuel and Iron Corporation and Two Locals of United Steelworkers of America*. Washington, DC: National Planning Association, 1951.

## Dissertations

Boemeke, Manfred F. "The Wilson Administration, Organized Labor, and the Colorado Coal Strike, 1913–14." PhD diss., Princeton University, 1983.

DeStefanis Anthony, R. "Guarding Capital: Soldier Strikebreakers on the Long Road to the Ludlow Massacre." PhD diss., College of William and Mary, 2004.

Henry, Robin C. "Criminalizing Sex, Defining Sexuality: Sodomy, Law, and Manhood in Nineteenth-Century Colorado," 74–76. PhD diss., Indiana University, 2006.

McGovern, George S. "The Colorado Coal Strike, 1913–14." PhD diss., Northwestern University, 1953.

Power, T. "Steel Unionism in Eastern Canada." BA thesis, Saint Francis Xavier University, 1942.

# Contributors

**Brian Clason** is a 2008 graduate of Colorado State University, Pueblo, with a BS in History; he is also a 2010 graduate from Colorado University, Denver, with a masters in administrative leadership and policy studies. Outside of historical research, Brian has ten years of experience in public education reform with a strong focus on at-risk and urban populations. He is currently a school administrator with Denver Public Schools with previous experience in teaching history, literacy instructional coaching, and advocating for educational interests of pradjudicated and adjudicated youth.

**Anthony R. DeStefanis** was born and raised in Providence, Rhode Island, where he graduated from Rhode Island College. He received his PhD from the College of William and Mary in 2004. He is currently an associate professor of history at Otterbein University in Westerville, Ohio, where he teaches courses in U.S. labor and working-class history, immigration, race, and ethnicity, and social protest movements. His book, tentatively titled "Guarding Capital: Soldier Strikebreakers on the Long Road to the Ludlow Massacre," will be out next year.

**Sarah Deutsch** is professor of history at Duke University. She is the author of three books, most recently *Women and the City: Gender, Space, and Power in Boston, 1870–1940* (2000), and numerous articles, including "Labor, Land and Protest since Statehood," in Marta Weigle, ed. *Telling New Mexico: A New History* (2009). She has served as program cochair for annual conferences of the American Studies Association and the Organization of American Historians, as dean of the Faculty of Social Sciences at Duke, and as chair of the Executive Committee of Delegates of the American Council of Learned Societies. Her current book project is "Making a Modern West, 1898–1942."

**Robin C. Henry** is an associate professor in the history department at Wichita State University. She received her PhD in U.S. history from Indiana University. Henry teaches courses on women and gender history. She has introduced and continues to teach a graduate course on gender and sexuality in U.S. History. Dr. Henry also served on the Committee on the Status of Women for the Organization of American History from 2009 to 2011.

**Ronald L. Mize** is director of the Center for Latino/Latina Studies and Engagement (CL@SE) and associate professor in the School of Language, Culture, and Society at Oregon State University. He previously taught at Humboldt State University, Cornell University, University of Saint Francis, California State University San Marcos, University of California San Diego, Southwestern College, and University of Wisconsin Rock County. He earned his PhD in Sociology and Rural Sociology at University of Wisconsin Madison. He is the coauthor of *Consuming Mexican Labor: From the Bracero Program to NAFTA* (2010, University of Toronto Press) and the coauthor of *Latino Immigrants in the United States* (2012, Polity Press), and over forty scholarly publications. His research focuses on the historical origins of racial and class oppression in the lives of Mexicanos/Mexicanas residing in the United States and the degree to which contemporary immigrant labor is informed by the political economy and cultural incorporation of Latinos/Latinas in the United States. Mize's maternal side of his family are multigeneration Mexican Americans who resided in CF&I's company town in Sunrise, Wyoming.

**Fawn-Amber Montoya** is currently an associate professor of History and coordinator of Chicano Studies at Colorado State University (CSU), Pueblo. She received her MA and PhD from the University of Arizona. She completed a two-year doctoral fellowship at Texas Tech University. Her research focuses on the U.S. Southwest with an emphasis on ethnicity and gender. Dr. Montoya is also actively involved in the Chicano Movement project through the CSU–Pueblo, University Archives. She served as the cochair of the National Association for Chicano and Chicana Studies Chicana caucus in 2012–2014. In 2011, she was awarded the CSU, Pueblo, University Wide Award for Excellence in Service and in 2010 received the award for Outstanding Student organization advisor. She is the Bessemer Historical Society's 2012/2013 scholar in residence and the co-chair of the Ludlow Centennial Commemoration Commission established by Executive Order of the Governor of Colorado.

**Maria E. Montoya** is an associate professor of History at New York University. She is the author of numerous articles and of the book, *Translating Property: The Maxwell Land Grant and the Conflict over Land in the American West, 1840–1900*. She is the lead author on a forthcoming U.S. History textbook, *Global Americans: A Social and Global History of the United States* coming out from Cengage Learning. She is also finishing a manuscript on the western industrialists John D. Rockefeller, Josephine Roche, and Henry Kaiser. She is looking at their roles in defining the spheres of work and home life during the early twentieth century.

**Greg Patmore** is professor of business and labour history and director of the Business and Labour History Group and the Co-operative Research Group in the School of Business, the University of Sydney. He also chairs the School's Ethics Committee. His main research interests are labor history, comparative labor history, Rochdale consumer cooperatives, employee representation, and the impact of industrialization and deindustrialization on regional economies.

**Jonathan Rees** is professor of history at Colorado State University, Pueblo. He is the author of *Representation and Rebellion: The Rockefeller Plan at the Colorado Fuel and Iron Company, 1914–1942* (University Press of Colorado, 2010) and *Refrigeration Nation: A History of Ice, Appliances and Enterprise in America* (Johns Hopkins University Press, 2013). His essays have appeared in *Inside Higher Education*, *Slate*, and the *Atlantic*.

# Index